Silence in the Face of Injustice

A Vision of Mercy and Hope

Gary W. Hardy, PhD

Cadmus Publishing
www.cadmuspublishing.com

Silence in the Face of Injustice
Gary W. Hardy, PhD

This book or parts thereof may not be reproduced, stored in a retrieval system, or transmitted by any means–electronic, mechanical photocopy, recording or otherwise–without the express permission of the author, except as provided by United States copyright law.

Unless otherwise noted, the Scripture quotations are from the Holy Bible, New King James Version®, copyright © 1982 by Thomas Nelson Inc., Used by permission. All rights reserved.

Cover design by Francisco Moraga

Copyright © Gary W. Hardy PhD, 2021

All rights reserved

ISBN 978-1-63751-506-8

LCCN 2021921061

Foreword

I am a disciple, a follower, of the Lord Jesus Christ; rescued, protected, disciplined, and chastened. I have a tendency to run away from my Father's house; I often fall down, but I get back up—usually with a lot of help from others. I walk, stumble, run and fall; yet each time, just when everything appears hopeless, His mercy appears. And He leads me on this amazing journey of grace.

I have failed and been cast aside, scorned, reviled, despised, and hated. I have been enslaved, trapped, bound, and often subjected to harsh and brutal control. Yet all of these things, these various trials and difficulties, began before I was arrested and imprisoned. Long before. I enjoyed many liberties before coming to prison, but I was already shackled and chained by sin. Paradoxically, while the prison took my liberty, I found a greater freedom. It is not the freedom of the world, however, but the freedom of the spirit. The freedom of being "in Christ" that, once obtained, can never be taken away.

In 1979, at twenty-two years of age, I prayed a prayer in the finest Baptist tradition to invite Jesus to come into my heart. I had no desire to follow Him, to deny myself or pick up a cross and follow Him; that wasn't part of my plan. I became a good church member, attended more services than most people, taught Sunday School when asked, and even served as a deacon in a local church. I considered myself a "born-again Christian"; and to any outside or casual observer, I performed the part well. Yet I fooled my wife, family, friends, and even myself. In reality, I was nothing but a fraud. My faith—if it indeed could be called faith—was in the "church" rather than in the true gospel of Jesus Christ.

Yet all of that changed in 2005, when I finally *came to Christ* rather than inviting him to *come into me*. *When I came to Him* in the cold and loneliness of the jail's suicide watch cell, *the Holy Spirit came to me*. Everything began changing. All things were becoming new. The things of the world began slowly fading or falling away, while other things were being painfully stripped away. I began hungering and thirsting for more of Christ, for His kingdom and His righteousness. My prison became His palace and the place of my preparation for service.

I believe it is presumptuous and probably blasphemous to believe that anyone may be saved merely by saying a prayer to invite Jesus to come into his or her heart. People who believe and teach such things base their teaching on a single verse, Revelation 3:20: *"Behold, I (Jesus) stand at the door and knock. If anyone hears my voice and opens the door I will come in to him and dine with him and he with me."* This verse (as with many such verses taken out of context) is part of a longer passage of instructions to the *church* of the Laodiceans. The members of this *church* had already believed the gospel, they were already disciples; they were simply being challenged for walking in disobedience and being "lukewarm" in the faith (see Revelation 3:14-22). Unfortunately, such false and misleading teaching permeates modern evangelism and is sadly the primary "conversion track" for many jail and prison ministries. Consequently, many people—inside and outside of prison—believe they are converted or saved, yet while they may have a form of godliness, they are denied its power. (2 Timothy 3:5) Many "good" people in the church today believe they are of His flock, yet do not have a real relationship with their Shepherd. Such a false "belief" is epidemic.

Surveys show that many Americans who identify as Christians rarely experience genuine spiritual transformation. Their spiritual journey generally begins with an awareness of the concept and some concern about the implications of sin, but rarely with any desire to do anything about it. If they attend church, it is often only at Christmas and Easter. While nearly two thirds of Americans describe themselves as "Christians," they have no particular spiritual or religious practice.

The remaining one third, in some form or another, identify themselves as being "born again," that is they acknowledge that they are sinners, have asked God for forgiveness, and embrace Jesus as their Savior. Many people in this group become immersed in religious activity with the hope of becoming a better person. Approximately 18 percent of all Americans fit this profile. Ten percent more reach the point of spiritual discontent—that is they believe there is something "more" to the Christian life. But half of these become so overwhelmed that they quit pursuing spiritual things and settle for the "life" they already have. Overall, this describes 94 percent of the American population. The remaining 6 percent live their lives very differently.

Those who choose to walk further on this spiritual journey—the 6 percent—experience complete brokenness over their own sin and desire to grow spiritually, to **be like Christ**. The focus and passion of their life is to love God and one another in accordance with Christ's commandment, *"A new commandment I give to you, that you love one another; as I have loved you, that you also love one another. By this all will know that you are my disciples, if you have love for one another."* (John 13:34-35) Surprisingly, many of these disciples may or may not attend a local church; rather they *are* the church—the body of Christ. They are more spiritual than religious. They strive to live each day and each moment in accordance with what they say they believe. They are possessed by the Spirit of God, and His indwelling presence guides their thoughts and actions each day. They live a life characterized by fully loving God and each other. No one needs to ask them *what* they believe; it is evident in **what they say and do** in their public and private worlds.[1]

I began this chapter by claiming to be a disciple—a follower—of the Lord Jesus Christ. I do not *practice* Christianity, at least not in the commonly understood sense. Rather, I strive to live each day and each moment as a follower of Christ, in fellowship and service with my brothers and sisters and, as one of my good friends describes, as a man whose story is one "of the abundance of the mercy and grace of an extraordinary God, in the life of an ordinary man who got himself in an extraordinary amount of trouble."

This book is not written for unbelievers or for the "casual" Christian; however, if you identify as such, I pray you will continue on the journey that the apostle Paul describes as "pressing on towards the goal." If you have not yet experienced brokenness over your own sin and do not have a burning desire to come after Christ, and a willingness to deny self, take up a cross, and follow Him, this book *may* not be written for you. Yet I invite you to read it anyway. On the other hand, if you are one of the few, the 6 percent, "those who love God and are called according to His purpose," then I invite you to prayerfully read this work, chew on it, question it, challenge it, pray about it, and pray about how you may become involved in **speaking out—not continuing to remain silent—in the face of injustice**. This book is a work of His mercy and grace and a milestone on my journey of faith. May you and each reader be blessed by the contents of this book.

Contents

Prologue 1
Introduction 5
1 – Silence in the Face of Injustice 13
2 – The Culture of Fear 27
3 – Complexities 36
4 – Victim Profiles 55
5 – Offenses and Offenders 63
6 – Effects of the Sex Offender Registry 85
7 – Roles and Responsibilities of Sex Offenders ... 104
8 – Roles and Responsibilities of the Church 121
9 – Transforming the Conflict 145
10 – Ekklesia 161
11 – The Vision 173
Epilogue 185
Acknowledgments 190
About the Author 194
Appendix A – Population and Prison Statistics 195
Appendix B – Age of Consent for Various States . 197
Appendix C – Sex Offender Probation Terms 199
Appendix D – Recommended Reading for Ex-Offenders 200
Appendix E – Recommended Reading for Justice 202
Bibliography 203
NOTES 210

Prologue

Suicide was the only option, or so he thought. After the revelation that a duplicitous and dishonest lifestyle had brought dishonor to his family, divorce from his wife, and dismissal from his employer, and even disenfranchisement from the local church, suicide appeared to be the only reasonable choice and the only possible escape from the shame. He had not intended for things to get this far. Yet driven by his own delusional thoughts, such as "No one will ever know," "No one needs to know," and "It's no one else's business," his dishonest and deviant acts had escalated beyond his ability or willingness to control them. He wasn't just slightly off course; he was drifting, hopelessly lost, and without a functioning moral compass to help find his way back home. He saw no hope of redemption, nor did he imagine that any opportunity for reconciliation or restoration was possible. He saw only the endless pain and suffering, the retribution and revenge of the criminal justice system, and a near certainty of spending the rest of his miserable life in a cold and lonely prison cell. Suicide appeared to be the only reasonable choice.

Three days after a suicide attempt, and in a drug- and alcohol-induced stupor, he awoke in a hospital's intensive care unit only to be arrested and taken to jail. After enduring the impersonal but invasive processing of the jail's receiving protocol, he was transferred to the jail's mental health ward. Stripped of his clothing and given only a small "modesty" towel, he entered a "suicide watch" cell. The steel on steel clanging of the closing cell door sent waves of terror and shame rippling through what little was left of his soul. Waves of fear and terror shredded his broken and desperate heart. The weight and hopelessness of the situation came crashing down. He knew the truth: more truth than anyone would ever know. Such knowledge had driven him to attempt suicide. He found himself plunging deeper and deeper into the endless abyss of darkness and despair. Everything was gone. Everything! He was certain that a dishonorable death would be far better than the ultimate reality of life and death in a lonely prison cell.

The mental health ward of the county jail houses prisoners who are (or have been) suicidal and/or are suffering from serious mental illnesses. Inarguably, anyone who considers suicide qualifies as seriously mentally ill. In his heart, it wasn't so much that he was seriously *mentally* ill as much as it pained him to admit that he was seriously *spiritually* ill. Sitting in the suicide watch cell, desperate and alone, he cried out to God, but initially heard nothing in return but silent judgment. The silence was all too frequently shattered by the desperate and painful cries echoing endlessly down the hall from the dozens of other broken and hurting men housed in the jail's mental health ward.

The years of attending Sunday school, morning and evening church services, and the church's annual Vacation Bible School, served him well during his time of isolation. Some of the Bible passages he had embedded in his memory now began filling his mind. Might it be that his crying out to God for help was at last being answered? From among these distant memories, he recalled the "Shepherd's Psalm"—a Psalm of David when he too was in torment:

> *The* LORD *is my Shepherd; I shall not want. He makes me to lie down in green pastures; He leads me beside the still waters. He restores my soul; He leads me in the paths of righteousness for His name's sake. Yea, though I walk through the valley of the shadow of death, I will fear no evil; for You are with me; Your rod and Your staff, they comfort me. You prepare a table*

PROLOGUE

before me in the presence of my enemies; You anoint my head with oil; my cup runs over. Surely goodness and mercy will follow me all the days of my life; and I will dwell in the house of the LORD forever. (Psalms 23:1-6)

Meditating and reflecting on these sacred words while rolling them over and over in his mind brought a peaceful and spiritual rest at last. Fear and dread began melting away. He remembered and recognized that the Lord is, was, and always would be his own personal shepherd. The Shepherd who cares for and protects His sheep. The Shepherd will not allow anything harmful to happen to those whom He loves. They are always under his care. And even when they run away, he relentlessly pursues them, rescuing them, bringing them back into the fold and under the protection of the flock. Slowly a light began shining, even in the deepening despair of his suicide watch cell. His tormented soul began crying out in prayer for the first time in many years. A glimmer of hope appeared. Glimpsing such hope began softening his heart. This softness and openness would eventually bring him to repentance and help change what he thought and how he made decisions.

He did not receive the life sentence he'd expected. Nevertheless, there were severe consequences for his crimes. He received a twenty-year prison sentence to be followed by lifetime probation and was ordered to register as a sex offender. While serving his time and because of the amazing grace of God, he began experiencing hope, and began considering prison as more of an opportunity rather than only a punishment. By God's grace and favor, he was soon given the opportunity to begin tutoring other prisoners in the prison's literacy and GED programs. In addition, providential circumstances opened other doors, allowing him to renew his own academic pursuits and to begin earnestly studying the Scriptures.

This book and ministry is the fruit of that grace. I am the man who thought suicide was the only option. I am the one who gave up on life, only to have God "*...[deliver] me from my strong enemy, from those who hated me, for they were too strong for me. They confronted me in the day of my calamity, but the LORD was my support. He brought me out into a broad place (prison); He delivered me because he delighted* *in me."* (Psalms 18:17-19)

This book is all about grace—the grace God gives to His children, empowering us *to be who He calls us to be, and to do what He calls us to do, according to His purpose and for His glory.* These things are only a portion of the blessings an extraordinary God continues to pour into my life through His continual presence and the abundance of His mercy and grace. All the glory and praise goes to God. I am but an ordinary man who got himself in an extraordinary amount of trouble, and I am being delivered by extraordinary grace. This journey of grace and mercy continues. I invite you into this adventure.

Introduction

Sexual violence affects people from every walk of life. Victims of sexual violence include people of every age, gender, ethnicity, spiritual belief, and socioeconomic class. Moreover, since over 90 percent of victims know their attacker (abuser), no one is immune from being victimized or from having a close family member or friend fall prey to some form of sexual abuse. Sexual violence wounds people, families, neighborhoods, and communities. But in some ways, such offenses are also symptomatic of the ongoing fragmentation of families, the disintegration of communities, the decline in social morals and values, and the increasing brokenness in this world.

The endless onslaught of "breaking news" reports a young child being molested by a family member or neighbor, a teenage runaway being kidnapped and sold into prostitution, a student being sexually assaulted on a college campus, a jogger being brutally raped in a neighborhood park, and a teenage girl committing suicide when the sexually explicit selfies she sent to her boyfriend began circulating among her classmates at school. In addition, there are reports of high school athletes being sexually assaulted by other players as part of a team initiation, and of a teenage girl being sexually abused by a local youth pastor. Incidents like these happen all too frequently in many American cities. In addition, around the world—as well as in many

American neighborhoods—millions of innocent children, teenagers, and young adults are kidnapped and taken as victims of human trafficking, prostitution, and sexual abuse.

Every one of these stories means one more person tragically suffers. A child's innocence is stolen. A teenager's virtue is corrupted. A rape victim's security is shattered. Sex offenses are personal and intrusive violations of the victim's body and soul. And while the physical wounds may eventually heal, the emotional, mental, and spiritual brokenness and pain lasts for a lifetime. Yet sexual offenses are more than just personal; they destroy intimate relationships, they shatter the lives of the victim's family and friends; and they send shock waves of fear and terror rippling throughout the community. These crimes are an incursion of evil into what appears to be a just and civil society.

Child molestation, rape, and other violent offenses are horrific and heinous acts. Unfortunately, all too often the media's *sensationalization* of these truly horrific crimes tends to produce false and misleading stereotypes by implying that every sex offender is a dangerous predator. Some offenders are—and remain—dangerous predators. Unfortunately, the inaccurate assumption that *all* offenders are dangerous or predatory produces an ever-increasing pandemic of fear and a shrill cry for justice. Indeed, not all offenders offend equally. The eighteen-year-old who got his fifteen-year-old girlfriend pregnant did not offend in the same way as a predator who made the headlines. Yet according to current laws, both must wear the label of "sex offender."

One of the most common myths concerning sex offenders is that they cannot change. This is why some have erroneously presumed that the recidivism rates are "frightening and high," (they're not.) Some people believe that sex offenders can be "managed," but few believe they can be "cured." Theologian Henri Nouwen discusses the differences between "cure" and "care": "What we see, and like to see, is cure and change. But what we do not see and do not want to see is care, the participation in the pain, the solidarity in suffering, the sharing in the experience of brokenness. And still, cure without care is as dehumanizing as a gift given with a cold heart. *Care is the basis and precondition of all cures.*"[2] The state believes—and the media

INTRODUCTION

portrays—that sex offenders must be managed, that they cannot be cured. But the state does not "care." Yet if professing Christians and church leaders do not believe sex offenders can be cured, is such a belief based on fear or because they do not care? Those who believe that sex offenders cannot change deny the power of the gospel, deny the power of grace, and thereby deny the power of Christ. If the leper was healed, the demoniac restored, and Lazarus raised from the dead, is there anything impossible with God?

The culture of fear, rather than a culture of truth, robs millions of U.S. citizens of their liberty, and many of their constitutionally-guaranteed rights and freedoms. This virulent fear gives us permission to abolish reasoning and abort justice, while substituting extreme injustice for justice. Fear does not suddenly overcome truth. Fear increases in vigor and strength by the persistent erosion and deliberate propagation of half-truths and alternative facts. The human atrocities involved in the medieval crusades, the Holocaust, and other such horrific abuses of human rights did not occur, nor achieve their full effect, overnight. These malevolent brutalities began with the deliberate propagation of fear and a corruption of the truth. These destructive campaigns were based on what is now recognized as the belief in absolute absurdities rather than verifiable truths and reason. Yet the absurdities deviously propagated by powerful and misanthropic demagogues employed fear as a weapon to justify the destruction of millions of innocent people. Those who believed the absurdities promoted by the powerful demagogues, willingly and ignorantly committed what are today recognized as great atrocities, even though their actions at the time appeared to be perfectly reasonable and acceptable.

This book examines whether the American justice system is based on reason and truth or on virulent fears. We will examine how the deliberate propagation of fear has led to the prosecution of the criminal wars and oppressions resulting in the mass imprisonment of millions of U.S. citizens while costing American taxpayers billions of dollars. Moreover, we will examine how the failed War on Drugs is being transformed into a war on sex offenders and how the mass imprisonment and unique restrictions imposed on those who have committed a sexual offense—especially the public registration of all sex offenders—creates a systemic injustice driven by a culture of fear rather than by the pursuit of justice and truth.

In examining the culture of fear, we will explore the forces propagating such fear and propose new strategies and possibilities for a more effective and restorative justice. We will consider important issues such as:

- *Whether the sweeping legislative reforms have increased or decreased public safety*
- *Whether fear-based generalizations and the use of stereotypes promote justice or injustice*
- *How the media's sensationalism of horrific crimes affects the pursuit of justice*
- *Whether justice for someone convicted of engaging in consensual sex with an underage girlfriend (or boyfriend) ought to be the same as justice for someone convicted of rape or child molestation*

In addition, we will explore:

- *The differences in various types of victims of sexual offenses*
- *The differences in various types of offenders*
- *Whether the sex offender registry promotes justice or injustice*

Then, we will examine:

- *The responsibilities of those who have committed a sexual offense*
- *How recovery and life transformation are possible*
- *Examine the effectiveness or ineffectiveness of the organized church in advocating for justice*
- *Consider the role of the true church—the* ekklesia—*in restoring truth and justice.*

We will also examine the relationship between the sex offender and the local church. Almost all Christians would agree that the Bible teaches that we are saved by grace through faith. But almost all of those same Christians would probably balk at the idea of a believing Christian brother (or sister) being a registered sex offender. Yet Jesus did not say, "*For God so loved the world that He gave His only begotten Son, that whoever believes in Him should not perish, but have everlasting life* (John 3:16), unless he or she is a sex offender who got caught."

INTRODUCTION

And finally, we will outline possible strategies in transforming the conflict and reestablishing justice for all. Such strategies include:
- *Establishing a compassionate dialogue amongst all stakeholders*
- *Involving the true church (ekklesia) in a covenant of compassion towards all who are prison*
- *Applying ancient methods of healing in restoring individuals' lives and communities*

Ultimately, this book poses the question whether, given the apparent alarming increase in sex crimes throughout this country, our current system of justice is helping or hindering the healing of victims and helping or hindering the healing, recovery, and restoration of ex-offenders. If it is proven that the present system of justice is hindering, what changes should be made, and how do we begin implementing such changes to begin transforming the conflict?

Dealing with sex offenders is not an insurmountable problem, although, in light of the pandemic of fear, finding a successful pathway for justice for both the victims of sexual abuse and offenders is certainly a difficult problem. Problems that seemingly cannot be—or are highly resistant to being—peacefully resolved are difficult because of their complexity. Nevertheless, even complex problems may be transformed if "the people who are part of the problem work together creatively to understand and improve it."[3]

Sexual offenses inflict physical, emotional, psychological, and spiritual wounds. Physical wounds may heal with time. Psychological and emotional wounds may heal through timely and extensive counseling. But spiritual wounds require spiritual healing. Furthermore, sexual offenses not only inflict spiritual wounds, they often arise from the offender's own spiritual wounds and brokenness. Spiritual healing does not come from religious dogma and doctrine, but rather through forgiveness, mercy, and authentic caring relationships. We need more compassionate mercy and amazing grace. Such grace is the domain and habit of spiritual people, or those among the "*ekklesia*."[4] These spiritual people and spiritual leaders are society's mediators and practitioners of grace.

There is a great deal of work to be done. In the eighteenth century,

British statesman Edmund Burke is reportedly to have said, "The only thing necessary for evil to triumph is for good men to do nothing." It has also been said that, "Silence in the face of evil is in itself evil; God will not hold us guiltless. Not to speak is to speak and not to act is to act."[5] How long can citizens in a just and civil society afford to maintain the status quo and the silence, and yet to hope to maintain a just and civil society?

In the onslaught of media sensationalism, the public—regular citizens like you and me—and our elected officials and legislators too often remain silent. In the midst of mass imprisonment and oppression, members of the spiritual community too often remain silent. And even when confronted with their crimes, offenders too often remain silent. The silence in the face of injustice raises the question of **why we are remaining silent**.

The ultimate goal and purpose of this book is to help end the "silence in the face of injustice" and to "gather up the fragments that remain." (John 6:12) These "fragments" are our brothers and sisters, those who are broken, deeply wounded and abandoned in prisons, and those who are isolated and shamed on the sex offender registry. In addition, I hope to encourage and challenge us to embrace the mission of the United Nations Declaration of Human Rights, affirming that the "inherent dignity and the equal and inalienable rights of all members of the human family is the foundation of freedom, justice, and peace in the world."[6] I believe we must attempt to develop a dialogue and strategy so that there are *no more victims*; however, we must work equally towards insuring that *no one is disposable* and that *no one is lost*.

This book consists of four sections. The first section presents the "Present Problem." Chapter 1, "Silence in the Face of Injustice," offers a perspective on our present justice system and describes how injustice has become the standard practice. Chapter 2, "Culture of Fear," exposes the cancer of fear and its impact on our decision making and justice. Chapter 3, "Complexities," examines some possibilities for dealing with the dynamic, generative, and social complexities concerning sex offenders and begins exploring strategies for transformation.

The second section, "Perspectives on People," exposes the

INTRODUCTION

stereotypes and generalizations surrounding the commission of a sex offense and the effect these prejudices have on convicted sex offenders. Chapter 4, "Victim Profiles," differentiates between the various types of victims and describes some of the physical, emotional, psychological, and spiritual effects of sex offenses. Chapter 5, "Offenses and Offenders," explores the various types of sexual offenses and presents the stories of five individual sex offenders who in many ways do not fit the publicly accepted or promoted stereotypes. This section closes with Chapter 6, "Effects of the Sex Offender Registry." This chapter provides an overview of the national requirement for state sex offender registration laws and exposes some of the devastating impact these schemes inflict on the lives of offenders, their families and friends.

The third section, "Roles and Responsibilities," begins identifying the responsibilities of various parties and exploring ideas and opportunities for transformation. Chapter 7, "Roles and Responsibilities of Ex-Offenders," challenges sex offenders and advocates concerning their own duties and obligations. Chapter 8, "Roles and Responsibilities of the Church," exposes the church's present response to former sex offenders in light of Scriptural teachings and presents some possibilities for change.

The final section, "Prayerful Possibilities," prepares us to dream the impossible. Chapter 9, "Transforming the Conflict," calls for a new kind of leadership and identifies some of the tools necessary to mediate the conflict. Chapter 10, "The *Ekklesia*," contrasts the limitations of the organized church with the Scriptural possibilities of the *ekklesia*—the body of Christ. Chapter 11, "The Vision," presents what is possible when dreams come true and the only question remaining is, "What took us so long?" It presents hope in the impossible becoming possible.

This book invites all who are willing to participate to join in the dialogue to examine the complexities of these difficult problems. In addition, I will demonstrate that, because of media sensationalism and the "stickiness" of the existing messages, i.e., that all sex offenders are dangerous predators, and because of the legislator's resilient timidity concerning these issues, the only reasonable hope for transformational change is for a new kind of leadership, that is for *mediators* to rise up from the *spiritual* community.

It is my hope and prayer that many will read this book with an open and prayerful heart and, most importantly, with an open mind. I am, and have been, deeply and personally affected by the material presented here. Yet it is neither my intention nor my desire to overwhelm you or even attempt to prove the "rightness" of my position on these matters. I believe it is more about the *posture* one takes rather than a *position* one holds. Therefore, I am asking people in various positions—especially professing Christians and leaders in the body of Christ—to set aside their fears and any preconceived ideas, and to join in a humble posture of prayer to seek the abundant mercy and grace of God. Join me in coming to the throne of grace that together we may obtain mercy and find more grace to help in time of need. (Hebrews 4:16) Please give me the space and grace to continue on this journey, serving our Lord and my friends and brothers and sisters in Christ who have been broken and cast aside. I do love God and His people and above all, I want us to get this right.[7]

1 – *Silence in the Face of Injustice*

Silence in the Face of Injustice presupposes the existence of injustice. One man's justice may be perceived as another man's injustice, just as differing life experiences, cultures, and other factors generally prevent any two people from agreeing on everything. Such natural and reasonable differences, taken to an extreme, often form the foundation for conflicts and difficult problems. On a community level, the differences and divisions in this country generate misunderstandings that often lead to dangerous and violent conflicts. Such perceived differences lead us to create artificial labels and identities by which we define others and ourselves. These false identities prevent or hinder clear communication; consequently, families, communities, and nations are destroyed. These differences of opinion and artificial identities obscure our ability to see the things we have in common, and often generate divisions that threaten the community and derail many opportunities. One such difference of opinion is *justice* versus *injustice*. Which is which? Who gets to decide? How can we overcome these differences?

The differing perspectives and understandings of justice, or for that matter differing perspectives on *any* issue, provides opportunities for an intentional conversation—a "dialogue." The conversations or dialogues among those who *agree* on various issues create opportunities to increase the participants' understanding; but a compassionate and constructive dialogue among those who strenuously *disagree* on any issue has the potential to *build* understanding and create community. Dialogues, therefore, offer opportunities to help us "learn to kindle and sustain a new conversational spirit that has the power to penetrate and dissolve some of our most intractable and difficult problems."[8] Is it possible then, by beginning a *dialogue* rather than simply relying on our own self-imposed artificial identities and assumed differences, that we may begin building the foundation and infrastructure necessary to help us differentiate between justice and injustice?

Human beings are intrinsically selfish, particularly when they believe they have been wronged or harmed. Therefore justice does not come naturally to us; we must pursue and protect it. As humans, our propensity and inclination for selfishness and corruption inevitably leads us to an unrestrained and unbalanced justice. So when justice is unprotected, corruption leads to injustice. Injustice rages against justice from within a culture laden with fears, prejudices, and ignorance. Fears arise from lack of knowledge or from the intentional and/or malevolent manipulations of ideas and opinions by those who seek to gain or profit from such fears. Unscrupulous leaders, pundits, and demagogues prey on people's fears; and the greater the fear, the greater the potential for injustice, and—for such unscrupulous manipulators—the greater the opportunity for profit.

Prejudices arise when we "pre-judge." People often fall prey to sensational mythologies, urban legends, or sensationalized "alternative facts" that twist and contort the truth. It has been said that, "prejudices are vagrant opinions without any visible means of support"; yet we color our "justice" with such vagrant opinions that they passively allow justice to degrade into injustice. Our unwillingness, or failure, to examine carefully the facts or evidence of any difference or misunderstanding obscures or conceals the truth, thereby arousing and justifying our prejudices. These prejudices then increase and inflame injustice. Consequently, the greater our prejudice, the greater our potential for injustice.

Ignorance arises from an intentional or even unintentional lack of knowledge or understanding. Yet injustice arises as easily from intentional or unintentional ignorance. Criminal offenders are not excused because of their "ignorance of the law." It then stands to reason that those who establish and enforce the law and promote the practice of justice are also not excused because of their ignorance. Even more, because of the sacred responsibility given to them as lawmakers and law enforcers, they must exercise great diligence to discern knowledge and truth, rather than being swayed by popular opinions or unduly influenced by their own ignorance.

People are entitled to their own *opinions*, but not their own facts; justice established on opinions and ignorance creates a dangerous injustice. More than two decades after President Abraham Lincoln issued the Emancipation Proclamation, fellow abolitionist Frederick Douglass wrote, "Where justice is denied… where ignorance prevails, and where a class of people are made to feel that society is an organized conspiracy to oppress, rob, and degrade, then neither persons nor property will be safe." Can justice prevail in the face of ignorance, or does ignorance permit injustice and thereby passively allow such wrong to prevail?

How do we define justice? "Justice" is the "administration of what is just." And what is just is that which has "a basis in or conforming to fact or reason." "Injustice" is "the absence of justice, the violation of right or of the rights of another."[9] Justice is denied or perverted (and injustice imposed) when fear, prejudice, and ignorance are allowed to outweigh facts or reason in the administration of what is just.

Based on such definitions and ideals, can we call the American criminal justice system "just" when this country, with only *5 percent* of the world's population incarcerates *25 percent* of the world's prison population? America, with a promise of "liberty and justice for all," imprisons far more of its citizens than most other countries. Are Americans the most evil people on earth, or only the most unmerciful, unforgiving, and judgmental? In fact, as illustrated in the charts below, the United States incarcerates more of its citizens than the G8 (the "industrialized" nations), and even more than the top twenty recipients of U.S. foreign aid.[10] If America is the "land of the free and the home of the brave," why are so many of its citizens in prison?

Chart 1

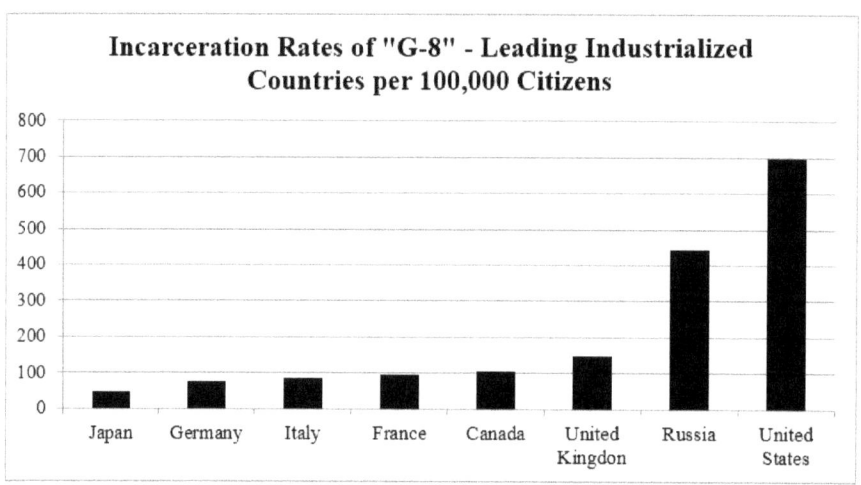

Chart 2

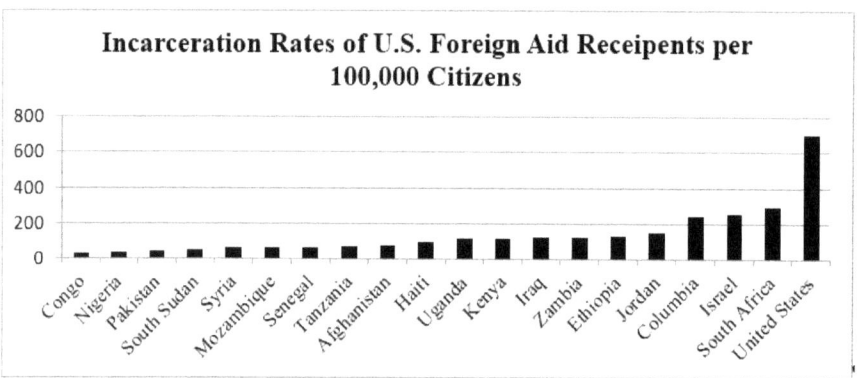

Many Americans, including many living in the Southern states, profess that the United States was founded on "Christian principles" and that the Holy Bible was in many ways the basis for our early justice system. It is not my intent to entertain that particular discussion or debate in this book. Nevertheless, what is disturbing and disappointing is that most of these Southern states in the so-called "Bible Belt"[11] have the *highest* rates of incarceration in this country. This raises a difficult question: if the gospel of Jesus Christ—the good news of forgiveness, mercy, and love—is being preached and taught in the churches on Sunday, what gospel is being practiced outside the churches and in the marketplace and halls of justice throughout the rest of the week?

Listed below are the rates of incarceration and *national rankings* for Bible Belt states.[12]

Table 1–Bible Belt States[12]

State	Rate of Incarceration *	Rank**
Louisiana	776	1
Oklahoma	715	2
Alabama	611	3
Mississippi	609	4
Arkansas	591	6
Texas	568	7
Missouri	530	8
Georgia	503	9
Florida	496	10
Kentucky	489	11
Virginia	457	12
Tennessee	425	17
South Carolina	414	18
North Carolina	352	30
Kansas	328	34
Average	524	

* Rate of incarceration per 100,000 residents
** National ranking of all fifty states

In an interesting comparison between the Bible Belt states and the original thirteen colonies, Bible Belt states imprison their own citizens on average over 160 percent more than the original thirteen colonies. Is it possible that the culture in the original thirteen colonies remains focused even today more on "freedom and justice for all," whereas the culture in the Bible Belt is today still affected and influenced more by the cultural remnants of slavery, servitude, and white supremacy? Is there a gospel for the states seeking freedom and a gospel for the states seeking to incarcerate and enslave? Do the Bible Belt churches preach and practice a "different gospel" from their cousins in the eastern states?

Table 2–Original Thirteen Colonies[13]

State	Rate of Incarceration *	Rank **
Georgia (BB)	503	9
Virginia (BB)	457	12
South Carolina (BB)	414	18
Delaware	411	22
Pennsylvania	387	23
North Carolina (BB)	352	30
Maryland	339	31
Connecticut	312	35
New York	260	40
New Jersey	228	43
New Hampshire	217	44
Rhode Island	204	47
Massachusetts	179	49
Average	327	

BB – Also a Bible Belt state
* Rate of incarceration per 100,000 residents
** National ranking of all fifty states

If justice is the administration of what is just, and what is just has a basis in or conforms to reason, why does American justice appear so much more unreasonable and unmerciful than that of the rest of the world? And why are so many professing Christians and church leaders of a supposedly "Christian" nation supporting injustice—or simply remaining silent concerning the continuing mass imprisonment of their brothers and sisters?

Fear, prejudice, and ignorance abolish reason and prevent justice. Injustice prevails when exceptions made in the justice system violate the individual rights guaranteed in the Constitution of the United States. For example, Section 1, Article 9 of the U.S. Constitution stipulates that no Ex Post Facto[13] law shall be passed. One of the most notable and dangerous exceptions to this constitutionally guaranteed protection requires that anyone *ever* convicted of a sex offense must also register with the authorities as a sex offender. Because of the public nature of the sex offender registry, former sex offenders are subjected to public shaming and harassment and often threatened with vigilante violence.

The legal justification for the enactment of such an *exception* is that sex offender registration is supposedly not a criminal sanction per se, but rather a civil requirement needed for public safety.[14] Yet does justice or injustice prevail when a violation of a civil law results in criminal charges and imprisonment?

Ex Post Facto laws are only one example of the exception-making being practiced in what many scholars have termed the "war on sex offenders."[15] In the growing war and oppression against sex offenders, a grave danger exists. In the *Harvard Civil Liberties Law Review*, Associate Professor Corey Rayburn Yung notes that such exception-making creates policy lock, an erosion of civil liberties, collateral damage and allows these exceptions to become laws.[16] These exceptions create *injustice*. Laws and policies that endanger justice for ex-offenders also endanger justice for everyone. Injustice for one is injustice for all.

The framers of the Constitution of the United States—the supreme law of the land—purposefully established a foundation of government for all of the people "to establish justice… (for) ourselves and our posterity." Embedded in this foundation are the three branches of our government—the legislative, executive, and judicial. A system of checks and balances protects and prevents any one branch of government, or one individual, from becoming too powerful or from being able to seize power for selfish or nefarious purposes. Justice is now under attack. This attack is not coming from foreign powers, unwelcome immigrants, or terrorist groups. It comes from the epidemic of fear and the internal corruption of justice—our acquiescence to injustice—and by the deliberate silencing and subjection of the *judiciary* to the *legislative* and *executive* branches of government.

The silencing and subjection of the judiciary began when a bloodless and silent coup occurred within the United States without a single shot being fired. For over two hundred years, the American justice system rested on the principles embedded in the three basic divisions of government. The legislative branch enacted laws, the executive branch prosecuted lawbreakers, and the judicial branch, including judges and juries, listened to and weighed the evidence. If the defendant was found guilty, the judge pronounced an appropriate and just sanction. Nevertheless, all of that changed after the coup. The effects of the coup are devastating and have changed the fundamentals of the American system of justice—where there is no longer justice for all. And no "justice for all" endangers justice for everyone.

The bloodless and silent coup occurred when the legislative and executive branches, comprised of *elected* (as opposed to *appointed*) officials, conspired to appear tough on crime while seeking re-election on so-called "law and order" tickets. Self-seeking politicians fed the media with stories of extreme crime and danger while the media themselves eagerly compiled sensational (but not necessarily true) stories intent primarily on creating a pandemic of fear while increasing their own readers and viewers (and profits). Why do we stand by and believe such things, and why are we so blind to injustice? The mass media thrives on creating fear, and thereby profits by not revealing the truth.

Americans are often too gullible and easily persuaded without ever thinking things through. They respond to carefully conceived and constructed arguments and slick forms of persuasion. It doesn't matter if the story is true, but what matters is whether it is believed. Does it persuade? *If it is persuasive, it doesn't matter whether it is true*. Such superficial persuasion rips the life out of the context of truth and justice. When nothing can be discerned as true, justice is destroyed, ethics disintegrate, and civilization returns to barbarism.[17] Consequently, in the corruption or absence of truth, injustice abounds.

Spurred on by such irrational, but potent, fears, legislators often engage in superficial persuasion by enacting laws based solely upon their prejudices, passions, errors of opinion, and in accordance with their own local interests and selfish views.[18] When the executive and legislative branches completed the bloodless coup, the power in the judge's courtroom shifted. The so-called "Truth in Sentencing" laws removed the sentencing power from the judges and delivered it to the legislators and prosecutors (executive branch) largely through the creation of minimum[19] mandatory[20] and presumptive[21] sentencing schemes and "three-strike"[22] laws. Such laws only conceal the truth, and abort justice by inducing defendants to accept plea agreements created by politically motivated prosecutors rather than allowing an *impartial judge* to decide an appropriate sentence.

One of the principle results of such a power shift is that in 95 percent of criminal cases judges no longer "judge"; instead, they merely pronounce the sentence stipulated by the prosecutors and agreed upon (even reluctantly) by the defendants. Retired Arizona Appellate Court Justice Rudolph Gerber laments that while "English common law allowed its judges an inner moral compass to assess the justice of their rulings… in our state (Arizona) that moral compass has been deflected by unsophisticated 'tough' solutions to crime that discourage honest queries about … basic fairness."[23] Injustice masquerades as justice, including minimum, mandatory, presumptive sentencing, and plea bargains, while prosecutors wage the ever-popular War on Drugs and other criminal oppressions and wars.[24]

Mandatory and presumptive sentencing laws became popular in the latter part of the twentieth century. Under the previous "indeterminate" sentencing protocols, some prisoners who had been granted parole, i.e., early release, committed a new criminal offense. The media sensationalized these offenses while accusing the judges of indiscretion and leniency. Yet the media rarely, if ever, presented all of the facts. Prisoners were granted parole before serving their entire sentence based on the decision of the *parole board*—not the sentencing judge. The parole board, not the judge, granted them their early liberty. Nevertheless, the ensuing media sensationalism created an epidemic of fear, leading to hastily-conceived and -enacted legislation favoring minimum, mandatory and presumptive sentencing schemes and thereby seizing power from the judiciary. According to Justice Gerber, "mandatory sentencing schemes now dominate felony sentencing and create serious injustices; disproportionate severity of sentencing to crime; reduction in trials by an increase in plea bargaining; prosecutorial, rather than judicial control of sentencing; (and a) lack of individualized [and just] sentences."[25]

Legislators and prosecutors, i.e. the officials selected by a fearful electorate, react to such fear with promises to be "tough on crime" and to "lock 'em up and throw away the key." These elected officials, i.e. politicians, now wield more clout than judges in criminal sentencing and establishing justice. The coup is complete. Gerber notes, "The prosecutor decides, not only *which* offenses to charge, but also *whether* to seek enhancement or aggravation, *whether* to offer a plea, what it will be, and *whether* a sentence is stipulated (agreed upon by the prosecution and defense without the involvement of the judge before sentencing). No judicial or legislative controls or procedural rules limit these choices. The office decisions of prosecutors, *who are often recently graduated from law school*, are discretionary, disparate, unregulated, and hidden from public scrutiny and judicially unreviewable."[26] In 1990, the Arizona Court of Appeals observed, "Suffice it to say that today we express our concern that a junior office in the *executive* branch of county government (deputy county attorney) is given great power and discretion to affect sentencing in a state court while denying the state *judicial* officer who presides over that court any discretion in what has traditionally and inherently been a function of the court."[27]

One of the stark new truths about the American criminal justice system is that very few criminal cases go to trial.[28] Beginning in the 1980s, the overly aggressive prosecution of criminal defendants—especially in the War on Drugs—overburdened the judicial system. This burden led to the rapid expansion of the prison system and the creation of the Prison Industrial Complex.[29] Since 95 percent of defendants enter guilty pleas, trial courts reach condemnation without adjudication. Moreover, even when defendants consider going to trial, prosecutors threaten to employ draconian sentencing (minimum mandatory and presumptive) mandates and various enhancements to threaten a greater sanction (sentence) to discourage it.[30]

The use of plea bargains also creates injustice by circumventing the original legislative sentencing guidelines. Therefore, the *executive* branch (prosecutors) has also seized control from the *legislative* branch of government. Justice Gerber remarks, "Plea bargaining negotiations reinforce an attitude of manipulation where defendants discover that our bargaining bazaars operate by threat, bluster, and push-pull gymnastics matching their own criminal wiles.... Rehabilitation is thus seriously compromised from the start, because plea bargaining reinforces in the criminal the very manipulative mentality we seek to eradicate, namely that the letter of the law does not need to be followed."[31] "Plea bargains have become so coercive that many innocent people feel they have no other option than to plead guilty."[32]

Why have plea bargains become the "system"? With the advent of the War on Drugs and the billions of federal dollars supporting the war at a local level, law enforcement departments and legislatures quickly became intoxicated with the power, perks, and privileges of their fancy new toys.[33] Since 1986, billions of government dollars have been allocated to fund the War on Drugs and other law enforcement programs at the expense of other government programs—such as education, medical care, and other social programs—and have necessitated an increase in taxes.

Owing to the illegitimate transfer of power from the judiciary to the prosecutors (executive branch), the U.S. prison population has swollen from approximately four hundred thousand prisoners in 1978 to over two million by late 1999. As previously noted, America has the highest incarceration rate in the world. Yet Justice Gerber notes, "The most shocking aspect of our incarceration mania is not the *quantity* of persons we incarcerate but their *quality*. While we are putting more hard-core and violent types behind bars than ever before, we are also imprisoning more non-violent offenders."[34]

And owing to plea bargains, it is estimated that as many as sixty-five million Americans (or roughly 20 percent of the U.S. population) now have criminal records. This is approximately equal to the *combined* present populations of *all* of the Midwestern states. In addition, citizens who have felony records face harsher sanctions and penalties for any subsequent offense. Fear fuels the belief of "once a felon, always a felon." Individuals with criminal records face a lifetime of consequences, affecting their future education, employment, housing, and more. "The United States is experiencing a criminal justice (injustice) crisis.... By accepting the criminalization of everything, the bloat of the criminal justice system, and the rise of the plea bargain, the country has guaranteed that millions of Americans will never have a shot at leading ordinary lives."[35] The difficulty in obtaining employment, housing, and education, and in just living an ordinary life, is significantly increased for former sex offenders. Many communities have created exclusion zones throughout the city so that former sex offenders have no place to live.

In forty-eight states, an individual with a felony conviction loses the right to vote. Although periods of disenfranchisement vary by state, the alarming escalation of arrests and increasing number of convictions obtained by plea bargains prevent millions of United States citizens who have *served their time* from participating in, or having a voice in, the democratic process. Is it not an abuse of power when an offender who has completed his or her sentence can no longer vote for elected officials? Is it not a serious conflict of interest when politicians use the power of law to prevent those they have convicted and imprisoned from later opposing them or even supporting an opponent at the ballot box?

The executive—rather than the judicial or even the legislative branch of government—is now in control of "justice." This is precisely what the writers of the Constitution wanted to avoid by establishing the system of checks and balances. When the executive branch seizes control of the government, the government ceases to be a democracy that engages in debate and discourse based upon evidence and reason. The government "of the people, by the people, and for the people" is in danger of falling under the control of demagogues. Demagogues are political leaders who gain power and control by appealing to people's *fears, emotions, prejudices, and ignorance* rather than the rationality and reasonability of the evidence. And there is perhaps no better way to stimulate the public's fear than by the sensationalized stories of sex offenders.

Sex offenses are indeed serious offenses; however, fear-based legislation often presumes that *all* sex crimes are dangerous, predatory or particularly heinous. Consequently, defendants accused of a sex crime are threatened with lengthy minimum mandatory sentences and enticed to accept plea agreements. Differentiating between penalties for sex offenses and non-sex offenses may be appealing from a philosophical point of view, especially if the media hype is to be believed, yet it is both illogical and fiscally irresponsible. When we respond to reports of a sex offense in fear, we tend to lash out at the people we fear rather than those who are truly dangerous. Consequently, longer sentences are imposed, and such sentences often result in life in prison.[36]

Tragically, many "lifers" serving time for a sex offense received such a sentence because they refused to accept a plea agreement for an offense they did not commit (presumption of innocence). They exercised their Constitutional right to go to trial to prove their innocence. Nevertheless, although they were found guilty at trial, some truly are innocent. How many people have been convicted of a crime only to be exonerated dozens of years later? Too many! In the mid-eighteenth century, British jurist William Blackstone affirmed, "It is better that ten guilty persons escape than one innocent suffer." How many innocent people have we allowed to suffer in and out of prison because the *fear* of sex offenders has led us to abolish reason and pervert justice?

In recent years, American legislators have criminalized many behaviors, allowing police to arrest millions of people each year—almost eleven million in 2015 alone.[37] Stephen Bibas, Professor of Law and Criminology at the University of Pennsylvania Law School, contends that the criminal justice system has become a "capacious, onerous machinery that sweeps everyone in" and plea bargains, with their swift finality, are what keep the machinery running smoothly.[38] Legislators have added so many criminal codes that in 2013 Appellate Judge Neil Gorsuch (now on the United States Supreme Court) publicly raised concerns. "What happens to individual freedom and equality—and the very conception of law itself—when the criminal code comes to cover so many facets of daily life that prosecutors can almost choose their targets with impunity?"[39] In 1980, approximately 1.8 million Americans were in jail, prison, or under the jurisdiction of probation and parole. By 2015, that number skyrocketed to nearly seven million, an increase of over 375 percent![40] The number of people in jail and prison or under supervision, on probation or parole, in the United States today is roughly equivalent to the entire population of the state of Arizona!

Does the American criminal justice system—from the establishment and enforcement of the law to the prosecution and imprisonment of those who are accused of violating such laws—produce justice? Americans pledge allegiance to a republic with "liberty and justice for all." Citizens enjoy the right to remain silent when accused of a criminal offense. Yet by choosing to remain silent in the face of *injustice*, justice is denied to others. Their willing or negligent silence allows injustice to prevail, and violates the fundamental precepts of this country and the pledge "of liberty and justice for all."

Ultimately the only reasonable answer, or at least a place to start, is through beginning a dialogue. Justice will only be restored when all of the stakeholders commit to creating and participating in a constructive and compassionate dialogue, opening themselves up to the complexities of the problems at hand, and begin solving the tough problems—such as mass incarceration and injustice—through mediation rather than force. Dialogue among those who strenuously disagree builds foundations and gives birth to mutual compassion, transforms difficult conflicts, and creates a caring and just community. But first, we must face and examine our greatest enemy—the culture of fear!

2 – *The Culture of Fear*

Fear! Demonstrations, riots, Ebola, West Nile virus, pipe bombs, gang violence, biological warfare, immigrants, Muslim extremists, ISIS, "breaking news"—these are just a few of the fears we face each day. Are these imaginary or legitimate threats, or are they perhaps simply what others want us to fear for their own agenda or profit?

Americans live in a culture of doubt and fear, while living in one of the safest and most prosperous times in history. It is reasonable to be fearful when bad things actually happen. If the house is on fire, we fear for the health and safety of our loved ones. Yet once we know they are safe, we realize that fear serves no useful purpose. It will not extinguish the flames. A student may be fearful of an upcoming exam, yet only preparation and reason—not panic and procrastination—will calm such fear. Each day Americans live and react in fear, most of which proves to be baseless. It has been suggested that 95 percent of the things we worry about never actually happen, and there is little or nothing we can do about the 5 percent that does happen. Bad things do occur. Yet it is how we appropriately *respond* in such situations rather than how we impulsively *react* that makes a difference in how we survive and grow in spite of such things.

Since the 1990s, "fear mongers have knocked the optimism out of us by stuffing us full of negative presumptions about our fellow citizens and social institutions. The United States is a wealthy nation. We have the resources to feed, house, educate, insure, and disarm our communities if we resolve to do so."[41] Living in fear then is a choice; unfortunately, it is also contagious. Why is fear so contagious? "Why do we spend tens of billions of dollars and man hours each year on largely mythical hazards like … prison cells occupied by people who pose little threat or danger to others, or programs designed to protect young people from dangers that few of them will ever face."[42]

Neil Strauss notes, "We are living in the most fear-mongering time in human history. The main reason for this is the tremendous amount of power and money available to individuals and organizations that can propagate and perpetuate these fears…. To mass media, insurance companies, Big Pharma, advocacy groups, lawyers, politicians, and so many more, your fear is worth *billions*. And fortunately, for them, your fear is very easy to manipulate. We are hardwired to respond to fear above everything else. If we miss an opportunity for abundance, life goes on; if we miss an important fear cue, it doesn't."[43] In addition, the Prison Industrial Complex—consisting not only of private for-profit prisons, but also various vendors that supply it—thrives on the perpetuation of a sense of impending danger and fear. The Prison Industrial Complex has a guaranteed income and increasing profits, as long as fear, and the subsequent epidemic of mass imprisonment, can be maintained.

Fear is a powerful emotional response. It triggers the emotional brain long before the logical brain has a chance to respond rationally. As an emotion, fear begins in the unconscious mind. The stimulus is assembled, labeled, and categorized with other similar experiences. For example, when walking in the dark across the backyard, we may catch a glimpse (stimulus) of what appears to be a snake in the grass. If we are deathly afraid of snakes (as many of us are), this stimulus triggers the emotional response of fear. Our heart rate increases, our palms began sweating, and we prepare to flee as our fight-or-flight response system takes control of our body. Yet as soon as we recognize it is only the garden hose, our logical (conscious) mind takes over and calms our fear. In fact, we may even laugh at ourselves for having such an irrational response to a simple garden hose, and hope no one else saw our fearful reaction. So how can we use our logical (conscious) mind to resist being manipulated by those who create and spread fear for personal, political, and corporate gain? The first step is to understand that although "the emotion may look like fear, sound like fear, and smell like fear… it is actually something quite different."[44]

According to neuroscientist Joseph Ledoux at the New York University for Neuroscience, most of what we fear, such as the corruption of government officials, cyber terrorism, corporate tracking of personal information, terrorist attacks, and criminals, such as identity thieves, robbers (and sex offenders), has nothing to do with fear. "What we are talking about is *anxiety*, not fear." Fear is a response to a present threat; anxiety is a more complex and highly manipulatable response to something one anticipates might be a threat in the future. It is a worry about something that hasn't happened and may never happen."[45]

Anxiety is an experience of uncertainty, whereas fear is danger that seems certain. Someone may suffer anxiety towards snakes, but they do not constantly live with the physical and emotional sensations accompanying fear. Nevertheless, people (especially the media and advertising industry) often engage our propensity to be fearful as a lever to exploit us for personal, political, financial, and corporate gain. Promoting a danger that seems certain becomes a tool to manipulate others, through social media and other group situations, to whip others into a frenzied state. An enhanced state of alarm exists when like-minded people feed on each other's emotions. Such social dynamics create a "groupthink phenomenon in which group members excessively seek group concurrence, suppress dissent to maintain group harmony, and blindly convince themselves that the group's position is correct. Groupthink is a process that can lead groups (unfortunately including lawmakers) to make hasty and often bad decisions."[46]

As an example, *The Chapman University Study on American Fears* indicates that 70 percent of the country is afraid of terrorism, the economy, government corruption, identify theft, and a whole range of fantastical imaginations. In the 2016 U.S. presidential election, then-candidate Donald Trump warned, "We're not going to have a country if things don't change." Trump's rhetoric fanned the flames. "They (immigrants, including Hispanics, Muslims, and others) are bringing in drugs. They're bringing in crime. They're rapists. It's only getting worse. You walk down the street, you get shot." Trump's answer was to "Build a wall. Ban the Muslims. Obama founded ISIS. Hillary is the devil. Death, destructions, violence, poverty, weakness! And I (Trump) alone can make America safe again."[47] Or can he? Is America unsafe? Are we being "choked with fear"? Why are we so afraid of things that may or may not happen?

Candidate Trump was tapping into many of the fears propagated and promoted by the media. Yet in *The Culture of Fear*, sociologist Barry Glassner notes, "Americans are living in the safest place and at the safest time in human history."[48] "Around the globe, household wealth, longevity and education are on the rise, while violent crime and extreme poverty are down. In the United States, life expectancy is higher than ever, our air is the cleanest it's been in a decade… and *violent crime has been trending down* since 1991."[49]

Journalist Kurt Anderson notes, "For most of the twentieth century, national news media felt obliged to pursue and present some rough approximations of the truth rather than to promote a truth, let alone fictions …. (Yet today) they believe that incorrect and preposterous assertions circulated in the mass media have become the price of freedom of speech."[50] Fear-mongering "news pundits" on both the right and the left work to keep their constituents riled up in a fanatical and frantic state of fear and unrest. Americans are now immersed in an unending onslaught of propaganda and "alternative facts" fueled by biased radio and television news commentators and anyone with a social media presence. The inmates have escaped from the asylum and they are running loose on the internet. Anderson continues:

> Before the web, *cockamamie ideas and outright falsehoods could not spread nearly as fast or widely, so it was much easier for reason and reasonableness (and justice) to prevail.* Before the web, *institutionalizing any one alternate reality required the long hard work of hundreds of fulltime militants. In the digital age, however, every tribe, fiefdom, principality, and region of Fantasyland—every screwball with a computer and*

internet connection—suddenly had an unprecedented way to instruct and rile up and mobilize believers, and to recruit more. False beliefs were rendered both more real seeming and more contagious, creating a kind of a fantasy cascade in which millions of bedoolzed Americans surfed and swam....Before the web, it really wasn't easy to stumble across false or crazy information passing itself off as true.[51]

Consequently, before the web, "alternative facts" such as that anyone who commits any sexual offense is a dangerous predator, that sex offender recidivism rates are "frightening and high", or that requiring certain people to register could protect the community and neighborhoods from harm and other "cockamamie ideas and falsehoods" did not even come to mind. And if they did, reason was free to combat unreason and truth could overcome fear. Yet today, "the internet entitles and equips all the proponents of unreason and error (and fear) to a previously unimaginable degree."[52] We are drowning in a culture of fear, of our own making, and are being fed to a frenzy by the demagogues profiting from such fears.

The culture of fear originates and thrives on media sensationalism. The unrelenting and pernicious onslaught of sensationalized "news" stories creates and sustains this pandemic of fear. The "truth" is presented by the media in such a way as to create an illusion of impending danger by exaggerating as many catastrophes, collisions, and crimes as possible. When local news is insufficient, bad news is imported from anywhere in the world. Yet why do such tragedies dominate the local evening news for days in so many American cities? Could it be that we are addicted to fear, or could it be that the media stands to gain by inducing and manipulating us to "stay tuned?" Television news and news magazines, e.g., *Dateline, 20/20, Crime Watch*, et.al, survive and thrive on scares and cause unrest in your neighborhood and around the world.

Suddenly, things that never mattered before, and things that were not even on the radar, become of critical and life-changing importance. Supposedly, "white" Americans are becoming an endangered species, as every criminal is considered as one who is dealing drugs, raping and taking away many jobs. Family members who were once at peace with each other are suddenly taking sides over issues in which they have no personal involvement or knowledge, or issues that previously posed no danger, but now seem to be of critical and life-threatening importance. Consequently, we live in a society choked with fear.

Chris Bader, one of the architects of the Chapman University *Survey on American Fears,* notes, "The longer we delve into fears, the more I see fear as a response to uncertainty. If there is a crack in human psychology into which *demagogues* wiggle, it is by offering psychological relief from the anxiety created by uncertainty. Because when people are unsure—or made to feel unsure—and not in control of their safety, their finances, families, possessions, communities or future, their natural inclination is to grasp for certainty. This is where a good scapegoat comes in."[53] Politicians, business leaders, entertainers, and media and entertainment moguls are being exposed each day for their sexual impropriety and abusive behaviors. Could sex offenders be the scapegoats we need in order to assuage our own consciences from our growing decline in conventional sexual morality?[54]

Americans have a long history of creating scapegoats—someone else to blame for many of their troubles. For example, there is an appalling history of how the early settlers and government of this country dealt with Native Americans. Because of suspicion and rumors, many of these indigenous people were rounded up, robbed of their lands, and forced to relocate to "reservations." In addition, in the spring of 1942, following the Japanese attack on Pearl Harbor, the U.S. government subjected the Japanese American population to various atrocities. The government justified the mass incarceration of Japanese Americans as a "military necessity," arguing that it could not distinguish loyal Japanese Americans from disloyal ones.[55] A more recent example comes shortly after the 9/11 attacks. Muslim Americans were subjected to discrimination and violence, as they became scapegoats for much of the anxiety and fear of others. In addition, violence spilled over to Sikhs, who are not Muslim, due to the misconceptions that their turbans identified them as Muslims. Innocent people were killed and injured tragically because they *looked* Muslim. Such cultural xenophobia provides multiple examples of

America's obsession with fear and of the prejudice and ignorance that leads to injustice. And while there are many issues capturing our imaginations and feeding our fears, one of the greatest fears comes with only two words: SEX OFFENDERS.

If the media is to be believed, dangerous predators are lurking in school classrooms, in youth sports organizations, in scouting and in church groups, and behind every tree or bush in the neighborhood. While sex offenses *are* serious offenses, and they do significant and serious harm to the victims, not everything we call a sex offense is a "serious" offense. Also, while a few sex offenders are "dangerous predators," most are not. For example, in 2009, the Georgia Sex Offender Registration and Review Board surveyed Georgia's seventeen thousand registered sex offenders and found that 65 percent of the registrants (over eleven thousand) were of little or no threat and ought to be released from supervision and registration requirements. Eight hundred and fifty were considered "dangerous" and one hundred of those were deemed "predatory." Nevertheless, the legislators refused to make any changes.[56]

The bottom line—literally, the bottom line in terms of *profits*—for the news organizations is that sex offense stories make great news accounts. They encourage viewers to stay tuned and to seek further updates. These stories capture the attention and imagination and stimulate fear.

What drives such media sensationalizing? Perhaps one reason for media sensationalism is competition with other media. For the past several decades, producers of television shows, movies, internet content, and video games have increased the sexual content of and began featuring explicit demonstrations of sexual images and behaviors in their products. Such demonstrations are an appeal and an appeasement to society's more prurient and salacious desires. "Sex crime" dramas detailing the accounts of the *Special Victims Unit* (SVU) as well as various "news magazines" e.g., *20/20, Crime Watch Daily,* and *To Catch a Predator*, feed viewers' imaginations and fantasies as well as creating and heightening certain fears. The internet and movie streaming services (Netflix, HULU, et al.) allow affordable and anonymous access to almost every form of pornography and stories of sexual violence. Many people who may be embarrassed at being seen coming out of a theater showing a sexually explicit movie may now view such material in the privacy of their own home.[57] Unfortunately, their children and teenagers often have the same access and can view this same material. In addition, given the instant news environment of the internet, traditional news organizations need to find a way to attract and retain viewers. There is no better bait than a sex story—especially one that reports on a *sexual offense*.

For example, local news in Arizona will report a story of a sexual offense as "breaking news," regardless of its locale, source, or veracity. The story of a teacher being charged with sexual conduct with a seventeen-year-old student in Florida may even lead the Arizona evening news, even though neither the victim nor the perpetrator have ever been to Arizona nor have any Arizona connections. What is the purpose or relevance of such reporting? What can it be other than to incite fears and create suspicion of every teacher or other person who might work with children and teens? Po$$ibly, it attract$ viewer$ and increa$e$ rating$!

The media's sensationalized fear-mongering costs the American public tens of billions of dollars each year in unnecessary imprisonments and supervision, not to mention the labor required to maintain a sex offender registry that most experts recognize as "unjust and ineffective." Fear cannot stand in the face of truth. But unfortunately the news media is less interested in reporting the truth than they are in maintaining viewers, readers, and profitability. Consequently, the only "truth" that is reported is the "truth" that will create and sustain fears, and increase ratings and profits.

Unless a criminal is banging on your door, living in fear is a useless response. We do not live with a rapid heart rate, sweaty palms, or standing ready to flee. Fear is a response to a *present* threat; anxiety is a manipulatable response to something one anticipates might be a threat in the *future*. It is a worry about something that hasn't happened and may never happen. Fear—whether real or imaginary—must be dealt with in the moment. Anxiety is managed and even conquered with *increased information and truth*. Therefore the best way to deal with the possibility of a sex offender living in the neighborhood is not by living in fear, but by seeking more information and living in truth. Perhaps one way of lessening—or even eliminating—the anxiety of having a sex offender move into the neighborhood is by beginning a conversation with the individual and learning more about them, rather than relying on the media's sensationalized news reports.

In Section 2, "Perspective on People,", we will begin looking at individual stories and some of the devastating effects of injustice; but first, the next chapter in this section, "Complexities," examines some possibilities for dealing with the dynamic, generative, and social complexities concerning former sex offenders and entertains and explores strategies for transforming injustice into justice.

3 – Complexities

The *culture of fear* creates webs of complexities and difficulties that are not easily resolved, and are even more difficult to transform. Fears and anxieties interweave and entangle with one another. They self-perpetuate, creating more fears and inflaming existing ones. The resulting inferno devastates and destroys everything in its path, including many relationships and opportunities to do good. But perhaps even more, it sears our ability to feel, blinds our ability to see, and prevents us from hearing the painful cries of others.

Without feeling, seeing, or hearing we are sense-*less*. We lose the ability to be present to ourselves and become useless to others. Without feeling, our minds are confused; we possess no understanding of spiritual things; we become alienated from God and isolated from the very thing—the very One—who can help us. (Ephesians 4:17-19) Blinded by fear, we cannot see the pain and suffering of others, nor the cause of our own troubles. Deafened by fear and anxieties, we cannot hear the cries of the helpless, or the cries emanating from within our own broken and hurting souls, nor can we experience the joy of serving. Our daily lives become as hopelessly entangled as a ball of string. Every situation or difficulty appears to be an insurmountable problem. The good news is that there is a way out, a way of disentangling these things, and a way to feel, to see, and to hear. But we must first seek to understand the problem(s) we face before we know what to do. We must fearlessly and carefully examine the challenges and difficulties we face.

Mediation expert Adam Kahane suggests that problems become difficult and resistant to change because they are *complex* in three unique ways. These include:

- *A high **dynamic** complexity, i.e., the cause and effect are far apart in space and time and are hard to grasp from firsthand experience*
- *A high **generative** complexity, i.e., they unfold in unfamiliar and unpredictable ways,* and
- *A high **social** complexity, i.e., the people involved see things very differently.*

Therefore, the problems become polarized and stuck.[58]

We do not solve difficult problems well. Unfortunately, amidst a growing sense of powerlessness, force is often used to solve difficult problems. In America today, divisions between red or blue, liberal or conservative, black or white, alt-right or alt-left, or a myriad of other artificial distinctions render us unfeeling, blind, and deaf—senseless. Clinging to fear, prejudices, and ignorance hinders the resolution of the simplest of issues, and prevents and destroys any opportunity for the transformation of these complex or intricate matters.

There is a better way to work toward eliminating injustice and establishing "justice for all" and to identify legitimate fears and transform challenging problems. It involves utilizing skills that not commonly used, but which many people possess and which everyone is capable of developing. Complex problems may only be solved if *all of the people* who are part of the problem work together creatively to understand the situation and improve it.[59]

Those who choose to continue embracing their own fears, their own prejudices, and to remain ignorant will inevitably remain part of the problem and miss their opportunity to be part of the solution. By choosing to remain entrapped in their present pain, they forfeit their own present potential. In choosing to remain silent, they remain mired in the mundane and miss the miraculous. It need not be so.

One of the world's leaders in creative conflict resolution, Adam Kahane, states, "We get stuck by holding tightly to our own opinions, plans, identities, and truths. But when we relax and are present and open up our minds and hearts and wills, we get unstuck and we unstick the world around us."⁶⁰ The way we talk and *listen* expresses our relationship with the world. When we fall into the trap of telling and *not listening*, we close ourselves off from being changed by the world and we limit ourselves to being able to change the world only by force. But when we talk and *listen* with an open mind, an open heart, and an open spirit, we bring forth our better selves and a better world.⁶¹

The key to effective communication is not simply to discuss various issues. It is not planning or proving a point by engaging in angry rhetoric and partisan debates. When opponents engage in a conversation, there may be a bit of discussion, but rarely any *dialogue*. Very little time is spent listening; rather, we wait for an opening to respond. *People do not listen—they reload.*⁶²

Any conversation towards a more merciful justice or considering evidence-based reforms in the criminal justice system tends to create animated and adversarial discussions and debates. These discussions proceed along a familiar course, with each side quoting their experts and using hard data (i.e. statistics) to back up their claims. Yet even the root of the word "discussion" means to "shake apart,"⁶³ leading towards a "decision" to "cut off."⁶⁴ Discussions naturally seek closure and completion, whereas dialogues open *new* possibilities and seek *new* options. "Decide" means to resolve difficulties by cutting through them. Yet, all too often, something important may be cut off and carelessly or even unintentionally discarded.

Dialogue, however, explores the nature of choice and facilitates the choosing and selecting among alternatives. Differentiating between discussion, debate, and dialogue⁶⁵ is far more than simple semantics; it is the pathway to transforming conflicts instead of forcing a one-sided victory or compromise. Engaging in dialogue has the potential to evoke new insights and to reorder our knowledge, particularly in the "taken for granted" assumptions that people bring to the table.⁶⁶ One such assumption is about sex offender recidivism. (Recidivism is the tendency to return to criminal behavior, and therefore to prison.)

One of the greatest impediments to establishing a constructive and compassionate dialogue is false and misleading information.

Unfortunately, much of the information inflaming the public's fear and anxiety concerning sex offenders is based on faulty and misleading statistics. This is probably a good time to share my views on the use of statistics. I dislike them. They are often misleading and frequently useless. A very wise man (my father) often said, "Statistics don't lie, but many people lie with statistics." Advocates on *both* sides of complex problems often use and abuse statistics to support their own fearful, prejudicial, and ignorant claims. Such claims can be misleading and useless.

The most frequently cited statistics used by both sides in justifying their fear and crying out against injustice are *recidivism* rates. *Both sides are guilty of prejudice.* Victim advocates, legislators, and even United States Supreme Court Justices cite recidivism rates as being "frightening and high"—as high as *80 percent*. Yet sex offenders and their advocates tend to quote *only* the lowest published rates of *3.5 percent*. Neither side is listening. Neither side is seeking the truth. Both sides are seeking to "win" a debate rather seeking to engage in a constructive dialogue.

So where and how did such great discrepancy in recidivism rates begin? How can some people maintain that recidivism rates are "frightening and high" while others assert that they are extremely low? In 1985, Robert Longo, a rehabilitation counselor in the Oregon prison system, was interviewed for an HBO special, *Rapists: Can They Be Stopped*. Many of Longo's innovative treatment methods (methods that have today been largely debunked and discarded by the treatment community) were featured in the program. Yet because of the notoriety he gained from the program, the editors of *Psychology Today*[67] invited him to write an article for their publication. In the article, Longo states, "Most untreated sex offenders released from prison go on to commit more offenses, indeed as many as *80 percent* do." Longo suggested *later* that it was an *estimate* based on the numbers he was seeing *in his program* for *some subpopulations of sex offenders* who didn't finish treatment. His assertion was not even meant as an estimate of rates among re-offense in his own program, which he said ranged from *10 – 15 percent*. The point of the piece, and his undocumented assertion, was to show that *effective treatment works*.[68] But the truth was never disclosed. The fear of an 80 percent recidivism rate by sex offenders—whether founded in fact or not—was sufficient to lay the foundation for lawmakers to begin abolishing reason and perverting justice.

In 2002, United States Supreme Court Justice Anthony Kennedy wrote, "The recidivism rate of untreated offenders has been estimated to be as high as *80 percent*" and that a treatment program "gives inmates a basis… to identify the traits that cause such a *frightening and high* risk of recidivism."[69] The following year, in *McKune v. Lile*, Justice Kennedy once again offered the majority opinion of the court, "[the state] could conclude that a conviction for a sex offense provides evidence of a *substantial risk* of recidivism. The legislature's findings are consistent with the grave concern over the high rate of recidivism among convicted sex offenders and their dangerousness as a class. The risk of recidivism posed by sex offenders is *'frightening and high.'*"[70]

In a research paper, *"Frightening and High": The Supreme Court's Crucial Mistake About Sex Crime Statistics*, Arizona State University Distinguished Professor of Law Ira Ellman notes:

> *Residency restrictions [based on sex offender registration]…are severe enough to exclude registrants [sex offenders] from most available housing in their community, preventing them from living with their families. Separate 'presence restrictions' in many communities bar registrants from using public libraries or enjoying public parks with their families. Their registration formally excludes them from many jobs, and as a practical matter keeps them from many more. The registration requirement typically extends for decades and in some states, such as California, for the rest of their lifetime, with no path off of the registry for most registrants. Challenges to the registration requirements and the consequences that flow from it, are usually turned back by the courts and politicians who often quote Justice Kennedy's dramatic language describing the recidivism rate for sex offense as 'frightening and high.' A Lexis search of legal materials found that phrase in ninety-one judicial opinions well*

as briefs in 101 cases.

The use of the terms "frightening and high" originated with Longo's unsubstantiated inference and has *no basis in truth or fact*. Ellman's research exposed Longo's article in *Psychology Today* as the source for the confusion. "But," Ellman continues, "the statement [alleging an 80 percent recidivism rate] is a bare assertion: the *Psychology Today* article contains no supporting reference for it. Nor does the author [Longo] possess the scientific credentials that would qualify him as an expert on recidivism at trial. He is a counselor, not a scholar of sex crimes or re-offense rates, and the cited article is not about recidivism statistics. It is about a counseling program he ran in an Oregon prison."[71]

Ellman also asks, "So, what is the re-offense rate for those convicted of a sex offense? One cannot calculate a recidivism rate without first defining 're-offense', without specifying the time period to employ, and without considering whether one needs to distinguish among different groups of offenders said to have committed a sexual offense."[72]

As an example, "Sex offenders vary in their risk for sexual recidivism. Previous meta-analyses found that the average *sexual recidivism* rates of identified sexual offenders are in the 7 percent to 15 percent range after five to six years of follow-up."[73] In addition, an additional study of 7,740 sex offenders from twenty-one samples showed the risk of sexual recidivism was *highest during the first few years after release and decreased substantially the longer individuals remained sexual-offense free in the community.* The five-year rate for *high-risk* sexual offenders (defined by Static-99[74] scores) was 22 percent at the time of release but *decreased* to 4.2 percent for the offenders in the same static risk category who remained offense free in the community for ten years. The recidivism rates of the low risk offenders were consistently low (1 percent to 5 percent) for all time periods.[75] Unlike Longo, Hanson and his associates (the group who presented the meta-analysis) are all scholars in the field of recidivism research and their finding were published in the *Journal of Interpersonal Violence*.[76]

Their analysis corresponds closely with the findings of the Georgia Sex Offender Registration and Review Board's survey of Georgia's seventeen thousand sex offenders. In their comprehensive study, they recognized that 65 per cent of the registrants (over eleven thousand) were of *little or no threat* to the public and recommended that these ex-offenders ought to be released from any supervision and registration requirements. In addition, 850 were considered "dangerous" and a hundred of those were deemed "predatory."[77] Clearly, statistics do not lie, but it is easy to lie and create misunderstandings and divisions through the use and abuse of statistics.

Victim advocates and legislators are not alone in their abuse of statistics. For in attempting to prove their point and justify their position, sex offenders and their advocates are equally guilty. Sex offenders generally quote *only* the 3.5 percent recidivism rate found in the *Bureau of Justice Statistics* report, *Recidivism of Sex Offenders Released from Prison in 1994*. This report lists (among other things) the following recidivism rates:[78]

Table 3

	All	Rapists	Sexual Assaults	Child Molesters	Statutory Rapists
Percent rearrested for any new sex crime within three years	5.3%	5.5%	5.5%	5.1%	5.0%
Percent reconvicted for any new sex crime within three years	3.5%	3.2%	3.7%	3.5%	3.6%

rates. However, longer follow-up periods have the tendency to yield *decreasing* recidivism rates. In fact, the longer an individual remains offense free in the community, the more likely it is that he or she will continue to remain so. This affirms Ellman's assertion that we cannot calculate recidivism without first defining "re-offense," the time period, and different groups of offenders.[79] *Different definitions, different times, and differing groups being considered are going to yield different results.* That is the inherent nature, corruption, and intentional (and unintentional) deception involved in the use and abuse of statistics.

Victims and their advocates, including legislators, politicians, and even United States Supreme Court Justices, often use and abuse statistics to confirm their own fears, prejudices, and ignorance and to inflict and expose extreme injustice on sex offenders and their families. Yet ex-offenders and their advocates also use and abuse their own statistics to confirm their own fears, prejudices, and ignorance.

By focusing only on the low recidivism rates, they minimize the great harm done to the victim(s) and to the community.

Nevertheless, in seeking to use *only statistics* in supporting their cause, both sides fail to prove their point or win their position. Statistics prevent each side from *feeling* the other's pain; they prevent them from *seeing* the harm; and they prevent them from being able to *listen* to each other. The path to transforming the conflict—the tough problems—will begin when both offenders and victims began talking and listening to each other. That is the hope and overall purpose of this book.

Working through the complexities of tough problems is not about winning or losing. It is about transformation. It is about dialogue. Dialogue empowers people to learn from and with each other. It offers a route for understanding and effectiveness that goes to the heart of the meanings we make and the thinking and feeling that underlies what we do.[80] What if we created an opportunity for a dialogue among all the parties concerned and actually began listening to each other?

The American criminal justice system is far from perfect. Innocent people are too often convicted, and too often the guilty go free. What happens to society when innocent people endure injustice? What happens when guilty people are subjected to injustice? When we remain committed only to endless discussions or mired and entrenched in contentious debates, we forfeit the opportunity to engage in a meaningful and compassionate dialogue. Unless we choose to pursue a courageous dialogue, both innocent and guilty people are destroyed. Former Vice President Al Gore writes, "The persistence and sustained reliance on falsehoods as the basis for policy, even in the face of massive and well-understood evidence to the contrary, has reached levels that were previously unimaginable; therefore, reason, logic, and truth play a sharply diminished role in the way our legislators now make important decisions."[81]

Establishing and maintaining a compassionate dialogue is perhaps the only way to solve tough problems. Undoubtedly, sex offenses cause significant and serious physical, emotional, psychological, and spiritual harm to their victims. But, on the other hand, the pandemic of fear driving the societal dehumanization and exclusion of ex-offenders from opportunities for redemption and reconciliation also causes significant and serious harm. There is no one "right" answer.

Why does anyone commit a sexual offense? No one is born a pedophile or a rapist, and rarely does anyone ultimately seek to offend. Rather, sex offenses more often than not grow out of a deep woundedness and from traumatic experiences that are often unspoken and unhealed. For example, extensive research shows that when compared with others, sex offenders suffered more than three times the odds of childhood sexual abuse (CSA), twice the odds of physical abuse, thirteen times the odds of verbal abuse, and more than four times the odds of emotional neglect, and were very likely to have come from broken homes.[82] Indeed, most observers note that 85 – 90 percent of all male prisoners grew up in a home without a father or a positive male role model.

The multiple maltreatments (sexual, physical, and emotional abuse, and neglect), along with other forms of family dysfunction, suggest that many offenders were raised in a disordered social environment.[83] Such adverse family environments provide a fertile breeding ground for someone to begin developing the propensities leading toward committing a sexual offense. Abuse, neglect, and family dysfunction often lead to mistrust, hostility, and insecure attachment, which then contribute to social rejection, loneliness, negative peer associations, and delinquent behavior.[84] As difficult as it may seem, broken people break things. If we begin viewing former sex offenders as being broken, do we help them heal by placing them in a cage and condemning them to a lifetime of societal exclusion and shame? Certainly not! Moreover, we must also face the fact that viewing victims only as victims and never seeing them as broken people who can heal does not serve them any better. We need to examine our views of both the offender and the offended for both to heal fully. By changing the system in regards to offenders, we also change how we view victims. The two are inextricably tied together. Long prison sentences often also mean long victimization, but little justice for anyone.

Just as there are two sides to every issue, there are both the offenders and the offended. The question is not about how we win, but how we *come together and heal*. Changing the justice system on such a difficult issue may take a miracle. How do we find or work to create such a miracle?

The greatest miracles often come through the greatest difficulties. The greatest victories often arrive through the most impossible circumstances. When there is no dialogue, the status quo wins. And seeking only to maintain the current status quo allows injustice to prevail. Can good people fail to, or refuse to, engage in dialogue regarding complex and testing problems and consistently remain silent in the face of injustice and still be considered "good"?

The miraculous option—in which neither side "wins" nor "loses"—is when people on both sides begin setting aside their personal fears, prejudices, and ignorance and begin working together to change the status quo. The "miraculous" option becomes possible when all of the parties affected begin talking and listening to one another until they find a way forward—a way that neither of them had previously seen or even considered possible.

Sex offenses encompass a high dynamic complexity, i.e., the cause and effect are far apart in space and time, and so they are hard to grasp from firsthand experience. The immediate *effect* is the offense; however, long-term effects ripple throughout the lives of the victim(s), their families, and community members. The effects are far-reaching and debilitating. The effects on the offender consist of an arrest, trial, conviction, and imprisonment, as well as a lifetime of suffering and shame. These effects are also far-reaching and debilitating. But what is the *cause* of the offense?

The effects of the offense are obvious; however, the cause is much more difficult to discern. Unfortunately, the criminal justice system places little emphasis on determining the *cause* of the offense as they are primarily concerned only with the effect, i.e., "what happened." Deviant and predatory behaviors are not a normal state. No one is born to commit a sexual offense. As previously noted, there is no "pedophile gene," and no one is born a rapist. Why then do these things happen? Why do some people choose to offend? Why do some people suspend empathy or concern for anyone other than themselves? Offenses occur as a matter of choice, of deliberate decisions emanating from various thoughts and feelings. But what is the *cause*? What is the relation between American society's growing obsession with sexual freedom, and perversity and an increasing incidence of sexual violence? Perhaps a few reasons to consider are the changing views of sexual practices in American culture, the epidemic of broken and single parent families, the effect of the sexual saturation in all forms of media content, and the "modern values" being portrayed in television, movies, and the internet.

Jonathan Grant suggests, "Our culture's romantic idealism encourages us to boldly explore the boundless playground of sexual relationships. Yet we quickly succumb to 'exposure' when faced with the corrosive elements of our culture's hypersexuality and its fatalism about lasting commitments. This combination of factors has turned romantic relationships from places of adventure and exhilarating risks into crevasses of death and despair."[85] It is often out of these "crevasses of death and despair" that the foundation is formed or strengthened that often leads to the unthinkable—the commission of a sexual offense.

Grant posits, "The growing influence of the [secular] worldview over the last century or so has resulted in sex being progressively separated from the social contexts that had traditionally given it its essential meaning. Sex has been redefined as a separate, autonomous entity in its own right, and an independent commodity that can be reclassified under any category."[86] Against such growing separation of sex from traditional boundaries has been the growing dissolution of marriage—not only from divorce but also from others simply cohabitating without the benefits of marriage. Such relationships are inherently unstable, yet often produce children. The "hook-up" culture, and unprotected sex, produces even more children. The epidemic of broken and single-parent homes increases the frequency of child abuse, not only from physical, emotional, and psychological trauma, but all too frequently from the sexual abuse of children and teenagers. Such abuse comes from contact offenses with "family" members and/or early exposure to sexuality (including pornography) that young minds simply do not possess the capacity to understand.

Changes in entertainment content and media also impact the modern view of sexuality. What are the subtle and not so subtle messages concerning sexuality that are being conveyed today through television shows such as *The Big Bang Theory*, *Good Behavior*, *Animal Kingdom*, *Mr. Robot*, *Claws*, *Will* and various reality shows where sex without strings, without responsibility, and without consequence, are frequently portrayed as *normal*?   What about movies and television shows that leave nothing to the imagination regarding nudity, sexuality, or deviant and bizarre sexual practices? In 2017, the USA cable channel featured a primetime showing of the sexually explicit and degrading movie *Fifty Shades of Grey* featuring sadistic and masochistic sexual practices between "consenting adults." It was supposedly censored for television, yet very little was left to the imagination.

Pornography is becoming ubiquitous throughout every aspect of our culture. In 2011, pornography was a business worth thirteen billion dollars a year in the U.S., and ninety-seven billion a year worldwide.[87] Wendy and Larry Maltz define pornography as "any sexually explicit material that is intended to be, or is used as, a sexual outlet. The goal of pornography is to create a connection between the user and the material (usually for the economic benefit of the maker) instead of with a human being."[88] One researcher notes, "Softcore pornography is being replaced by a pornified culture in which advertising, music, TV shows and mainstream movies are constantly and excessively sexualized. Whether you are an intentional user of pornography is irrelevant when pornographic images constantly bombard users of mainstream media."[89] The effect is particularly noticeable (and troublesome) among children and young adults. "The impact of these shifts is significant as young people's lives move from Dr. Seuss to porn without them even realizing it."[90]

There are many connections between the acceptance and tolerance of pornography and the acceptance and tolerance of the sexual exploitation of women and children. Prostitution is often referred to as the world's oldest profession, but is much more accurately referred to as the "world's oldest oppression." Vednita Carter, founder of *Breaking Free,* notes a strong link between prostitution and pornography: "Pornography is prostitution on paper." [91]

The complete cause of American society's growing obsession with sexual freedom and perversity is beyond the scope of this book. Yet is it possible that by immersing our children and ourselves in the toxic brine of immorality and sexual practices, without boundaries or restraint, we are somehow contributing to the problem of sexual offenses? Is it possible that some of the fear and prejudice driving the fear of sex offenders is somehow related to a residual societal guilt and the need for a convenient scapegoat to assuage our consciences from our own sexual perversity? Why are we not surprised when powerful politicians, high profile athletes, religious leaders, business leaders, and others are caught up in deviant, if not illegal and offensive, sexual behaviors? Yet many of these politicians and media executives are the same ones calling for greater punishments and restrictions for all sex offenders.

Obviously, someone who commits a sexual offense makes a decision to offend. There comes a moment when they suspend empathy for anyone other than themselves. What begins as a sexual "sin" degenerates into a sexual "offense," and there is no way to undo what has been done. One counselor notes that the line between a sexual sin and a sexual offense is a very thin one. Those who engage in sexual sin are only a decision or circumstance away from committing a sexual offense. One such example is what constitutes "legal" and "illegal" pornography, or what is commonly called child porn or Child Sex Abuse Images (CSAI).[92] What does it say about our cultural obsession with sex, youth, and self-image when the largest single genre of "legal" pornography material consists of sexually graphic and explicit images of *young teenage girls* who have just turned eighteen years of age? While it may be considered a sexual *sin* to view legal pornography—including "barely legal" images of teenage girls—with internet access, affordability and anonymity, it is far too easy to intentionally or even unintentionally obtain images of child or teen sex abuse as well. The line between a sexual sin and a sexual offense is crossed very easily, and perhaps more often than we may realize or admit.

In regard to pornography and other sexual conduct, there are differing opinions and standards about the legal age of consent. Nevertheless, to suggest that it is somehow socially acceptable to objectify an eighteen-year-old young woman (or man) for sexual gratification and pleasure, but that a similar image of anyone younger is somehow unacceptable, obscures a legitimate and important question of morality and ethical behavior with an arbitrary legal standard. Psychologist Karen Franklin differentiates between *pedophiles* (those sexually attracted to pre-pubescent children—generally under the age of twelve) versus *hebephiles* (those sexually attracted to post pubescent—but *underage* teens),

> *The absurdity of describing erotic attraction to adolescents as a mental abnormality [or necessarily criminal behavior] is that most heterosexual men are sexually attracted to teenage girls (who happen to be at the peak of their reproductive fertility.) This fact is established by multiple research studies over the past several decades. Such findings are of no surprise to the moguls of popular culture or to the advertising industry [that] use provocative images of teen girls and boys to sell everything from clothing to cars.*[93]

Companies such as Abercrombie and Fitch, Victoria's Secret and others advertise sexy lingerie for teens and preteens. National talent competitions, including *American Idol* and *America's Got Talent*, often feature and promote young singers and dancers performing very adult and sexually suggestive songs and dance routines. A popular music video featured teen pop idol Miley Cyrus swinging naked on a "wrecking ball." What message does this send to viewers of all ages concerning body image, healthy relationships, and sexuality?

This raises the following question: at what age is sexual abuse through objectification and self-gratification acceptable? At what age is the *sexual abuse* inflicted upon men and women in the "legal" sex trade, e.g., those engaged in legal prostitution, exotic dancers, porn actors, and so on, no longer causing emotional, physical and psychological harm? Is it legal for some and illegal for others? Has society degraded to the point that certain forms of sexual abuse are acceptable, but others are criminal acts? Are we—especially members of the modern day church—in danger of being without excuse, judging another, and condemning ourselves because we are practicing the same (or strikingly similar) sins? (See Romans 2:1.)

The dynamic complexity of this issue stems from the fact that the cause and effect are far apart in space and time so they are hard to grasp from firsthand experience. As we have seen, the causes of sexual offending are not readily apparent. Moreover, unless an individual has been an offender or a victim, they possess no firsthand experience. We know that sex offenders often hate their sin. They experience guilt, sorrow, and massive amounts of shame, depression, and despair. They frequently make promises to themselves and to God to stop their deviant and destructive behavior. But without counseling or treatment, these promises are rarely, if ever, kept. Many of them suffer acute depression, self-hated, and they either attempt or commit suicide.

Many sex offenders are sex addicts, although certainly most sex addicts are not sex offenders in the criminal sense. Nevertheless, for both addicts and many offenders their core beliefs extend from the four faulty core beliefs identified by Patrick Carnes in *Out of the Shadows*. Carnes notes,

- *First, an addict believes, "I am a bad and unworthy person."*
- *Second, "No one would love me as I am."*
- *Third, "My needs are never going to be met if I must depend on others."*
- *Fourth, "Sex is my most important need."*[94]

Why are we criminalizing behaviors and oppressing an addict, rather than providing an environment to help them heal and recover as well as holding them accountable for their actions? Why do sex addicts who cross the line and commit a sex offense not seek professional or community help? Is it perhaps because mandatory reporting laws do not allow secrets to be kept or held in confidence? Counselors, medical professionals, school officials, and others are legally required to notify the authorities when they become aware that an offense has been committed (such as a teenager becoming pregnant) or that a minor or other vulnerable person may be in danger. Consequently, the threat of judgment, condemnation, and incarceration hinders potential offenders or actual offenders from receiving or ever seeking help.

In 1992, Vermont began offering a help line for those who were tempted to commit a sexual offense. The idea began when Fran Henry, a woman who had been sexually abused by her father in the 1960s, sought counseling and treatment. In the course of her treatment, she confronted her father and realized that she did not want to see him in jail, but she wanted to make it less likely that other children would suffer. She began visiting men in prison who had been convicted of a sexual offense and asking, "What would have stopped you?" Many indicated that counseling would have been helpful and thought they would have stopped if someone had picked up on the warning signs and confronted them sooner. Unfortunately, the mandatory reporting laws—intended to protect children—very likely place even more children at risk by lessening the chance that any offender or potential offender would self-report any incident or temptation.

In the 1980s, Johns Hopkins University offered a program for sexual offenders at a clinic in Baltimore. Yet during the following decade, state laws were passed requiring the police to be notified about any incidents of child abuse disclosed during treatment. The clinic saw the rate of referrals to its program decline to zero as patients stopped disclosing previously unknown offenses. A paper published in 1991 concluded that no children were being protected by the law and that therapy was being made less effective.[95]

The path to transforming the dynamic complexity of this issue is a very difficult one. Yet the way to transformation begins when the advocates for both offenders and victims find the courage to set aside their fears and prejudices and begin countering their ignorance with knowledge and began talking and *listening* to each other. This process and the possibilities of this vision will be discussed later in this book.

In addition to being dynamically complex, sex offenses are also generatively complex, i.e. they unfold in unfamiliar and unpredictable ways. The generative complexity of the problems with sex offenders depends on whether we choose to continue the injustice or if we boldly and courageously choose to engage in a dialogue. Problems include low generative complexity if they continue in familiar and predictable ways. For example, victims and their advocates maintain that what seems to work in the present, i.e., injustice, will continue to work in the future. *Revenge and retribution feels good for a season, but it never leads to healing, reconciliation, and restoration.* The cost of allowing such injustice to continue is increasing prison populations, and the spending of millions of tax dollars in imprisonment, probation costs, and law enforcement man-hours required to maintain an ever-increasing sex offender registry, not to mention the loss of human and social capital from those we incarcerate.

Injustice rises from a lack of knowledge and a pandemic of fears. Injustice does not overcome fear; it is enhanced by it. Ultimately, the only reasonable answer comes through beginning a dialogue. Justice will only be restored when all the stakeholders commit to joining in a constructive and compassionate dialogue and begin solving the tough problems through mediation rather than force. Of course, what appears to be a low generative complexity, i.e., things pretty much remaining the same, quickly becomes a high generative complexity with its future suddenly becoming unpredictable and unfamiliar when participants find the courage to begin a dialogue. What happens if we open ourselves up to change and seek to begin transforming the conflict through mediation rather than force?

Legislators attempt to cope with the unfamiliar and unpredictable in familiar and predictable ways by making and enforcing laws to punish offenders. They fail or refuse to recognize that there are two ways to "unstick" a problem. One way is to act unilaterally, i.e. to impose a solution by violence or force. This maintains the status quo. The second is for the actors (the stakeholders) to start talking and listening to each other with the hopeful intent of finding a way forward together.[96] The authoritarian approach does not work for solving complex problems, because complex problems can only be solved with the *participation of the people* who are part of the problem. Everyone needs to be empowered to come to the table.

In addition to being dynamically and generatively complex, sex offenses are also socially complex, i.e. the people involved see things very differently. Consequently, the problems become polarized and stuck. Many individuals and organizations on each side of this issue engage in passionate, but partisan debates. Victim advocates include the Center for Missing and Exploited Children, Chris Hanson's *To Catch a Predator* and *Crime Watch*, and many others. Those who advocate for sex offenders include the National Association for the Reform of Sex Offender Laws (NARSOL), Women Against the Registry, Citizens United for the Rehabilitation of Errants (CURE), and others. Each of these organizations spends time and effort advocating on behalf of their particular group. Yet relatively little time is spent talking with or listening to each other.

A problem has **low** social complexity if the people who are part of the problem share common assumptions, values, rationales, and objectives. A problem has **high** social complexity if the people involved look at things very differently.[97] Obviously, given the level of fear, prejudice, and ignorance on one side and the secrecy and deviancy on the other, stakeholders involved on both sides of sexual offenses see things very differently. If they didn't, there wouldn't be any conflict. Problems of high social complexity cannot be peacefully solved by authorities from on high. Presently, legislative answers driven by fear, prejudice, and ignorance only lead to injustice. On the other hand, it is socially unthinkable and irresponsible to allow the molestation of children and innocent victims to continue without consequence. All of the people involved must participate in creating and implementing a solution.

One such example of high social complexity occurred in South Africa when Nelson Mandela and indigenous tribal leaders, and F.W. De Klerk and other South African government officials, began working together to overcome Apartheid—the rigid racial division between the governing white minority population and the non-white majority population. If the complexities of Apartheid may be unwound and peacefully resolved, can the inherent complexities involving sex offenders also not be resolved?

Social complexity requires us to talk, not just with people who see things the same way we do, but also especially with those who see things differently, even those we don't like. We must stretch way beyond our comfort zone.[98] One of the greatest difficulties facing both sides is the desire or insistence on *being right*, i.e., if I am "right" everyone who disagrees with me must be "wrong." Kahane mentions, "Such a desire to be completely clean (or always being right) is like an obsessive-compulsive disorder where the patient is always washing his hands. It is not healthy to try to keep yourself away from everything unclean in the world."[99] Those who are unwilling to enter into the pain and suffering endured by sex offenders and victims alike will never be able to help them heal.

Working to transform problems that involve social complexities requires us to learn to listen reflectively. It is not enough to be able to hear the chorus of voices; we must also hear the contribution of our own voice. It is not enough to be able to see others in the picture of what is going on; we must also see what we ourselves are doing. It is not enough to be observers of the problem situation; we must recognize ourselves as actors who influence the outcome. We must commit to becoming involved.[100] It has been said, "If you are not part of the solution, you are part of the problem." Actually, it is better said, "If you not part of the problem, you can't be part of the solution."[101]

Part of the way forward includes people—good people—who have previously chosen to remain silent, to begin caring. The kind of caring described by theologian Henri Nouwen: "Real care is not ambiguous. Real care excludes indifference and is the opposite of apathy… [The basic meaning of care is] to grieve, to experience sorrow, to cry out with. We feel quite uncomfortable with an invitation to enter into someone's pain before doing something about it."[102]

Most of all, complexities involve people. In the case of sex offenses, they involve victims and offenders. The next section, *Perspectives on People*, exposes the stereotypes and generalizations of both victims *and* offenders surrounding the commission of a sex offense and the effect such stereotypes and generalizations have on sex offenders and their families.

4 – Victim Profiles

Innocent victims of sexual abuse are wounded emotionally, psychologically, and physically. For them, sex abuse is personal. It means that someone else touched them—assaulted them in an intimate way that was not wanted and could not be stopped.[103] Sexual abuse violently intrudes into their privacy. It destroys their sense of safety and security. In fact, sexual abuse touches the soul in ways that are never forgotten. Innocent victims come from every walk of life. Every age, gender, ethnicity, income level, political, or religious belief is represented. Their commonality is in their suffering, yet there is great diversity even in their commonality. Those who have undergone sexual abuse and offense are not necessarily the stereotypical victims represented by the media. Not all are molested as children. Not all are violently raped. They are all indeed victims; however, they are not all the same. And in the interest and pursuit of justice, we must learn to differentiate between the degrees of victimhood so that justice may be applied and injustice avoided.

Innocent victims of child molestation and predatory rape comprise the stereotypical victim profile of a sexual offense. Those who commit these offenses often fit the stereotypical sex offender profile. Victims of child molestation and predatory rape endure great physical, mental, emotional, psychological, and spiritual harm. Many may never fully recover or heal from such wounds. These heinous and predatory crimes very reasonably create a universal public outcry, but far too often, the media sensationalism of such crimes helps produce and perpetuate an all-encompassing epidemic of fear.

Innocent victims are the stereotypical victims; but do such stereotypical profiles serve to increase our understanding and promote justice? What if everyone who is labeled as a victim is not entirely *innocent*? Not all sex offenses are the same, and not all victims of sexual offense are the same. There are, in fact, at least three categories of direct victims: *innocent*, *consensual*, and *complicit*. Among the *innocent*, two classes are neither culpable nor responsible for the offense. The first class is prepubescent children who perceive no sexual interest of their own other than perhaps an innocent self-awareness and personal exploration. They do not willingly participate in any molestation and assault. They are entirely innocent victims of such cruel and heinous acts. The second class is those who are subjected to predatory and violent sexual assaults in their homes, in the park, or in other public and private places. Frequently, their only contact with the offender is immediately prior to and during the offense. Many such victims are sexually assaulted by an unknown predator, although many victims of date rape as well as victims of *illicit* and *unethical consent* (discussed below) also fall into this category. All of these *innocent* victims are unwillingly subjected to heinous and vile predatory sexual assaults.

The second category of victim is *consensual*. Consenting victims are minors in the early or late stages of puberty who are often willing participants in the "offense." Since minors are legally incompetent to give consent, we refer to them as *incompetent consenting*.[104] In some instances, the victim has often confessed to initiating the sexual contact. Unfortunately, most state laws expect the older participant (defendant) to exercise extraordinary judgment and self-control in escaping the passion of the moment and to diligently avoid any temptation or sexual contact with the victim. Unfortunately, most young men (men are usually the offenders) often choose not to exercise such personal restraint, even though they are perfectly capable of doing so. As a side note, while some neurobiologists suggest that the human brain is not fully developed until the age of twenty-five, this does not justify or explain the seemingly unreasonable and unrestrained sexual behavior of teenagers, college students, and other young adults. Many young men (and women) in this generation (or any recent generation at the same age) are capable of making sound, reasonable, and mature judgments even in their late teens and early twenties. There are some who are (or were) capable of sexual self-control, in spite of the sexual saturation of modern American culture.[105] While everyone is responsible for their own choices and decisions, it is also important to consider the many cultural differences and standards in establishing justice.

Instances of *incompetent consent* usually occur when the offender and the victim are relatively close in age. They are often engaged in a dating relationship and are mutually attracted to each other. Identifying "offenders" in this category is much more difficult. Laws vary widely from state to state.[106] For example, thirty-five states set the minimum age of consent for sexual activity as age sixteen. Therefore, in many of these states, a twenty-one-year-old (or older) and a sixteen-year-old may engage in consensual sexual conduct without legal consequence. Yet in at least thirteen states (including Arizona), the very same conduct is a *felony*. In addition, twenty-four states allow a fourteen-year-old and an eighteen-year-old (maximum four-year age difference) to engage in *consensual* sexual conduct without any criminal ramifications. However, in twenty-six states (including Arizona[107]), such conduct is a *felony sexual offense* and is often categorized, prosecuted, and punished as a "dangerous crime against children."[108] Unfortunately, even engaging in certain *incompetent consensual* sexual conduct results in the offender being listed on the sex offender registry. In many cases, such registration is for a lifetime, whereas the *exact same sexual conduct* in other states is legal.

It is important to note that not all *consenting* victims are *incompetent consenting*. Extreme care must be taken to ascertain the source of the "consent." In the worst case, consent is not really consent, but the result of careful and intentional grooming by the offender. These are identified as *illicit consent*.[109] In such instances, consent is gained through illicit means, such as lowering the victim's resistance and inhibitions with alcohol or drugs, or with various promises and presents.

There is an insidious and predatory aspect of such manipulative grooming. In such instances, the offender never has noble intentions. They seek only to gain the confidence and permission of the victim through various persuasive and controlling techniques. They offer promises and presents before the sexual assault, but resort to various forms of intimidation and threats afterwards. In such cases, not only has the victim's innocence been stolen, but they are also emotionally traumatized into believing or feeling that they are at least partially responsible for the offense. Such traumatization escalates the harm and exacerbates the victim's suffering and pain.

A sexual offense of *unethical consent*[110] occurs when the offender is *significantly* older (usually more than four years) or holds a position of power and control over the victim. Some teachers, coaches, scout leaders, step-parents (and even parents), religious leaders, and other older adults often systematically control, manipulate, and groom their victims with the ignoble intentions of committing a sexual assault. These victims are not consenting through an independent and informed decision, but rather through deliberate and intentional manipulation by the offenders own prurient and deviant desires. These types of offenses bear a great similarity to child molestation and predatory rape (*innocent* victims) in that there is a clear distinction between the victim and the offender (predator).

The third category of victim is *complicit*. Some minor victims intentionally misrepresent their age either by possessing a fake ID, misstating their age on the internet, or by engaging in certain adult activities such as gambling or drinking alcohol in public places. In addition, minors often post and share sexually explicit pictures of themselves without inducement or force or sexting. They are unaware that they are themselves then technically and legally guilty of creating and distributing child pornography. If the sexual conduct from such *complicity* is consensual, i.e., no coercion or force is involved and there is no criminal intent (mens rea)[111], is the *complicit* victim actually a victim with no culpability or do they bear some measure of responsibility for their situation or circumstance?

There is no doubt that *innocent* victims fit the stereotypical profile of victims. Those who molest a child or commit a predatory and violent rape or who systematically groom their victims into submitting to their own deviant desires commit a classic sexual offense, i.e., molestation, rape, and devious seduction. Moreover, *illicit* and *unethical consenting* victims, such as those who are maliciously groomed or from whom consent has been obtained by illicit means, are certainly *innocent* victims. Not only has their innocence been compromised, they are often emotionally traumatized by believing or feeling that they are somehow responsible for the offense. Yet it is less clear or even reasonable that a minor who lovingly, intentionally, and mutually engages in sexual conduct is truly a victim, (*incompetent consent*) especially when the victim and the offender are relatively close in age.

The purpose of criminal law is to protect the public from harm by inflicting punishment upon those who commit various criminal acts. Within the philosophy of criminal law various theories are employed to justify or explain the goals of punishment, including retribution, rehabilitation, and restoration. Obviously, innocent victims deserve justice. Yet does this mean that those who commit a molestation, rape, or devious seduction ought to be imprisoned for life and permanently discarded or barred from normal participation in society? Should their punishment continue long after their prison sentence has been completed? Does true justice require revenge and retribution or must a just and civil society also seek to offer some form of redemptive, rehabilitative, and restorative justice? If it is important that we work together to insure that there are "no more victims," must we not also work towards an understanding and belief that "no one is disposable?" No one is beyond redemption.

Of course, there is no justification for any sexual offense— provided it is truly an offense, i.e., there is no *incompetent consent* or *complicity* by the victim. Nevertheless, when there is legitimate *incompetent consent* or the victim is *complicit*, it is difficult to imagine justice is served through a justice of punishment with retribution and revenge. In fact, in most cases such extreme justice leads to injustice. Nevertheless, where the elements of an offense against an *innocent* victim are present, i.e., child molestation, predatory rape, or devious seduction, then justice must intervene. Yet in light of current legislative and prosecutorial conduct—wherein the *prosecutor* decides not only which offenders and offenses to charge but also whether to seek enhancement or aggravation, whether to offer a plea and what it will be, and whether a particular sentence is stipulated[112]—then the injustice proffered by the *elected* officials (legislatures and prosecutors) serves only to enforce injustice even over the judiciary's objectivity and wisdom.

It is also worth noting that many offenders were once victims of various offenses and childhood trauma themselves. There is no *causation*, i.e., being a victim of sexual offense does not predict that someone will offend, nor is it justification for any offense. Nevertheless, researchers found significant *correlations* between individuals who have been sexually abused or suffered childhood trauma and who commit sexual offenses later in life. As noted, ex-offenders had significantly more incidents of childhood sexual abuse, emotional neglect, and a high probability of coming from broken and dysfunctional homes.

As noted in the previous chapter, "The growing influence of the (secular) worldview over the last century has resulted in sex being progressively separated from the social contexts that had traditionally given it its essential meaning."[113] In such separation, we are immersing our children and ourselves in the toxic brine of sexual immorality and deviant sexual practices without boundaries or restraint. The harmful conflation of broken and wounded offenders, as well as the permissiveness and moral laxness of American culture, exposes a myriad of teenagers and young adults—especially *complicit* and *incompetent* consenting victims—to an environment where sexual offending may be inevitable.

When someone is labeled as a *sex offender* and their name and other identifying information appears on the sex offender registry (and corresponding neighborhood flyers), there is no notation as to whether their victim was *innocent*, *incompetent*, *illicit* or *unethical consenting*, or *complicit*. Certainly, there are *innocent* victims and, as noted above, at least some of what may appear as "consent" may not be consent at all. Nevertheless, in the case for true *consent* (age notwithstanding) or in the case of *complicity* on the part of the victim, has any true victimization occurred? How can a minor who willingly and knowingly (without any other inducement) participated in a sexual act become a victim solely at the hand of the offender? This is not to suggest that such relationships are appropriate or healthy. In fact, sexual conduct and promiscuity at such a young age is usually regrettable. In addition, minors who willfully and knowingly engage in *complicit* (deceptive) behavior and sexual conduct are in many ways actually "preying" on the offenders. This is not to suggest that a young woman who misrepresents her age to deceive and entice an older man into a sexual relationship should *necessarily* be charged with a criminal offense, although each case must stand on its own merits. Nevertheless, it does suggest that counseling is strongly indicated and that her family and social interactions ought to be carefully examined as an alternative to the criminal punishment of the "offender."

In these latter cases, *incompetent consensual* and *complicit,* it is reasonable to question whether the offender is alone responsible for any serious physical, emotional, or psychological harm. Moreover, in the case of *incompetent consent*, how much harm is done when the *offender* (usually the male) is charged with a sexual offense, imprisoned, and forced to register as a sex offender for the rest of his life? What is the impact of such extreme injustice on the victim? Do they feel responsible for getting the offender "in trouble"? As long as the offender is in prison or subject to parole or probation supervision, they will generally not be allowed to have any contact with the victim, nor will he (or she) be allowed to function as a parent to any children who may have been conceived during such crimes. This leads to a question: which is a greater risk in a just and civil society—irresponsible young men who boast of multiple "baby mamas" of legal age, yet who offer little or no support in helping to raise such "unplanned" children—or an eighteen-year-old young man who impregnates his fifteen-year-old girlfriend with her intentional and loving participation and *incompetent consent* and who then commits to helping to support and raise their child? The man who is a "deadbeat dad" is subjected to financial justice, but the loving teenage father who is labeled as a "sex offender" is subjected to an extreme and criminal injustice.

Sex offenses against innocent victims inflict great physical, mental, emotional, psychological, and spiritual harm. Some victims never fully recover or heal from it. Such heinous and predatory crimes create a universal public outcry. Yet just as not every victim fits the same victim-profile, not everyone who commits a sexual offense fits the same stereotypical offender-profile. Are all sex offenders the same? In the next chapter, we begin exploring the different types of offenders and hear some of their own stories.

5 – *Offenses and Offenders*

In the previous chapter, we described the various types of victims and mentioned how some sex offenders were once victims of various forms of abuse themselves. In the introduction, we posed the question of what we must know and understand before we know what to do. Therefore, this chapter focuses on knowing and understanding those whom we label as sex offenders, without fear, prejudice, or ignorance coloring our opinion, so we can begin a dialogue about what we must do.

Before discussing the various types of offenders and sharing some of their stories, it is important to consider the various types of offenses. All sex offenses are sexual sin; however, just as not all victims are the same, not all offenses are the same. Sexual offenses may be divided into at least seven different types: child molestation, predatory rape, sexual conduct with minor, immature and opportunistic crimes, reverse predation, boundary violators, and sex addicts.

The sexual molestation of a child is a heinous and vile act. It occurs when a child—a prepubescent victim (usually under the age of twelve)—is subjected to any sexual contact or abuse. The victim is innocent. Child molestation victims endure great physical, mental, emotional, psychological and spiritual harm and many never fully recover or heal. The offender deliberately abuses his power and authority, manipulates the situation, and robs the child of their innocence. Child molestation is the most universally hated of all sexual offenses. Unfortunately, regardless of the nature of the offense, the image of the child molester prevails in most media stereotypes of *anyone* accused of a sexual offense. Yet not all sex offenses involve the molestation of a child, and to presume so is horribly unjust.

Predatory rape is defined as when the victim is unknown to the attacker or, if known, has not consented to sexual contact. It is often more a crime of power and anger than sexual gratification. Nevertheless, such offenses are no less destructive, vile, or heinous. As with victims of child molestation, victims of predatory rape suffer great harm and may never fully recover or heal. Predatory rape and child molestation represent many of the *innocent* victims of sexual offenses; however, these crimes represent only a portion of every crime classified as a sexual offense. For example, in the Arizona Department of Corrections, as of 2010, less than one-half of the prisoners being held for sexual offenses were charged with child molestation or sexual assault (rape).

The offense of sexual conduct with a minor creates the most confusion because of many distinctive factors. In each instance, the act is immoral and ill advised. But not every case involving sexual conduct with a minor is the same. As noted in the previous chapter, age of consent laws are often confusing and vary significantly between states. In some instances, a single year may make a difference between an *illegal* and an *immoral* act. In addition, there are the instances of *incompetent consent* in which the victim initiates the conduct and is an eager and willing participant. Nevertheless, there are also instances where a minor victim is maliciously and intentionally targeted and subjected to a sexual assault and suffers serious trauma. Unfortunately, media reports of sexual conduct with a minor do not differentiate between various types of offenses, and unfair generalizations are often made which leads to injustice.

Immature and opportunistic offenses, such as offenses labeled as sexual conduct with a minor, represent a wide variety of circumstances and victims. Many offenses of this nature *lack any criminal intent*. Such offenses occur more from immorality and immaturity than

OFFENSES AND OFFENDERS

criminality, e.g., young adults (18 – 21) and older minors often become sexually involved with younger minors (14 – 17) in the workplace or neighborhood. In addition, varying age of consent laws, cultural norms, and morals contribute to the confusion. In some instances, children engaging in exploratory sexual conduct with other children, e.g., playing doctor or house, are in principle guilty of a sexual offense and technically violate child molestation or sexual abuse laws. As ridiculous as this may sound, too many children have been charged with a sexual crime for their immature and opportunistic actions, even while their actions lacked any specific criminal intent.

Reverse-predation sexual offenses occur when *victims* intentionally misrepresent their age either by possessing a fake ID, by lying about their age on the internet, or by engaging in certain adult activities in public. In each of these instances, the "victim" engaged in a deceitful act with criminal intent; yet they are seldom, if ever, charged with a criminal act. They are viewed as the victim of a sexual offense. In addition, teenagers posting and sharing sexually explicit pictures of themselves or others (sexting) are technically guilty of creating and distributing child pornography. However, the person in possession of such sexually explicit images (selfies) are often charged with a crime while the person who created (and sent) the image is viewed as an innocent victim.

Boundary violators represent a very serious form of sexual offense. These violations occur when a parent, step-parent, other family member, teacher, coach, youth leader, or anyone else in a position of trust or authority commits a sexual assault. There is no argument for *incompetent* consent. The victim is unduly influenced and groomed by the offender. The offender uses their power and authority, or manipulates the victim for their own deviant sexual gratification. Such abuse is a flagrant violation of personal and sexual boundaries. These offenses represent a violation of the victim's sexual innocence and are a violation of trust. These offenses inflict great harm.

Not all sex addicts are sex offenders, and not all sex offenders are sex addicts; nevertheless, many sex offenders are sex addicts. Sex addiction does not excuse or justify a sexual offense; rather it is an important contributing factor. Many sex addicts/offenders engage in internet-based crimes, i.e., luring a minor for sexual purposes, and the downloading of child-abuse sexual images (child porn). Sex addicts may also often habitually engage in prostitution, exhibitionism, and voyeurism.

All of the above actions are sex offenses. Yet it is important to note that all of these are fundamentally different offenses. Therefore, if we are to act without fear, prejudice, or ignorance we must know and understand such differences as we seek equal justice under the law. But who are the offenders? What are the differences in their stories?

Justice requires judgment. A just judgment includes what happened, who was involved, and even more importantly, *why* it happened. A thief who steals food to feed his family violates the law, but may be less *morally* culpable than someone who steals out of laziness or greed. Justice includes considering both mitigating and aggravating circumstances before pronouncing judgment. The physical evidence may be the same in two different cases, yet the circumstances are usually different. Who are the individuals who commit these offenses, and what are their stories?

All of the following stories involving sexual offenses are based on actual cases of men I have met in prison. Names, places, and some details have been modified or combined to protect the identity of those involved. These stories are presented here because they are different from what is generally reported in the media. Nevertheless, similar stories happen every day. The media sensationalizes certain stories for their own advantage—stories such as the predatory kidnapping, rape, and murder of innocent and vulnerable children. For example, when a teacher, coach, or youth leader commits a sexual offense, every person in such a position may become suspect. Nevertheless, the overwhelming majority of adults who work with children and teens are good and honorable people. They cannot imagine molesting a child or grooming and sexually assaulting one of their students. Such crimes are unthinkable. In a similar manner, while there are still too many children molested, too many people who prey on vulnerable teenagers, and too many predatory and violent sexual assaults, such crimes represent only some of incidents that are now labeled as a sexual offense.

For the most part, the following stories are not likely to be reported in the media—at least not in this detail or perspective. These stories are not presented to minimize or justify what happened, but rather to help create an understanding that the story revealed in the media is never the whole story. They are presented here to invite an understanding of the "rest of the story" and to help lessen our anxiety. If we can set aside our anxiety, perhaps we can even find compassion and extend an invitation to begin a dialogue of redemption and healing for everyone.

Story 1 – Spring Break – 2005

Adam looked forward to spring break, not to party, but to plan and prepare for his future. Just a few weeks earlier, he'd received a letter of acceptance from a Big Ten University offering him a full ride scholarship and the opportunity to pursue his passion and dream to play college football, and then perhaps one day in the National Football League. His best friend, Scott, who was a year older, was already attending the same university on a football scholarship. Scott's influence had opened the door for the college scouts from the Big Ten to come to Adam's small Arizona town to recruit this talented running back. Adam was a three-year letterman, an Academic All-American, and heavily recruited by many of the PAC-12 schools, as well as others throughout the country. Yet more than anything, he wanted to follow Scott, who was his mentor, "big brother," and the one friend who had helped him during his sophomore year when Adam's father was tragically killed by a drunk driver.

Brian, Adam's father, had coached both the boys throughout their years in Pop Warner football and had continued teaching and challenging them when they began junior high and high school. Brian had always insisted that the boys complete their studies first, as football was a rewarding passion, but usually not a career. Getting a good education was the most important thing, regardless of what happened on the field. Adam was excited about following in his friend Scott's footsteps at the university in the fall. But a decision Adam made—actually a series of seemingly unimportant decisions he made—were about to change his life and the lives of many around him forever.

The seemingly unimportant decisions began when he decided to stay home during spring break rather than joining his mother and younger siblings on the family's Disneyland trip. He planned to continue his training and workouts for the upcoming football season. It wasn't unusual or unreasonable for Adam to stay home alone. He had turned eighteen years old a few weeks earlier and was a responsible and dedicated young man. He had not fallen into the party scene of using drugs and alcohol; in fact, if anything, his only real addiction was football. In memory of his father, during his latter high school years, he dedicated himself to excellence in the classroom and on the field. He earned the respect of his coaches, teachers, and administrators at the high school and was envied and admired by his teammates and other students. Nevertheless, the fateful decision to stay home would change his life forever.

Phone calls at one o'clock in the morning rarely bring good news. This one was no exception. Adam's best friend Scott was calling from across the country, desperately asking his younger friend for help. Scott's kid sister, Megan, was in trouble. Megan was a freshman at the same high school as Adam and was looking forward to her fifteenth birthday just a few weeks away. Her mother and father had gone through a bitter divorce several years earlier. Although Megan lived with her mother, she spent every other weekend with her father. Megan's relationship with her father was never comfortable, especially since her big brother had gone away to school. Her father was often angry or drunk, and often both. When he wasn't drunk, he played the role of a typical "Disneyland dad," showering his kids with gifts and trips rather than being a good and responsible parent. The first weekend of spring break was the time Megan was scheduled to spend with her father, so her mother had gone on a camping and fishing trip with her new boyfriend somewhere in northern Arizona.

When Megan showed up at her father's house after school, there was money for pizza and a note saying he would be home late. He was meeting with some clients after work. She knew this meant he would eventually come home drunk. The note said that she was not allowed to go anywhere or have anyone over. She could use the computer and watch movies until he got home. Megan ordered the pizza, did some homework, talked to some friends on her cell phone, watched some movies, and went to bed at eleven o'clock. When her father finally did come home at twelve-thirty in the morning, he was angry and drunk. She had never seen him this drunk or this angry. He accused her of having her friends over and drinking his beer. He began raging and swearing, accusing his teenage daughter for being just like her mother—nothing but a "worthless whore." Her father had never hit her, but she wasn't taking any chances. At the first opportunity, she grabbed her cell phone and ran outside, down the street and away from his rage, but barefoot and wearing nothing but her underwear and nightshirt.

Hiding behind the neighbor's bushes, she thought briefly about calling the police. Yet her father hadn't hit her. He hadn't committed any crime, although he had probably been driving under the influence since the car was parked half in the driveway and half in the front yard. Nevertheless, she thought calling the police seemed useless. Besides, with her mother out of town, she had nowhere else to go. Sooner or later, she knew she would have to go home and face her father, so calling the cops on him seemed like a very bad idea. So she called the only other person she knew she could call in the middle of the night—her big brother, Scott. Even though Scott was nearly 1,700 miles away, at least he would know what to do.

After a brief conversation with Megan, Scott called Adam—not knowing he was also home alone—and asked him to go and rescue his kid sister from their drunk and raging father. Thirty minutes later, Adam called Scott and assured him that Megan was safe and that they would figure out what to do later that day. Unfortunately, Megan had a huge teenage crush on Adam, and she had no problem being rescued by her idol.

Megan was scared and had many questions. How was she going to face her father? What was she going to tell her mother? How much trouble was she in? Nevertheless, she felt safe with Adam. Adam offered her his sister's room; but she was still scared, frightened, and alone, and wanted someone to comfort her. So naturally, she sought comfort in the arms of her hero and idol.

On some level, Adam knew this was a bad idea. Megan was young and attractive. Between Megan's seeking comfort from Adam and having a romantic attraction to him and Adam's poor decision-making, one thing led to another and they soon ended up in the same bed. Afterwards, they both agreed that it should have never happened and would never happen again.

Later that day, when Megan called her father when he was finally sober, she said she had spent the night at a friend's house. She went back home, and all was forgiven and forgotten until several weeks later when she discovered she was pregnant. She had to face the truth and tell her parents; at least her mother, as she feared her father would want to kill Adam.

She wanted to protect Adam. After all, it hadn't been entirely his fault. He had not forced her to do anything she didn't want to do. In fact, she had been the one who had initiated the sexual activity. Neither one of them had planned for things to go that far. Telling her mother was the most difficult part. Megan didn't have a regular boyfriend; in fact, her parents had said she couldn't even date until she was fifteen. But now, shortly after her fifteenth birthday, she was pregnant.

Her mother was understanding, but demanded to know the identity of the father. Who had impregnated her innocent child? Megan explained what happened, and her mother understood and blamed the whole situation on Megan's father. If he had not been irresponsible and drunk, this would never have happened. Nevertheless, that did not change the fact that her fifteen-year-old daughter was pregnant. Something had to be done.

Neither Megan nor her mother considered abortion. While adoption was a possibility, Megan was more interested in keeping her baby. In the meantime, however, she had to get to a doctor and began prenatal care. When the doctor's office learned how she had become pregnant, they were required to notify the authorities. A fourteen-year-old is not permitted to "consent" to sex. Therefore, in the eyes of the law, a crime had been committed and someone needed to be held responsible. And that someone was Adam. The police officer took her statement as she explained what had happened during the weekend of spring break. She admitted her own responsibility in the act; however, Adam was eighteen and an "adult" in the eyes of the law. Therefore, he was responsible for committing a *sexual offense*.

Shortly after discovering she was pregnant, Megan called Adam and talked to him. She didn't want to cause him any trouble. She knew her brother Scott and Adam were best friends and she knew of Adam's dreams of going to college and playing football. She didn't want to interfere with his plans, but felt that he had the right to know about the baby. In her mind, she certainly hadn't been raped; in fact, she had been an eager and willing participant. Nevertheless, the police had to interview Adam.

When the police officer interviewed Adam, his story matched Megan's account of that fateful night of spring break. The officer was sympathetic; Adam seemed like a good kid. Adam admitted to the sexual encounter, regretted it, and was even more concerned that he would soon be a father. In many ways, he was confused. Should he give up his college career, the chance to play football, and change his plans to help raise his child? So many decisions and so much pressure were now on this good student and outstanding athlete. Nevertheless, a few days after the interview with the detective, all of his questions were answered and all of his plans changed when he was arrested and indicted for multiple "sex crimes." The grand jury indictment included five sexual offenses categorized as "dangerous crimes against children." He was held in jail on a $75,000 bond pending trial. If convicted on all counts, he would receive a *minimum mandatory* sentence of over forty-one years in prison.

Adam's mother did not have anything to use as collateral—the money to bail him out—or to hire a criminal defense attorney. Consequently, Adam remained in jail while his case was assigned to a public defender. After several months of negotiating, the public defender assured Adam that he had no defense; in fact, he had certainly committed the crimes even though there was obviously no criminal intent. Adam had confessed to the sexual conduct; but since Megan was only fourteen at the time of the offense, the prosecutor wasn't as sympathetic. Therefore, his only reasonable option was to accept a plea agreement. If he had chosen to go to trial, the law *required* that each sentence be served consecutively, meaning he would be in prison until he was at least fifty-nine years old. If he was convicted—and he would be convicted—the law required that he spend his entire adult life in prison. But there was another choice.

The prosecutor offered Adam a "sweet" plea deal: seven years in prison and a lifetime on probation with "sex offender" terms, and the statutory requirement that he register as a sex offender for the rest of his life. To add insult to injury, while he was on lifetime probation, he could not have any contact with Megan (his "victim") or ever be alone with his child. Even if he were able to get off of probation, the civil consequences of being labeled as a sex offender would also prevent him from ever attending his children's school functions or participating in many meaningful ways as a parent.

Adam's dreams of a college education and of playing football in the Big Ten Conference vanished in one fateful night. By accepting the plea agreement, he would be released from prison when he was twenty-five, but forced to wear the scarlet letter of being labeled as a sex offender for the rest of his life. Those who paid attention to the flyers in the neighborhood or looked him up on the sex offender website would never know the truth; they would only see that he was a "sex offender"—a young man who had supposedly taken advantage of an innocent young girl. Is that the truth or is there more to the story? Is anyone willing to fight for justice, or has justice already been served? Is Adam a dangerous predator, a child molester, or a young man who succumbed to normal hormonal desires with an equally hormonal young woman?

Story 2 – Becoming a Captive by Celebrating Freedom

Sam loved teaching. He loved the martial arts. He especially enjoyed teaching others the ancient arts of self-discipline and self-defense. He opened his own training facility in Ogden, Utah while working part time as an instructor at Weber State University. At twenty-six years old, life was good. But then on one crucial day and one fateful trip to Arizona, his life changed forever.

Sam accepted an invitation to spend the Fourth of July weekend with some friends in Prescott, Arizona. There was a newly-refurbished hotel and casino, and the city hosted an awesome fireworks display.

OFFENSES AND OFFENDERS

July 4th was on a Thursday, so he decided to make it a long weekend, arriving in Prescott late Wednesday night and checking into the Sheraton hotel. Thursday afternoon, he saw Marta in the casino bar. She was beautiful, a strikingly attractive Hispanic woman with large brown eyes and long black and flowing hair. She introduced herself as a graduate student from Arizona State University and that she had come to Prescott for the weekend to get out of the stifling heat in the Valley of the Sun. They shared a few drinks and spent the afternoon at the blackjack tables where she gambled as well—if not better—than Sam. She accepted his invitation to the fireworks display and accompanied him back to his hotel room that night. They spent the weekend together—drinking, gambling, laughing, and enjoying each other's company in the bedroom. There were never any promises or plans about continuing the relationship. He was returning to Ogden and his business, and he assumed she was returning to Tempe to finish her graduate degree. But she had other plans.

Late Sunday evening Marta asked Sam to marry her. They could go to Las Vegas and get married and she could accompany him back to Ogden. She would transfer to Weber State University in Ogden and continue her studies so they could begin their new life together. He enjoyed their time together, but he was not interested in a long-term relationship—especially marriage. Spurned by his rejection, she became angry, threatening to report to the police that she had been raped. So it was up to him—he could marry her or she would go to the cops. He knew there was no evidence of rape. He had introduced her to his friends. Many people in the casino had seen them together, and there was no way anyone could convict him of rape. Nevertheless, Marta made good on her threat to notify the Prescott police and revealed to them that she was only sixteen years old and not twenty-three as stated on her fake ID. She very conveniently left out the part about her own drinking and gambling, but she readily admitted that she was a Mexican citizen and in the United States illegally. She also alleged she had been an innocent victim of Sam's unwanted sexual advances and abuse.

When the detective interviewed Sam, he admitted the *consensual* sexual conduct but denied any knowledge about her being underage.

She had been drinking and gambling alongside of him and using her fake ID at the bar and at the cashier to receive her winnings. How could he have possibly known that she was a minor? Neither the fact that she had misrepresented her age nor that she was in the country illegally (both felony offenses in their own right) were valid defenses. So, Sam was charged with multiple counts of sexual conduct with a minor and with sexual abuse.

He was offered a plea of two and one-half years in prison and five years' probation. Yet his conviction for sexual conduct with a minor included the requirement to register as a sex offender for the rest of his life. His career was ruined. No one would bring their child to a registered sex offender for self-defense lessons, and the university quickly fired him from his teaching position. The Fourth of July trip to Arizona, and few nights of passion had caused him to forfeit his liberty and much of his future.

Once he was released from prison, those who paid attention to the flyers in the neighborhood or looked him up on the sex offender registration web site would never know the truth. They would only see that he was a sex offender who had sexually assaulted a young woman. But is that the truth or is there more to the story? Is anyone willing to fight for justice, or has justice already been served? Is Sam a villain or a victim? Did his action ever rise to the level of "criminal intent" or simple sexual immorality? How could he be convicted of a crime which he had no reasonable way of knowing *was* a crime?

Story 3 – The Careless Caretaker

Steve's future could not have been brighter. He was doing what he loved, in a city and with the people he loved. He had served in the U.S. Air Force as a medic. He'd spent most of that time serving as a physical therapist at a U.S. military hospital in Germany, helping wounded soldiers in rehabilitation and recovery. After being honorably discharged, he returned to the States and settled in Flagstaff, Arizona, where he began working at the Northern Arizona Regional Medical Center. He loved the mountains, the trees, and most of all the winter ski season at the Snow Bowl. He worked as a rehabilitation specialist at the hospital with a part-time gig at the resort during the ski season. With a free lift pass included in his resort compensation, life was good.

His naturally outgoing and helpful personality afforded him many good friends. As a veteran and a diligent and disciplined worker, he earned the respect of his employer, co-workers, and others. He purchased a condo just outside of the city near the base of the mountains, but within easy walking distance of the hospital. He had an on-again and off-again intimate relationship with Pam, one of the emergency room nurses who lived in a condo in the same gated community.

Pam was a thirty-four-year-old single mother of an irrepressible and active fourteen-year old daughter, Karen, who thought she was more like twenty-four than fourteen and was more than a handful to raise. Karen's father had abandoned her and her mother when Karen was an infant, so she never knew him. Being a single parent was fine with Pam while Karen was growing up; but when Karen hit her teenage years, the normally-close mother and daughter relationship became strained. Karen wanted more freedom, but Pam wanted to protect her teenage daughter, so they settled into a loving but often tumultuous relationship, an all too common occurrence for mothers and teenage daughters.

Pam was excited when she was given an opportunity to move to the graveyard shift at the hospital. With the 10 percent shift differential, it meant an immediate raise. She needed the money, but could not imagine leaving Karen home alone at night. Although work was only five minutes away, leaving her fourteen-year-old daughter at home alone every night seemed like a very bad and even an irresponsible idea. But there was another option.

When Steve and Pam were "on" and even when they were not, Steve had established a good relationship with Karen. In the good times, Pam imagined that Steve would be a good stepfather, although, like many young men, he was more interested in doing his own thing and skiing than settling down into a serious relationship. In fact, it seemed that Steve and Pam were "off" during the ski season, but "on" when the weather warmed up and the snow disappeared from the slopes. At any rate, Pam decided to approach Steve about watching over Karen at night. They agreed that Karen could sleep in Steve's guest room, and then join her mother for breakfast at their condo in the morning. Everyone agreed. Steve had no problem watching over his guest. He liked the young girl and had taught her to ski, as she was such a natural on the slopes. Although she was sometimes a handful, Steve wasn't her father. Therefore, their relationship developed more as friends rather than as a teenager and part-time surrogate parent, especially since Karen maintained that she was too old for a "babysitter." But the friendship began turning into a relationship. It was a relationship Steve did not want, but did not turn away from and thought he could handle. He was wrong.

Karen quickly developed a teenage infatuation with her "friend." In her eyes, he was the mature and sophisticated ski instructor. He listened to her stories and problems, even late into the night and long after she should have been in bed. She began leaving him little "love notes" and adding personalized playlists to his smartphone, which Steve thought was "cute" but he was otherwise oblivious to what was really going on. Karen thought she was falling in love with her mother's sometimes-boyfriend.

One Friday night while watching a movie, Karen snuggled up next to Steve on the couch. One "innocent" kiss that night became much more than a kiss as the days and weeks wore on. Soon they were "sleeping" in the same bed. Steve felt incredibly guilty and even knew what he was doing was immoral and illegal, but chose not to stop. He thought he could keep it a secret and keep it under control. He knew he could get in trouble, but he had no idea of the extent of the legal consequences that would change his life forever. He justified his actions by telling himself he had not coerced, seduced, or forced her to do anything. She seemed to want it more than he did. Yet he was the adult and the one responsible. Even over her objections, he would suffer the consequences. But how bad could it be? In his mind, he thought it would be a slap on the wrist, a reprimand, or even a fine. As it turned out, it was much more than that.

The Flagstaff police detectives came to interview him at work after someone reported a troubling post on Karen's social media account. She said she had a wonderful boyfriend, a special lover who understood her and spent time with her. She even was allowed to spend the night at his house. When investigators searched her phone and email accounts, they discovered the intimate emails, explicit photos, and text messages that Steve and Karen had exchanged. Steve was arrested at work, his condo searched, and he was taken to jail and held on a $100,000 bond.

The Coconino County Grand Jury indicted him on seventeen felony sex offenses. They had all of the evidence they needed to convict him. If he had gone to trial, he would have died in prison—a very old and lonely man. The prosecutor offered him a plea agreement of twenty-four years in prison followed by lifetime probation with sex offender terms, and lifetime registration as a sex offender. He would be released from prison when he was fifty-eight, ready to retire but with no money for retirement. His career was over, his friends had abandoned him, and even his family had turned him away.

He knew that, even when he was released from prison, those who paid attention to the flyers in the neighborhood or looked him up on the sex offender registration website would never know the truth. They would only see that he was a sex offender. He would be forever seen as a man who had sexually assaulted an innocent young teenage girl. But is that the truth or is there more to the story? Does the punishment fit the crime? Is Steve a dangerous predator or a young man with poor boundaries and little common sense?

Story 4 – The Analyst Who Investigated Too Much

David was a soldier. A good soldier and an exemplary enlisted man, he had chosen to make the U.S. Air Force his career. He became a keen and gifted military intelligence analyst with a top-secret governmental clearance, and had been entrusted with some of the country's most sensitive information. However, David had a past; not anything he had done, but other things—secret things—that had been done to him. And he never forgot them.

His own father had abandoned the family when David was five years old. David had been an "accident." His three siblings were much older—the youngest being twenty-three when David was born. So rather than dealing with another child, David's father had simply disappeared. David spent a lot of time during his childhood years with

Matt, a family friend who lived down the street. In many ways, Matt served as the father David never had. But when David was ten years old, Matt introduced him to pornography. At first, Matt showed David only "adult" porn, but gradually introduced him to images of young boys and girls being sexually abused. He manipulated and coerced David into undressing and posing for pictures and began sexually abusing him. David hated the abuse, but loved the attention, and in some perverse way enjoyed the way it made him feel. How could something that he knew was so wrong feel so good? When David resisted, Matt threatened to retaliate and said if David told anyone no one would ever believe him. After four years of continuously sexually abusing David, Matt was killed in a traffic accident. Now fourteen years old, David was devastated by the loss of his "friend," and while the accident ended the sexual and physical abuse, the effects of the mental and emotional abuse tormented his soul.

Years of abuse had taken its toll. David became an isolated extrovert. Outwardly friendly but inwardly very much alone, he kept the secrets of the painful past buried deep in his soul. He analyzed everything. So the opportunity to enlist in the Air Force appeared to be a way he could escape—at least from the neighborhood—even if his past followed him. He gained recognition as a very bright and articulate young man and advanced quickly in rank and responsibility. Soon he was conducting intelligence briefings for some of the nation's top military commanders, even while the past memories churned in his soul.

When a fellow soldier was arrested and charged with possession of child sex abuse images (child porn), David wondered if any of the images might be of him as a young boy. Like many men his age, he had viewed more than his share of "legal" porn. In fact, the young women he viewed in the images gave him some of the relationship satisfaction he had been unable to obtain in real life. He'd dated several women, but had never been able to sustain an intimate relationship for more than a few weeks. But now he began wondering if he could find the childhood images that had been taken of him. Were they out there? Had anyone else seen them? Did anyone else know his secret? What if someone found out or recognized him?

He began searching parts of the dark web, looking specifically for child porn. Initially, he wasn't as much interested in the children in the images, but rather looking only for pictures of himself. Yet viewing these images triggered a flood of feelings and memories he had long since consciously forgotten. They stirred something deep inside of him—something he had suppressed, that confused him, but something to which he was inexplicably drawn. He wanted to get help by talking to a counselor or someone who could help him deal with his past and present addictions. But he thought there was no one in whom he could confide without being arrested and forfeiting his career. He loved his job; in fact, he was very good at it. But underneath the intelligence analyst, the demons raged.

He soon began searching for more and more pictures. Some of them disgusted him, but others excited him. He found himself spending hours on the computer, hours when he should have been doing his job. He had heard how others had been arrested when various internet service providers reported suspicious images flowing through their services. So it came as no great surprise when the detectives showed up at his door and arrested him; in fact, it was a relief. Perhaps he could get some help. Perhaps he could get some counseling. Perhaps he could finally free his soul from the demons that controlled him. But help would have to wait; a lengthy prison term waited.

After the detectives seized his computer, he was charged with seventeen sex offenses—"sexual exploitation of a minor." Instead of being charged in federal court where he would have faced a maximum sentence of ten years, he was charged in Arizona where the mandatory minimum sentence for possession of child porn is ten years per picture, to be served consecutively. If he proceeded to trial and was convicted (and there was little doubt that he would be convicted), he would be given a *minimum* sentence of 170 years. Initially, he thought about taking his case to trial because he wanted a chance to tell his story and explain what had happened to him as a child. He acknowledged his guilt and, indeed, had a great deal of remorse. But most of all, he wanted to find help. He wanted to find freedom from the demons that had possessed him for so many years. But deliverance would never come—at least not yet. First, there was prison.

His public defender advised against going to trial. Even with his story, the facts remained. He was in possession of hundreds of images of child porn. And in the eyes of the law, the story of *why* the offense had happened didn't matter, only the facts. If David lost at trial—and he would lose—the judge would have no choice but to sentence him to a minimum of 170 years in prison. His only choice was to accept a plea. His story, however, would never be told—at least not the whole story. The world would only know that he was guilty of possessing hundreds of images of child porn. They would never know his story or the abuse he'd suffered that began this horrible journey. Therefore, he accepted a plea agreement.

David was sentenced to twenty years in prison followed by a lifetime of probation with sex offender terms. He would be released when he was forty-eight years old and required to register as a sex offender for the rest of his life.

Those who would eventually see the flyers in the neighborhood or who looked him up on the sex offender registration website would never know the truth. They would only see that he was a sex offender—a man who was guilty of possessing child pornography. But is that the truth or is there more to the story? Does the punishment fit the crime? Is David a villain, a victim, or both? The system has taken care of him as a villain, but will anyone ever offer him help as a victim? Will he ever be free of the memories? Will he ever be free from the demons?

Story 5 – The Stepdaughter Seduction

Marshall was as serial monogamist—sort of. He was married to only one woman at any given moment; yet there had been five or six of them. Now in his mid-forties, he was no longer satisfied with women his own age, but he was attempting to preserve his own youthfulness with younger women—sometimes much younger. He earned a decent income in sales; yet child support and spousal maintenance obligations from previous marriages limited his disposable income. It also limited his ability to woo younger women with his wealth. His current wife, Robin, had a young teenage daughter, Marcy, who was just beginning to grow into maturity. And just as Marshall's relationship struggled with Robin, Marcy and Robin's relationship had its share of challenges. So when Marshall began focusing more attention on Marcy, she was all too eager for the attention.

During the summer when she turned fifteen, Marshall began inviting Marcy to accompany him on business trips and serve as his "assistant." She was eager to please her stepfather, especially when it included staying in nice hotels and traveling. She would agree to anything to get away from the constant conflicts with her own mother. Marshall soon began grooming her, making sexually explicit comments about her body and inquiring about her boyfriends. Marcy was uncomfortable with her stepfather's remarks. Yet she loved the attention; she felt special and grown up. She loved the many perks, especially traveling and staying in luxury hotels. When Marshall began making sexual advances, she was frightened and confused. After she gave in, he swore her to secrecy saying that if anyone ever found out he would lose everything, and she and her mother would be ruined. It would just be their "little secret."

For the next three years, the sexual abuse continued. She hated the abuse and she hated him. Yet she felt powerless to make it stop. He told her that if she told anyone, she would be exposed as a slut, her future would be ruined, and she'd never have a good relationship with a decent guy her own age. Finally, in desperation, she attempted suicide by taking an overdose of her mother's pain pills. After a brief hospitalization, she entered a mental health facility and eventually revealed to a counselor what had been happening at home. The counselor contacted the police who arranged a confidential confrontational phone call that led to Marshall being arrested and held on a $500,000 bond.

Marshall eventually accepted a plea for twenty-four years in prison followed by lifetime probation. When he is released from prison, he will register as a sex offender for the rest of his life. Thus far, Marshall has not accepted responsibility for his crime. He blames Marcy for "seducing" him and claims that he was unable to resist her advances.

When he is eventually released from prison, the flyers in the neighborhood and the sex offender registration website will note that he is a sex offender—a man who was guilty of sexual conduct and abuse with a minor. It is possible that during his remaining time in prison that he will choose to participate in sex offender treatment. It is possible that he will get past his religiosity, claiming that Jesus has forgiven him and that is all that matters. It is possible that he will come to accept responsibility for his crimes, to recognize why he did what he did, and develop empathy for his victims. It is also possible that he will remain stuck in denial and deception for the rest of his life. And it is possible that he will never "be well."

Summary

Many sex offenders are in some ways victims of circumstances. Some are guilty of youthful indiscretion (Adam), poor decision-making and inappropriate boundaries (Steve), or a situation in which there was no criminal intent (Sam). Yet others, (such as David and Marshall) demonstrated a deliberate indifference towards the law and have suspended any empathy towards innocent and vulnerable victims. Yet true justice must be based on the "truth, the whole truth and nothing but the truth." Therefore, any attempt to impose justice must take into consideration not only what happened, but also *why* it happened— in other words, the whole truth.

The deviant and predatory behavior of sex offenders is not a normal state. No one is born to commit a sexual offense. There is no "pedophile gene." No one is born a rapist. Healing begins for the individual victims, the offender, and the community at large when we work to begin uncovering the *why* of what happened and how healing and recovery are possible. Why do these things happen? Why do some choose to offend? Why do some suspend empathy or concern for anyone other than themselves?

Offenses occur as a matter of choice, of deliberate decisions emanating from various thoughts and feelings. Secret thoughts and suppressed feelings left unattended or unexposed distort the mind, confuse the heart, and scorch the soul. Sexual offenses do not just happen. In most instances, they are deliberate and calculated acts. No child is accidentally molested. No teen is carelessly groomed and seduced. Child sexual abuse images do not "just appear" on the computer screen, and no one is inadvertently or accidentally raped. Assaults against *innocent* victims, i.e., child molestations, deviant seductions, rapes, and the proliferation of child sexual abuse images (child porn) represent something much deeper and much more sinister than the acts may appear. These deviant and destructive acts are committed by those who are broken themselves—deeply wounded and hurting souls—and persons whose own sexual and emotional past is filled with suffering and pain. In many instances, not only do offenders hate the things they do or have done, they also hate themselves.

Sex offenders who commit deviant and destructive acts are in their own perverse way often seeking to medicate their inward suffering and pain. They live in their own form of hell while creating a corresponding hell for their victims. A desperate and deepening cycle of deviant conduct often drives their behavior. Their lives are chaotic on many levels. Their relationships are built on deceptions, finances are often manipulated and concealed, excuses are made, and work and school performance suffers. The addict slides deeper and deeper into the abyss of shame and despair, an abyss from which there appears to be no relief or escape.

Considering such stories and looking deeper into the lives of the people they represent, what is the responsibility and opportunity of a supposedly civilized society? Is it fair to judge and condemn? Is it just to dehumanize and demonize? Is it reasonable for society to impose retribution and revenge and to deny or limit opportunities for repentance, rehabilitation, and restoration? Is there especially an opportunity for the faith community—especially those who claim to love God and follow Christ—to see and hear with new eyes and hearts of compassion and to demonstrate the mercy of Christ? Is there an opportunity to offer forgiveness to one another, to reach out and forgive the unforgiveable, love the unlovable, and touch the untouchable, to offer healing and hope to the "modern day leper"? Is there room for "amazing grace?"

Stories involving child molestation and other forms of sexual abuse are horrible and heartrending. The stories in the media create and inflame fear, but they are seldom, if ever, the whole story. The stories presented above, and countless other similar stories, hopefully create a sense of curiosity and compassion that maybe, just maybe, what we hear is only one side of the story. Perhaps the better—and indeed the only—pathways to justice are through *compassionate listening*. Adam Curie, Senior Quaker mediator for England, says, "We must work for harmony wherever we are, to bring together what is sundered [broken apart] by fear, hatred, resentment, injustice or any other conditions that divide us… It begins with a concept of human nature based on the belief of a divine element within each of us, which is ever available, awaiting our call to restore harmony. We must remember this good exists in those we oppose."[114]

The past cannot be changed. A child once molested cannot be un-molested. The victims of sexual assault cannot be un-assaulted. An image of child sexual abuse distributed on the internet (and the memories it creates) cannot be erased. Nevertheless, the future can be changed. As with Dickens' Scrooge, we may change the future if we are willing to change what we see and hear in the present. We may change the present if we listen not only to the *first* story, but also to the *rest* of the story.

Fear presently dominates the conversation on both sides. People are afraid of having sex offenders live in their neighborhood, work in the community, attend their schools, or worship and serve alongside of them in their neighborhood church, synagogue, or temple. The sex offender registry imposes its own form of destructive and unjust violence. Is it possible to move forward with compassionate hope and justice for all if we continue condoning any form of violence? In the next chapter, we conclude this section by considering the consequences for former sex offenders—and for their families—of being listed on the state's sex offender registry.

6 – *Effects of the Sex Offender Registry*

In the preceding chapters, we examined the different types of victims and offenders. Clearly, some offenses are despicable, heinous, and vile acts perpetrated against prepubescent children, as well as other sexual assaults against *innocent* victims involving violence, intimidation, coercion, or threat. Some offenses involve offenders exerting their power, authority, and manipulation to satisfy their own selfish and deviant fantasies. On the other hand, offenses that involve clearly *complicit* or *consenting*[115] victims cannot be truthfully portrayed as "despicable, heinous and vile acts."

Offenses against *innocent* victims are reprehensible and result in the offender being listed on the sex offender registry. Innocent victims deserve justice; however, is a perpetrator being listed on the sex offender registry justice or simply a form of revenge and retribution in disguise? There are many difficult and deleterious consequences imposed upon ex-offenders and their families because of being listed on the state registry. This chapter seeks to expose some of those effects and discuss both the registry's lack of effectiveness and the imposition of the severe consequences of deliberately ostracizing citizens who should be reintegrated into society after having paid the price of justice. Unfortunately, the registry applies to everyone required to register, including those who are involved with *consenting* victims. This is a gross and indisputable injustice. Therefore, before examining the overall effects of the sex offender registry, we will examine the effects on those involved with *consenting* victims.

At the heart of the issue of *consent* is that age of consent laws vary considerably by state.[116] For teenagers and young adults, this means that what may be permissible in one state is a serious criminal offense in another. Unfortunately, what is *legal* conduct in one state may be ruled *illegal* in another. Therefore the only distinction between insensibility and indiscretion versus criminal sexual behavior may be determined more by geography rather than by an individual's specific conduct.

This raises a question as to whether justice is—or ought to be—bound and circumscribed by geography within the United States. Unfortunately, while the Constitution of the United States is the supreme law of the land, individual states retain the right to make and enforce their own laws including what is and is not deemed a sexual offense. Fortunately, in some states, "Romeo and Juliet" laws protect such star-crossed lovers from criminal prosecution; nevertheless, such laws are confusing and inconsistent at best. Moreover, if the star-crossed lovers are unfortunate enough to live in certain states, the older (usually the young man) is subject to criminal prosecution, imprisonment, and inclusion on the sex offender registry. How then does "justice for all" prevail when an offense in one state is not an offense in another, and sex offenders involved with *complicit* or *consenting* victims are required to register as sex offenders for life?

Tragically, many sex offenses do not involve *complicit* or *consenting* victims. Rather, those who commit some offenses are closer to the stereotypical profile of sex offenders who molest children or commit predatory sexual assaults. They are the source of the public's anxiety and fear.

How and why did the sex offender registry begin? In 2006, based on these more despicable, heinous and vile offenses, President George W. Bush signed into law The Adam Walsh Child Protection and Safety Act (hereinafter referred to as AWA). Legal scholar Corey Rayburn Yung notes, "This (law) fundamentally altered assumptions about the operation of the federal criminal justice system. This 'sea change'

EFFECTS OF THE SEX OFFENDER REGISTRY

elevated sex crimes from mere political posturing to the beginning of a *criminal war* on sex offenders."[117] As previously noted, based on the mass incarceration of citizens, Americans are not only perhaps the most unmerciful, unforgiving, and judgmental people, but they are obsessed with war. When not at war with other nations (and even when such wars exist), the American government creates "criminal wars." This feeds the political demagogue's obsession for power and control with attempts to exercise dominance and oppression over other citizens' rights and liberties. A few such examples are the failed attempts at Prohibition, the failing "drug wars," and the futile "War on Terror."[118]

It is important to note that the War on Drugs and the War on Terror are all wars against "things" (a noun), whereas the war on sex offenders is a demoralizing war and oppression against sex offenders. It is against *people*. These people are not from some foreign nation, nor are they invading our borders. They are our brothers and sisters, our fathers and mothers, extended family members, and some of our neighbors, friends, co-workers, and those who once worshipped alongside of us in local churches, synagogues and mosques. Unlike the wars on drugs, terror, or military wars, the criminal war or oppression against former sex offenders is not designed to eradicate the use of a substance, to fight for or to establish peace, or to increase the nation's wealth. Rather it is an oppressive and deliberately calculated war designed to imprison, subjugate, ostracize, humiliate, and destroy human beings. Who benefits from such oppression and war?

Power corrupts and absolute power corrupts absolutely. Far too often, man's lust for power removes the blindfold from the one holding the scales of justice. While fear abolishes reason and perverts justice, those who drink the intoxicating elixir of political power often compromise their own intellect and judgment. Candidates for political office, who once had noble intentions, ideals, and a desire to serve, become, once elected, intoxicated on the powerful potion of the privileges and perks of their new position. They begin compromising their once noble intentions, and their desire to serve transforms into a desire to be served.

Leadership and effectiveness in the government today are unfortunately driven almost entirely by the pursuit of power, privilege, and perks rather than service and sacrifice. Over fifty years ago, John F. Kennedy warned legislative leaders that the world would ultimately measure their success by whether they were people of courage, judgment, integrity, and dedication. Yet, even then, as today, corruption and compromise had conquered the halls of Congress and other legislative bodies. Honest and intelligent discourse and debate are dead (or on life support), and constructive and compassionate dialogue is usually nonexistent.[119] Public communication is divided into meaningless sound bites or tweets designed to inflame and are easily digested by a largely ignorant populace. "Twitter wars" have usurped the opportunity for thoughtful and polite public conversations and dialogues. Consequently, citizens are easily deceived by the power of the press and tweets rather than by engaging in a meaningful search for truth. Former Vice President Al Gore noted, "[During] the first 150 years of this country we knew nothing but the oriented word and the logical and reasonable debate of what was written and said in the marketplace of ideas. The Bible, hymnal, Declaration of Independence, Constitution, laws, Congressional Record, newspapers, books, and pamphlets were the source of information and knowledge. But over the past fifty years, the reliable source of this information and knowledge has eroded away and is being replaced with electronic media."[120]

It is probably unreasonable, then, to expect those politicians who gain power, privilege, and perks by sustaining the status quo to initiate dialogues for change, especially when such proposed changes could make them appear to be soft on crime, or even worse, make them appear to be sympathetic towards former sex offenders. Such a lack of courage exposes their unwillingness to consider the questions of justice, compassion, and reasonable approaches as cowardice, lack of ethics, and capacity for judgment. Their integrity is compromised by duplicity and their lack of dedication is revealed as a gross and paralyzing incompetence and prejudice.[121]

Laws are necessary to establish justice, to insure domestic tranquility, and to secure the blessings of liberty. Yet important and sound decisions cannot be gleaned from the bubbling cauldron of fear and panic. The impromptu decisions made in the heat of the moment rarely lead to success or justice. Laws conceived in the heat of the moment and created in the cauldron of fear do nothing to establish justice; in fact, they establish and perpetrate a grave injustice.

The AWA and other sex offender laws were created in the bubbling cauldron of fear. This fear did not primarily come from those with experience, except for those who were personally involved and whose lives were devastated by such horrific and vile acts.[122] Innocent victims and their immediate family and friends are right to be angry and to demand and pursue justice. But the *pandemic* cry for justice often emanates from the media's sensationalism of a relatively few horrific crimes and the presumption that all sex offenders are molesters and dangerous predators and are guilty of such vile offenses. Yet, as previously noted, there are many different types of victims, offenses, and offenders; but current legislation and prosecutorial practice rarely takes into account such differences. Rather, in response to fear, prejudice, and ignorance, hastily-enacted laws concerning sex offenders do little or nothing to provide protection for the public, but rather impose unjust systems of oppression, retribution, and revenge. And politically-motivated prosecutors are eager to prosecute every case. Laws created in the crucible of fear are an attempt to pursue justice in the legislature; however, the pursuit of justice is not the function of the legislative branch of government. Ideally, and in accordance with the Constitution, the pursuit of justice is the domain and privilege of the court, that is the judicial, not the legislative or executive branch of government as noted in chapter one.

The pandemic of fear and outcry grew from media sensationalism of the vile and despicable—but relatively few—acts by some offenders. We know that very few offenders commit dangerous and predatory acts involving innocent victims. Nevertheless, even a few—or even one—are too many. As previously noted, out of Georgia's seventeen thousand registered sex offenders, 850 (5 percent) were considered *dangerous* and a hundred (0.006 percent) of those were deemed *predatory*. In fact, "the Georgia Sex Offender Registration Review Board...concluded that 65 percent (over eleven thousand) of them posed very little threat."[123] Consequently, unjust and ineffective laws are imposing severe oppression on eleven thousand Georgia citizens.

Considering that there are over 850,000 former sex offenders listed on the *national* registry (encompassing all fifty states), it is likely that over half a million of them actually "pose very little threat." In addition, over two hundred thousand of these registrants committed their offense when they were children or teenagers! Are we establishing justice, insuring domestic tranquility, and securing the blessings of liberty when we unjustly oppress over half a million American citizens and their families, including many whose offenses involved *consenting* or *complicit* victims?[124]

The justice system distinguishes between a simple assault and premeditated murder; yet in both instances, an assault resulting in injury and perhaps death has occurred. The justice system distinguishes between a petty theft and an armed robbery; yet in both instances the victim's property has been illegally taken. The justice system distinguishes between possessing and using or dealing dangerous drugs, recognizing that one offender is using and the other is profiting from "illegal" substances. And while the prison sentences imposed upon predatory child molesters, i.e., *innocent* victims, *differ* from sentences imposed on offenders involved in sexual conduct with minors (especially those involving *incompetent consenting* or *complicit* victims) **the laws concerning sex offender registration are identical.** The only significant difference is how long the ex-offender remains listed on the registry and therefore how long they are then subjected to discrimination, ostracization, hatred, and tragically, even vigilante justice. In addition, each state determines who must register and for how long and whether the sex offender may later appeal to the courts for removal. How is "equal protection under the law" sustained when each state administers the federal requirements as they please?

Laws in most states restrict where anyone labeled as a sex offender may live, work, drive, and even just exist. Some regulations are written in such a way that simply being in the wrong place—even for an innocent or legitimate reason—may trigger a new sex crime charge and send the ex-offender back to prison. Some laws are so restrictive and onerous that entire cities are off limits. In worst-case scenarios, huge homeless populations form their own towns, creating groups of registrants (lepers) living in the woods, in parking lots, and under bridges.[125] In addition, laws in more than twenty states allow certain sex offenders to be detained by "civil commitment" and to receive "treatment" for an indeterminate time *after* their release from prison.[126]

The rights described in the *Universal Declaration of Human Rights* include the right to life, liberty, and security of person; to freedom of conscience, religion, opinion, expression, association, and assembly; to freedom from arbitrary arrest; to a fair and impartial trial; to freedom from interference in privacy, home, or correspondence; to a nationality; to a secure society and an adequate standard of living; to education; and to rest and leisure. The declaration also affirms the rights of every person to own property; to be presumed innocent until proven guilty; to travel from a home country at will and return at will; to work under favorable conditions; receive equal pay for equal work and join labor unions at will; to marry and raise a family; and to participate in government and in the social life of the community.[127]

Former sex offenders are all too often denied these basic human rights, for example:

- *Ex-offenders are often denied the right to attend a local church. Many states laws prohibit them from being around children at any place or at any time. Therefore, if children are at the church, ex-offenders may not attend. Moreover, as will be explained in Chapter 9, while a few churches entirely prohibit ex-offenders from being part of their fellowship, those that do allow participation usually impose substantial restrictions and limitations. Does this not deny or compromise the practice of the freedom of religion?*

- *Ex-offenders on probation or parole are not allowed to associate with any convicted felon. Therefore, friendships and relationships that began in prison—even in the context of sex offender education and treatment programs—may not be continued upon release from prison. Does this not deny or compromise the right of association?*

- *Ex-offenders are often subject to arbitrary arrest and, if not arrest, then certainly unwarranted suspicion. They are often denied freedom from interference in privacy, home, or correspondence. Many cities instruct the local police departments to contact ex-offenders once a month, coming to their home or place of employment simply to verify that they are living and working where they say they are. Such tactics are likely meant to intimidate and harass and drive them from the community. There is no apparent legitimate law enforcement purpose. Ex-offenders must register all online identifiers, email addresses, and websites, which restricts their privacy in correspondence. Does this not deny or compromise the right to privacy?*

- *Ex-offenders are denied employment in many companies, not because of their felony conviction, but because their felony conviction is a sexual offense. They are unable to obtain professional licenses and other business permits. Does this not deny or compromise the right to earn an adequate standard of living?*

- *An ex-offender's passport requires a designation as a "sex offender." This restricts their ability to travel and subjects them to unwarranted and unjust scrutiny and harassment at various ports of entry in the United States and other countries. Does this not deny or hinder the right to travel from a home country at will and return at will?*

- *Ex-offenders possess the right to marry; however, they may or may not enjoy the right to see their children. A sex offender's children can visit their parent in prison if the child is not the victim of the offense. However, an ex-offender on probation or parole is generally denied the right to see their children or even be alone with the child during the duration of their supervision, which might be a lifetime of probation. Regardless of probation or parole requirements, schools and/or local regulations will not permit a parent who is an ex-offender to attend his or her own children's activities at school, including plays, concerts, and ball games. Does this not deny or hinder their right to marry and raise a family?*

- *In most jurisdictions, ex-offenders on probation or parole are denied the right to vote. This applies to most convicted felons; however, many of them are given lifetime probation or parole, thereby restricting their right to* ever *be able to vote and to participate in government. Does this not deny or hinder their right to participate in government?*

- *In many jurisdictions, ex-offenders are banned from parks, libraries, shopping malls, arcades, and anywhere minors* may *be present. They face residency restrictions that effectively deny them the*

EFFECTS OF THE SEX OFFENDER REGISTRY

opportunity to purchase homes in safe environments, to raise families in good neighborhoods, and to participate in the social life of the community, and ban them from living within many cities. Does this not deny or hinder their rights of community?

- *Being listed on the registry subjects ex-offenders to terror and causes vital resources to be withheld from them. Ex-offenders on probation and parole are often deprived of the use of a computer or the internet, and are therefore denied access to the "marketplace of ideas and social communication."*[128]

- *Many offenders believe the gospel (1 Corinthians 15:3-4); are saved by grace through faith (Ephesians 2:8); are "washed, sanctified and justified in the name of the Lord Jesus and by the Spirit of God" (1 Corinthians 6:11); and come after Jesus Christ, deny themselves and take up their cross and follow Him (Mark 8:34). Despite becoming Christians, many continue living in fear of rejection, are subjected to continuing public shame and humiliation and are excluded or ostracized by their local church. Does this not deny their freedom to practice their religion?*

Sex offenders are required to register with the local sheriff and provide a range of identifying information including their name, address, date of birth, criminal history, photo, fingerprints, and DNA material, as well as any online identifiers and the name of any website where the identifiers are being used. What does the state do with the information it obtains from the offender? Some governments have considered requiring specially-colored license plates to identify sex offender's vehicles. Most recently, a new federal law requires a designation as a "sex offender" on the individual's passport. This will almost certainly subject sex offenders to unwarranted and unjust scrutiny and harassment at various ports of entry in the United States and other countries.

In 2017, during the national disasters causes by tropical hurricanes, the laws in Louisiana (a Bible Belt state) required that everyone on the sex offender registry requiring evacuation be placed in "special" shelters, taking registered parents away from their infant children and registered sons and daughters away from their elderly parents. And in Florida (another Bible Belt state) Sherriff Grady Judd gained national notoriety when he took to social media to declare that no registered sex offender would be admitted to any facility in Polk County where the general population was sheltered.[129]

Oklahoma, Louisiana, Tennessee (Bible Belt states) and Illinois define *parks* to include public state parks. Statewide laws forbid park usage, access, or loitering by anyone required to register as a sex offender. These states have taken steps to insure that children with a parent on the sex offender registry will not be allowed to enjoy—as a family—the wonders and beauty that their state's parks offer to all citizens and the educational value of their state's historical monuments.[130]

Almost all offenders are listed on the state's sex offender website regardless of their assessed level of risk. Laws in most states require mandatory community notification to surrounding neighborhoods, schools, and appropriate community groups concerning offenders assessed as *intermediate* risk or *high* risk and even some who are considered a *low* risk. Flyers are distributed in the offender's neighborhood with a photograph, the exact address, and a summary of the offender's status and criminal background. In addition, press releases and flyers with all of the offender's information are given to the local electronic and print media to be placed in local publications.

If the actions being taken against sex offenders (including draconian sentencing schemes, various exceptions to law, and continuing violation of fundamental constitutional protections) are not tantamount to war, do they not rise to the level of oppression or deny personhood? Does such unjust oppression support or deny the basic human dignity and privileges affirmed under the *United Nations Declaration of Human Rights*? Is it even prudent to open the door to the regulatory oversight of private citizens with such an unsavory Orwellian flavor and substance?

Is such oppression legally, morally, or spiritually reasonable in a just and civil society? How is this oppression not as evil as domestic abuse or sexual abuse? Does the current system of sex offender laws not seek to prevent personal freedoms, induce fear, terrorize, humiliate, withhold resources (or access to them), isolate, threaten, and demand obedience and subject individuals to physical harm by exposing them to vigilante justice?

Christian counselor and marriage therapist Darby Strickland describes *oppression* in terms of marital or domestic relationships. She describes the harm that comes from abusive domestic (oppressive) relationships and the oppressive behaviors that "prevent personal freedoms, induce fear, terrorize, humiliate, withhold resources (or access to them), isolate, threaten, demand obedience, or physically harm. Living in these circumstances harms the oppressed person's emotional, spiritual, sexual, relational, or economic wellbeing."[131]

Oppression—in any form and in any situation—occurs when one party seeks to dominate and control the other through a pattern of coercive, controlling, and punishing behaviors.[132] This is evident in cases of abusive domestic relationships and in cases involving violent or coercive sexual abuse. Oppression is the manipulation and domination of one person (or persons) by another. It captures the idea that someone is subject to another's harsh control. For example, dominating spouses hold their "loved one" hostage—and commit domestic violence offense—through emotional, financial, and threats of additional physical harm.

Sexual abuse and assaults are forms of oppression, and in many ways mirror the horrors of domestic abuse. In both instances, i.e. domestic and sexual abuse—especially if the sexual offender is well known to the victim—a flagrant violation of trust is created and it inflicts significant emotional, physical, psychological, and spiritual harm on the innocent victim. Undoubtedly, sexual offenses against innocent victims are committed by offenders engaging in oppressive, selfish, and destructive behaviors. They often manipulate and groom their victims by offering them gifts, enforcing secrets, and threatening physical harm to the victim or other family members. They seek and sustain domination and control of innocent victims through a pattern of coercive, controlling, and punishing behaviors.

The oppressed person—whether in domestic or sexually abusive situations—become ensnared, isolated, and dominated over time. They must contort and conform their lives to survive under the pressure of a brutal and controlling ruler (spouse or other oppressor). Stuck in the painful circumstances, the oppressed person becomes confused and loses the ability to see the situation clearly. Their oppressors convince them that they are to blame (for their problems) and responsible for the abuse they've suffered.[133]

Oppressors (and many sexual offenders) are often not grieved by their own sins and are not usually interested in change. They magnify the faults of others to justify their domination and control. Due to the destructive and dominating effect of the oppressor and the powerlessness of the oppressed, these patterns go beyond the typical interplay of two people. When power is concentrated in one person, it tyrannizes (and encircles) the oppressed. It squeezes tighter and tighter, causing more and more pain. It makes flourishing and thriving impossible.[134]

The word *oppression* may also be used to describe social or political realities where a more powerful group takes advantage of another weaker group.[135] Yet while such oppression of spouses and victims of sex offenses is abhorrent and evil, is it true justice to impose similar forms of oppression on those who are convicted of a sex offense?

How does AWA affect the individual's right to *personhood*? The current system of sex offender legislation not only creates and sustains systemic oppression against sex offenders, but it denies them many of the rights of personhood. On January 14, 1988, President Ronald Reagan released the following declaration:

> *America has given a great gift to the world, a gift that drew upon the accumulated wisdom derived from centuries of experiments in self-government, a gift that has irrevocably changed humanity's future. Our gift is twofold: the declaration, as a cardinal principle of just law, of the God-given, unalienable rights possessed by every human being; and the example of our determination to secure those rights to defend them against any challenge.*[136]

Burt Parsons, editor of *TableTalk* (a monthly publication of Christian Reformed theologian R.C. Spoul's Ligionier Ministries) opened the publication's April 2013 issue concerning *"Personhood"* with Reagan's quote. The publication's theme for the month concerned abortion and the ongoing debate and division—even among professing

Christians—about the rights of the unborn child and the mother's right to choose. The Roman Catholic Church, the evangelical right, and other conservative Christian groups and church leaders denounce the practice of abortion primarily on the basis of protecting the rights and dignity of the unborn child. Such a position has biblical and ethical support, but such a discussion is beyond the range and purpose of this book. Yet the rationale and arguments used by the writers in *TableTalk* are instructive in how the rights—or denials of rights—of personhood also affect former sex offenders.

In his contribution, *Proclaiming Life to the Captives*, Parsons writes:

> *In America and throughout the world, the church of Jesus Christ must rise up to defend the rights of individuals—children in the womb and* abused children outside of the womb, *kidnapped girls forced into sex trafficking, men captured and sold into slavery, and the aged, the infirm, or unwanted murdered through euthanasia and genocide. Our triune God is the Almighty Creator and Sustainer of life. He has bestowed* dignity *on every person, and He alone has defined* personhood. *The barbaric murder,* abuse and slavery *of our fellow human beings ought to bring us to tears, to our knees in prayer, and to action on behalf of the least of these as we preach the gospel to the nations and fight for the life of freedom of all individuals so that they might live and hear the gospel of eternal life.*[137]

Why does the church of Jesus Christ and its leaders not rise up to defend the human rights of prisoners? Why is there little or no recognition of the well-documented and published fact that many sex offenders are "abused children outside of the womb?"[138] Why are we quick to deliver mercy and compassion through "tears and prayers and action" to the victims of "barbaric murder, abuse, and slavery," but silently support draconian sentencing, mass incarceration, civil commitment, and the public and governmental oppression of many of the "least of these,"[139] such as those we label as sex offenders? If God has "bestowed dignity on every person and defines them as a person," why does the organized church endorse the dehumanization and demonization of our fellow citizens, our brothers and sisters? Once again, is there any explanation as to why the Bible Belt states boast the highest rates of incarceration?[140]

Most jail and prison volunteers come from evangelical churches whose congregations believe that prisoners need to hear about Jesus. Yet these same fellowships are far less inclined to *be Jesus*—to be His hands, His arms or His feet—when a prisoner is released. Prisoners (especially sex offenders) are unwelcome in the neighborhood and are often unwelcome or even prohibited from attending the same churches that send volunteers into jails and prisons to preach their "gospel."[141]

Dr. Justin Holcomb writes:

> *Human history is tragically full of examples of persecution and oppression that arise when those in power create their own definition of human personhood and rights as to exclude and misuse certain groups of people. Scripture is clear that God has given all human beings dignity, personhood, and rights. The biblical understanding of personhood provides the essential foundation for* ethical *decisions for how to treat people.*[142]

We do not need to look back through history—although such a view is helpful and instructive—to find examples of "oppression that arises when those in power create their own definition of personhood and rights as to exclude and misuse certain groups of people." As noted in Chapter 3, "Complexities," Americans have a long history of oppressing certain groups, such as Native, Mexican, African, Japanese, and Muslim Americans. The United States Congress, with the cooperation of all fifty states, drafted legislation in response to the fear of sex offenders, including the AWA. Being on the sex offender registry clearly excludes certain groups of people from human dignity, enjoying human rights, and the blessing of *personhood*.

Dr. Holcomb continues:

> *Sin inverts love for God, which in turn becomes idolatry, and inverts love for people that becomes exploitation of others. The fallen human heart finds*

> *ways to justify its hatred of other people and its desire to exploit them. The result is a multitude of unbiblical views of personhood found throughout human history that dehumanize and exclude people who are made in God's image...[U]nbiblical ideologies of personhood have existed such as tribalism, Social Darwinism, racism, Nazism, and views of superior personhood based on religion, wealth, gender, age, intellect, heredity, and many other factors. Without the Biblical understanding of human personhood and dignity as image bearers of God, society is free to degenerate to violence, oppression, and exploitation of the weak by the strong.* [143]

The injustices that occur when personhood is redefined and sex offenders are exploited are innumerable and heartbreaking. The Bible calls us to fight for justice and mercy for all people. (Read Exodus 23:2-3; Deuteronomy 24:17-18; Proverbs 21:3; Zechariah 7:9-10.) Jesus opposed the dehumanizing assumptions of his culture. He spent significant time with children, the poor, the diseased, Samaritans, tax collectors, lepers and other "sinners." (Read Matthew 8:1-4; 9:9-13; 21:28-32; Mark 10:13-16; Luke 6:7-19; 10:28-42; John 4:1-45.) Certainly, in some instances, the church has been known for love and sacrificial service to the poor, oppressed, and marginalized. Such service is a powerful apologetic for the gospel. Yet when the church and its leaders remain *silent in the face of injustice*, those who are subjected to such injustice are denied dignity and personhood.

In *The Voice of the Church*, R.C. Sproul, Chairman of Ligionier Ministries and a co-pastor at Saint Andrew's Chapel in Florida, lamented the success of Planned Parenthood and others in the fight for abortion rights. The effort to legalize abortion was wrapped in the flag of personal liberty. He said, "What was most distressing was the *silence of evangelical churches* committed to the authority of the Bible and the classic Christian faith."[144] Sproul and many other Christians took an unwavering stand against abortion rights in defending the human rights and personhood of the child in the womb. Sproul lamented that many evangelical pastors declined to take such a position, stating that, "If they took a stand against abortion on demand, they said it would divide the churches. What could be a greater evil than such division? Remaining silent on the most serious ethical issue that the United States has ever faced."[145]

Abortion on demand is a serious ethical issue in the world. The Roman Catholic Church has remained steadfast in their public opposition to abortion on demand, even if their membership remains divided. For the most part, "mainline denominations" back the feminist liberal position of "pro-choice." Unfortunately, far too often abortion and homosexuality are primarily the only "hot button" social issues on which many professing Christians (particularly those identifying as *evangelical* or *born again*) are willing to take a stand. Other issues, particularly mass imprisonment, the dehumanization and demonization of sex offenders, as well as "clothing the naked, feeding the hungry, and visiting the sick and imprisoned" (Matthew 25:31-46) receive far less attention.

Sproul asserts, "The church has an obligation to speak out. (2 Samuel 12:1-15; 1 Kings 21; Matthew 14) The church is not the state, but it is the conscience of the state that cannot afford to become seared and silent. The principle reason for the existence of any government is to maintain, sustain, and protect the sanctity of human life. When the state fails to do that, it has been demonized. And it is the sacred duty of every church and of every Christian to voice opposition to it."[146] Does the "sanctity of human life" include those outside of the womb as well as those still within it? Does it include mercy and compassion for those who break the law, and rehabilitation, reconciliation, and restoration for sex offenders? When the state and the church both fail to support such mercy and grace, are not both demonized?

To paraphrase Sproul, it is time for the churches to see the evil of mass imprisonment and the dehumanization and demonization of sex offenders, and to stand up and be counted—no matter what the risk or cost. When the church is silent in the midst of oppression and evil, it ceases to be a real church. Whenever human dignity is under attack, it is the duty of the church and the Christian to rise up in protest against it.[147]

In his essay, *Understanding Personhood*, Dr. W. Robert Godrey

notes:
> *We live in a world of much cruelty and violence. In Psalm 5:5-6, David highlights the three characteristics of the wicked: boastful and proud; full of lies and deceit; and bloodthirsty and violent. In their pride and self-deceit, they are willing to use cruelty to advance themselves rather than pursuing love and peace.*
>
> *Wicked individuals seek to justify their violence... (by) claiming that the victims of their violence are in some way inferior or less human than they are. (They) justify violence against those who are not like (them); they are not part of (their) family, tribe, nation, race or religion.*
>
> *The wicked justification of violence may well be at its worst when applied to science... Bad science is used by wicked men to make moral and religious judgments as if they were objective scientific conclusions. The real problem is not science, but the abuse of science. The horrendous effect of these pseudo-scientific justifications is dehumanizing violence born out of selfishness.*
>
> *As Christians, we must beware of becoming self-righteous in our reaction to those who dehumanize people. There were Christians who were taken in by Hitler and defended slavery. We must not dehumanize those with whom we disagree. We especially want to make it clear to those who have defended abortions or who had abortions that all those who come to Jesus in repentance and faith find forgiveness.*[148]

On one hand, sex offenders may be described as wicked, boastful, and proud, full of lies and deceit, bloodthirsty and violent. They often use pride, self-deceit, and cruelty to gratify themselves at the expense of their victims. They justify their sexual violence through denial, minimization, blaming others, and any a number of mind games and cognitive distortions. But are their oppressors any better?

Oppressors (those who create and enforce injustice), those who acquiesce in silence, or those who stand in support of the governmental oppression of many of the "least of these," are also often boastful and proud, full of lies and deceit, and show every appearance of being bloodthirsty and violent. Oppressors often justify their oppression by claiming that sex offenders are in some way inferior or less human than they themselves are. In their pride and self-deceit, they are willing to use cruelty to oppress sex offenders and advance themselves rather than pursuing love and peace through talking with and listening to one another.

The oppression may be worst when applied to science. The bad science of maintaining that sex offender recidivism is "frightening and high" is used by the media, politicians, and lawmakers to make moral, legal, and even religious judgments as if they were *objective* scientific conclusions. As noted, the whole idea of sex offender recidivism being "frightening and high" is false and misleading and a deliberate abuse of statistics. Unfortunately, the horrendous effects of these pseudo-scientific justifications create and endorse dehumanizing violence and oppression born out of selfishness and an effort to deny or destroy personhood.

Christians must especially beware of becoming self-righteous in our reaction to those we dehumanize (especially sex offenders.) German Christians were taken in by Hitler and many of the Founding Fathers of the United States once defended slavery. We must neither dehumanize nor attempt to demonize those with whom we disagree. After all, most Christians believe that even sex offenders may come to Jesus in repentance and faith and find forgiveness.

And finally, in the essay *Blood in the Streets*, R.C. Sproul Jr., states:
> *We... construct foolish drama by worrying about what we will eat, or what we will wear while missing the battle of eternity that is going on right before our eyes."*[149]*...We don't seek the kingdom merely when we read our Bibles or sing our hymns. We seek the kingdom when we... weep and mourn for the murder of our neighbors... we seek the kingdom when we welcome the least of these into our lives, our homes, and our families.*[150]

EFFECTS OF THE SEX OFFENDER REGISTRY

The effects of the sex offender registry are far-reaching, life-altering, and life-changing. Sex offender registration laws infringe upon the basic human dignity and privileges of sex offenders. They prevent or hinder the sex offender's personal freedoms, forcing them into isolation, while threatening them and demanding obedience while subjecting them to physical harm. They create an unjust and ungodly oppressive environment, if not an actual criminal war.

The sex offender registry is the result of leaders who have lost their perspective and their leadership ability. They have abandoned their vision to lead fearlessly and with sound judgment, dedication, and integrity. Such leaders conspire to unjustly deprive sex offenders of liberty, deny them equal protection under the law, and routinely subject them to cruel and unusual punishment. Their actions constitute unjust oppression and deeply affect the former offender's right to personhood. They employ power, authority, and manipulation to rob sex offenders and their families of their freedom and to deny them certain liberties. They seek to deny the sex offender the blessings of mercy and the power of God's amazing grace.

Whether the criminal justice position concerning sex offenders is legitimate law enforcement, a criminal war, or oppression, may be debated. There are numerous excellent texts concerning the deleterious effects of the law on ex-offenders. These are listed in Appendix E – "Recommended Reading for Justice." It is not, however, the purpose of this book to join in that debate. Rather the focus remains on creating or joining in a dialogue to "gather up the fragments that remain so that no one is lost."[151] The "fragments" are the broken people abandoned in prisons and those isolated and shamed by being exposed on the sex offender registry. Developing a dialogue and strategy to insure that there are no more victims, that no one is disposable, and that no one is lost, requires evaluating whether the criminal justice system is helping to heal and restore broken people or only inflicting more needless pain and suffering.

Part three will begin building on the foundations previously established by identifying the roles and responsibilities of ex-offenders and the organized church.

7 – *Roles and Responsibilities of Sex Offenders*

Justice may be blind, but injustice emanates from fear, prejudice, and ignorance. The practice of injustice, however, is not the exclusive domain of the criminal justice system or the media. Ex-offenders and their advocacy groups also play an important role in recognizing their own practice of injustice and therefore have a responsibility of working to establish justice for all.

True justice is blind; but as with many virtues, it may often be difficult to define clearly. Fear, prejudice, and ignorance never bring about justice, but are rather a few of the hallmark characteristics that surround injustice. Within the criminal justice system, injustice often flows from those in authority, i.e., legislators, prosecutors, and correction officials. Yet tragically, injustice is equally as prevalent and practiced within the community of ex-offenders and their advocates.

An offender who commits or attempts to commit any criminal act (especially a sexual offense), commits a grave injustice. The offender imposes injustice upon his/her victim, robs them of their innocence and inflicts various forms of terror. And while those who seek true justice must not *retaliate* against a sex offender, the offender must be held accountable. Accountability does not end with an admission or confession of the offense, although that is certainly a necessary step. Rather, accountability requires the offender to begin pursuing and practicing justice even as they have every right and expectation to receive true justice.

How then does an offender or an ex-offender begin practicing justice? Justice begins with the offender's true, honest, and complete *confession*. A confession is different from merely an admission of guilt and is a difficult, but very necessary and important place to begin. Very few offenders willingly and openly confess their criminal behavior. Thus admission and confession are different; very, very different!

Admission recognizes that the offense happened, that is that the law was broken, whereas confession recognizes the offense caused great harm and that the offender is responsible for causing the harm. Offenders usually offer an admission of guilt but they often refuse or hesitate to *confess*. Admission is frequently accompanied by *regret*, that is, a certain amount of sorrow for what happened. Yet such sorrow is more often for what happened or is happening to the offender. In an admission, there is all too often little, if any, consideration or sorrow for what happened to the victim.

Confession is accompanied by remorse or a "godly sorrow." The apostle Paul spoke of such sorrow when he wrote to the Corinthian church, "Now I rejoice, not that you were made sorry, but that your sorrow led to repentance (a change of mind). For you were made sorry in a godly manner... For Godly sorrow produces repentance leading to salvation, not to be regretted, but the sorrow of the world (regret) produces death." (See 2 Corinthians 7:9-10.) Confession involves repentance—a complete change of mind. It is not accomplished by merely an admission of wrongdoing, but by an empathetic and heartfelt sorrow for what happened to the victim. Confession means there are no legal appeals and no attempts to overturn a conviction on a technicality, or by some other means. True confession and remorse by the ex-offender helps create a common unity and opens a door for a dialogue to begin.

Some of the difficulty in a true and open confession arises from the present likelihood of *injustice* being imposed upon the offender. When the imposition of injustice by the government becomes the standard for "justice," the offender is often hesitant to confess. There is no guarantee or even a probability that the offender will receive justice, i.e., a reasonable and restorative sanction. For example, as previously noted, criminal justice sentencing is too often driven by minimum, mandatory, and presumptive sentencing schemes wherein the judge has little or no discretion at the time of sentencing. For example, in Arizona, certain sexual offenses are subject to minimum mandatory and *consecutive* sentencing. Consequently, unless a plea agreement for a lesser sentence is offered and accepted, an offender convicted at trial may face a minimum mandatory sentence of hundreds of years in prison. It is this fear that prevents many offenders from coming to the place of confession. There is a sense in the mind of the offender that the less the authorities know, the greater the chance of escaping a severe judgment. Therefore, while an admission of responsibility may be obvious, confessions do not come quickly, if they come at all.

Sex offenders do not think clearly nor exercise sound reasoning while planning or committing their offense. Offenses grow from corrupt values, distorted thinking, addiction, secrecy, and opportunity. Sex offenses do not "just happen." They are a deliberate and calculated decision or a matter of choice. Once a person is charged with a crime, they may choose a pathway to justice (accountability and confession) or injustice (secrecy and denial). It is much easier to choose the path of injustice over justice, that is, to make every effort to mitigate their sentence. However, does someone who chooses the path of injustice—an admission without any confession—have any reason to expect justice when potentially facing a lengthy or even a lifetime prison sentence? Decisions such as these are just a small part of the complexities involved in seeking reasonable justice for sex offenders without imposing injustice upon the victims.

Advocacy groups and ex-offenders often focus primarily on the injustice ex-offenders suffer, but they often show little or no regard for the suffering and endless pain endured by thousands of innocent children and other victims of sexual abuse. Offenders know when their sentence will end, but their victims often endure great pain and suffering throughout their lifetime. Is it in the interest of justice when ex-offenders and advocacy organizations focus almost exclusively on the sentences and sanctions imposed on the offender, but ignore the deviant acts and the harmful impact of such acts on the victims and their families? Moreover, is it in the interest of justice when ex-offenders resist or refuse to participate in treatment programs designed to prevent further offenses?

The following stories illustrate sex offenders who have *chosen* to practice *injustice*. As with previous stories in this book, the names and a few details have been changed to protect the innocent and for privacy.

The Advocate

Greg was nineteen years old when he had what he maintained was a consensual sexual relationship with a fourteen-year-old victim. Greg was ultimately sentenced to prison for six years and held in civil commitment for an additional four years. When he was released, he quickly joined various groups advocating for legislative reform. He said he wanted to educate the public how the legal system mistreated people like him, and to convince his skeptics that he was not a dangerous predator. Through his personal enthusiasm and charisma, he convinced officials of both local and national advocacy organizations that he had been the victim of a grave injustice. He publicly maintained that he had committed a singular offense, a *consensual* relationship with an underage victim; but that was not the whole truth. Not even close.

Sex offenders on probation or parole are usually prohibited from any unsupervised or unauthorized contact with minors. Contact includes physical, verbal, email, texts, chatting, and so on. No contact means *no* contact. Period. Yet at age thirty-four, fifteen years *after* his original offense and five years *after* his release from prison, Greg was caught exchanging sexually inappropriate texts and emails with a sixteen-year-old child in a different state. According to police reports, they found "pages and pages" of communications, including several where Greg invited the sixteen-year-old to come visit him and some suggesting that he (Greg) take a "business trip" to the victim's city. Another text message from Greg to his new victim recommended that he (the minor victim) begin using various phone apps for "conversations you do not want to be seen by others." In another email, he badgered the sixteen-year-old with messages such as, "Since you never answered the question about whether or not you care about me, it's pretty obvious what the answer is."

After his arrest for unauthorized contact with the sixteen-year-old, Greg emailed his friends and supporters in the advocacy organization, saying, "The probation officer's claim that I should be arrested and held without bond for a first-time technical violation where no criminal behavior is asserted is ludicrous. Suggesting that I be imprisoned for behavior that is neither harmful nor criminal is even more suspect."

Greg admitted to the *consensual* sexual relationship with the fourteen-year-old when he was nineteen. Yet the official record shows that he actually pled guilty to *multiple offenses* involving *multiple victims*, including an incident involving a nine-year-old when he (Greg) was only fourteen. A singular offense may have been excusable; however, offenders with multiple convictions and demonstrable unaccountability or without even a bit of remorse may well be the very definition of someone being a dangerous predator.

The depth of Greg's denial, and multiple cognitive distortions, raises questions as to whether Greg has ever been required (or has volunteered) to participate in a sex offender treatment program. (As noted in the introduction, I have participated in and benefited from such a program and have significant amount of experience in helping others begin moving towards justice.) Greg's continuing assertion of being a victim along with his refusal to be accountable for his own actions is outrageous. Such conduct denies justice to his victims and promotes injustice.

Perhaps equal, if not more disturbing than Greg's denials, is the refusal of the advocacy groups that initially supported him and championed his cause to consider holding him accountable. One such advocate noted, "There is no evidence that any of the exchanges (with the sixteen-year-old) led to any physical contact and as always, it is imperative that we keep an open mind when someone is accused of a crime." The advocate ignored the fact that Greg had knowingly and intentionally violated the court order to have *no contact with minors*. In addition, when one of Greg's friends, who was also an ex-offender and a board member of the national advocacy group, became aware of Greg's actions (in texting the minor), he challenged him, but Greg asserted that he was not doing anything wrong. The board member cut off any contact with Greg and asked others in the group for advice. To his surprise, he found that some people in the advocacy group didn't believe there was "anything to worry about."

Unfortunately, in Greg's case, through his continuing victim posturing, lack of accountability for his actions, and an ocean of regret but not even a thimble full of remorse, he demonstrated that he was seeking a selfish justice (read: injustice), even while denying justice to any of his past, present, and (likely) future victims. It is deeply disturbing that Greg defended his actions. Considering the evidence presented to the advocacy groups, it is outrageous that *anyone* would defend Greg's actions. How does denial and defense lead to justice? The answer is quite simple: it doesn't.

The Salesman

Rich was a forty-two-year old businessman in a Midwestern state. His life was becoming increasingly chaotic. Business setbacks had led to financial difficulties that had exposed marital problems. He began isolating and withdrawing from his family and friends while spending hours mindlessly surfing on the internet. Soon pornography provided an available, anonymous, and affordable escape. He began craving more personal attention than the pictures alone could provide, so he entered the world of cyber-sex (live chatting with any anonymous and willing participant). What began as a seemingly unimportant (and legal) decision placed Rich in a dangerous and risky environment. Yet with one lapse in judgment after another, his conscience and moral compass virtually disappeared.

Teresa—the other person in one of his anonymous "chats"—*said* she was sixteen years old—the legal age for consensual sex in Rich's state. So, driven by one poor decision after another, ignoring his own sense of morality, and seeking to satisfy only himself, the forty-two year-old man began a sexually explicit conversation with someone whom he believed to be a sixteen-year-old girl. It didn't seem to matter to Rich that Teresa was six years younger than his own daughter. The pressures in his life had risen to the point that he'd willingly abandoned sound reason and judgment. He convinced himself that he wanted to meet her. He was addicted and out of control (and out of his mind), suspending any sense of reason and morality and any respect for justice. Fear of being alone prejudiced him against common sense—even if his actions were not *technically* illegal. Intentional ignorance led him into the realm of injustice in which he cared nothing for the young woman he was attempting to seduce, but only for the momentary satisfaction of his own salacious and prurient desires.

Teresa's parents were alarmed when they discovered the email and the text messages on their *fourteen-year-old* (not sixteen-year-old) daughter's smartphone. In fact, as with any reasonable parent, they were enraged. They read the emails suggesting that this forty-two-year old stranger was planning a "business trip" to their state to meet their daughter. The local and state police were notified, and a warrant was issued for Rich's arrest.

Rich was charged and convicted of luring a minor for sexual purposes over the internet. Yet advocacy groups *applauded* when his conviction was overturned by the state Court of Appeals. His conviction was reversed because Teresa had *told* him she was sixteen-years-old (the legal age for consent in his state.) The court's rationale was that, since the defendant had never actually met the young girl in person, he had no way of discerning her actual age. His defense (on appeal) argued there was no criminal intent. Defense counsel celebrated saying, "Thankfully now innocent people will be protected by the court's decision." The court's ruling acknowledged, "Sexual solicitation of children is a grave concern; but the concept that wrongdoing must be conscious in order to be criminal and subject the offender to years of imprisonment has long been a foundation of our justice system." Yet the prosecutor countered with, "I fail to have a great deal of empathy for a forty-two-year-old man soliciting sex from (even) a sixteen-year-old girl."

Does the resolution of this case represent justice or injustice? Do the girl's parents believe the state has protected their daughter? Why does a forty-two-year-old man solicit sex from a sixteen-year-old girl (legal age or not)? Why is a sixteen- (or fourteen)-year-old girl seeking anonymous sexual contact over the internet? Where is the empathy and compassion for this young girl *from the advocacy groups*? Do offenders who refuse to accept accountability and responsibility for their actions seek justice for themselves or justice for all? Can one party receive justice while the other suffers injustice?

What about Teresa? While she may have "consented" to the offense, what role did Rich have in seducing her and grooming her into a sexual relationship? What is going on in her life? How are her actions affected by our sex-saturated culture? What is going on in the life of a forty-two-year-old man that he is willing to take such risks? Would he have broken off the conversation if he knew her true age? What would have happened if they had actually met in real life? Would he have sexually assaulted her? Will he resume this pattern of behavior? Will he seek and receive help? There are so many questions and so few answers, including, "Was justice served?"

The Pornographer

This case drew national attention when Michael, a fifty-two-year-old high school teacher, was convicted of possessing twenty images of child pornography (child sex abuse images) and given a minimum mandatory sentence of two hundred years.[152] The sexually explicit images of abuse were carefully organized, printed, and maintained in three ring binders in his home. Michael admitted to possessing the images, but refused a plea agreement for a minimum of seventeen years in prison[153] followed by lifetime probation. He justified his actions by arguing that the state could not prove the young children in the images were "real" children as opposed to computer-generated representations. He admitted to having thousands of images, many of which were of very young prepubescent children involved in degrading and sexual abusive situations, but he was attempting to escape justice on a legal technicality. Where is the desire for justice for the thousands of victims and their families?

The two-hundred-year prison sentence may well be excessive and unjust. Michael was a respected member of his community and profession. Yet although he appeared to be a happily married man and a good father to his four children, he was living a secret and deceitful life. Where was his empathy, accountability, confession, or remorsefulness? Michael demonstrated concern for himself, but a reckless and callous disregard for thousands of children. Is it reasonable for him to expect or receive mercy when he has not been merciful? Or is it right for him to expect a different justice when he himself has practiced injustice?

In transforming any conflict, true justice must prevail. And true justice must be available to all. Greg, Rich, and Michael, as well as the advocacy organizations supporting them, must also begin seeking justice for the victims as diligently or even more so than they are seeking it for themselves. This is the beginning of transformation and change and an open invitation to dialogue. What is the ex-offender's responsibility in seeking justice *for their victims*? Sexual offenses cause devastating harm, regardless of whether the victims were *innocent, consenting,* or *complicit.* How does justice prevail for each victim?

Offenders often deny responsibility in the case of a *complicit*[154] victim. Nevertheless, those who offend against such victims demonstrate poor moral judgment at best and certainly a lack of common sense. Admittedly, *complicit* victims have a *part* in the offense; however, while the criminality of the offender may be debated, the questionable morality and potential adverse social consequences of a quick "hook-up" is without excuse or moral rationality.

The overall societal decline of sexual morality, along with the ever-increasing exposure to sexually suggestive and explicit images and situations in all forms of media and entertainment, contribute to a sexually charged and permissive environment.[155] One night stands, hook-ups and "booty calls" have become acceptable parts of American culture, thereby allowing such sexual encounters with a *complicit* victim to seem reasonable and even desirable. The natural differences in the maturation of teenage young men and women helps influence the seemingly (in their own minds) rapidly maturing young women to begin seeking older and apparently more "mature" men to date. And the older men are eager and willing participants. Young women looking for love and young men looking for sex form a seemingly innocuous, but dangerous, opportunity for what society has determined to be a criminal offense, i.e. "sexual conduct with a minor."

Nevertheless, while the *complicit* victim is partially responsible, where is the compassion and sorrow for a young person (usually a young woman) who was so desperate for love and attention that they were willing to sacrifice their own body for another person's sexual pleasure? Besides, regardless of the victim's *complicity*, the "offender" most often engaged in certain elements of preparation, seduction, and enticement. Offenders often willingly or negligently ignore warning signs that, if recognized, would at least create questions as to the victim's actual age and identity. Moreover, what does it say about the offender's maturity and emotional stability that they would engage in sex with a stranger regardless of the consequences or cost?

Sex offenders who are convicted of "luring a minor for sex over the internet" may reasonably argue that they did not know the true age of their victim and therefore make a rational defense for the *criminality* of their actions.[156] Nevertheless, although sex offenders with *complicit* victims may not have intended to offend and may not bear the responsibility alone, they cannot deny their culpability in seeking to engage in something so personal (sexual conduct) with someone they hardly knew and often had no desire to know. This is not to say that such foolish irresponsibility ought to be a criminal offense, especially since there is generally no criminal intent.[157] It is, however, an act of questionable morality and indiscretion. While imprisonment and registration in such cases is certainly unjust, a reasonable and rational sanction (without imposing any criminal record) may be to require counseling and some form of treatment to help the offender understand why they were seeking anonymous sex with anyone over the internet. Such an individual could benefit greatly by participating in various self-help groups, including Sexaholics Anonymous, Sex Addicts Anonymous, Celebrate Recovery, and other such organizations.

As mentioned in Chapter 3, *consenting* victims fall into three different types: *incompetent*[158], *illicit*[159] and *unethical*.[160] Each victim suffers harm from the offense. The scope of the harm inflicted upon *illicit* and *unethical* consenting victims will be discussed below with the other *innocent* victims. Nevertheless, if justice is to prevail, offenders involved in sexual conduct with *incompetent* consenting victims must accept responsibility for the harm and become accountable for their actions without justifications, rationalizations, or other distorted thoughts.

One way a former sex offender may pursue justice is by participating in sex offender education and treatment programs. Sex offenses cause harm to both the victim and the offender. And while treatment is not always available in prison, various forms of counseling and treatment are available outside. In addition, there are numerous self-help groups including Sexaholics Anonymous, Sex Addicts Anonymous, and Celebrate Recovery.[161] Appendix D – "Recommended Reading for Ex-Offenders" lists additional resources for treatment and recovery.

Given the variety of age of consent laws,[162] sexual conduct with *incompetent consenting* victims is rarely a matter of *criminal* behavior. Of course, instances in which the victim is coerced, forced, drugged (by alcohol or other substances), or subjected to any scheme intended to compromise the victim's inhibitions and desires involves *illicit* consent and will be discussed below. Cases of *incompetent* consent are limited to instances where the offender and the victim are relatively close in age and in which the victim was a willing and eager participant, or even initiated the sexual conduct. Although this may be a narrow category (as opposed to the more easily defined offenses involving *illicit* and *unethical* consent), there are too many such instances of young adults and teenagers being caught up in sexual conduct of questionable morality and poor judgment but without any evidence of objection on the part of the "victim" or criminal intent on the part of the "offender".

Nevertheless, if justice is to prevail, individuals involved in such *incompetent* consent must accept responsibility for the harm and become accountable for their actions. Yet, as in the case of *complicit* victims, justice in such cases does not require—nor is justice being served by—imposing criminal sanctions such as imprisonment, probation, and registration; in fact, imposing such "justice" is actually *injustice*. Rather, justice may be served by requiring education and counseling for both the offender and the victim and by requiring *both* to accept responsibility for any children born from such conduct. Far too often, irresponsible young men have multiple "baby mamas" but offer little or no support to help to raise such "unplanned" children. Such "deadbeat dads" deserve *financial* justice.[163] Yet too often criminal justice (prosecution, imprisonment, supervision and sex offender registration) works to prevent an eighteen-year-old young man who impregnates his fifteen-year-old girlfriend—with her intentional and loving participation—from helping to support and raise their child. Rather than exposing an offender to such *criminal* injustice, why not simply subject the father to the *financial* justice of helping to support his child until their eighteenth birthday?

Justice is not established and domestic tranquility or liberty are not protected when offenders involved with *complicit* or *incompetent* consenting victims are subjected to imprisonment, probation and sex offender registration. Rather, a grave and serious injustice is being imposed. They are not dangerous predators. They are not child molesters. They are not rapists. They are extremely unlikely to reoffend. Why does the government waste millions of taxpayer dollars to prosecute, imprison, supervise, and require such an "offender" to register as a sex offender, often for the rest of their life? Is it possible that such injustice prevails because we live in a culture of fear and have created an epidemic of hysteria driven by the media? Or is it perhaps because most legislators apparently lack the willingness to overcome their own fears, prejudices, and ignorance to seek to govern courageously, with sound judgment, dedication, and integrity?

Unfortunately, there are no statistics available about which victims are *innocent*, *consenting*, or *complicit*. Arguably, offenders with *complicit* or *incompetent* consenting victims are not presently receiving justice. Nevertheless, too many victims are truly *innocent*. An innocent victim deserves justice; but is justice being served or is the *extreme justice* merely the injustice of a system driven by retribution and revenge?

Innocent victims are prepubescent children or teenagers who are forcibly molested, adults who are preyed upon and violently sexually assaulted, and teenagers who are sexually assaulted through *illicit* or *unethical consent*. These *innocents* do not willingly participate in the molestation, sexual conduct, or assault. They endure great physical, mental, emotional, psychological, and spiritual harm and may never fully recover or heal from such wounds.

An offender chooses to commit a sexual offense against an innocent and unsuspecting victim, at least in part, because of a willing suspension of empathy. The offense is an ultimate selfish and violent act wherein there is no regard for anyone other than one's self. One of the keys to developing empathy is by listening to stories of victims, preferably in safe and controlled confrontation or "victim empathy" groups. Unfortunately, because of the intimate and personal nature of sexual offenses, correction officials rarely use such victim impact groups, even though they have been known to have a tremendous positive effect on *all* of the participants.

In this chapter, I have chosen to share two of the stories from the book, *Under the Covers: A Message of Hope.*[164] This book features the personal and painful experiences of women and children who have been *innocent* victims of sexual abuse. It is important for ex-offenders to confess, not only their responsibility, but also to find a way to feel the pain and suffering they have caused. Here are two stories, in the victims' own words.

Dealing with Terror

When I was a child, I was violated by someone I trusted. This person looked so good from the outside that no one ever suspected him, and no one would believe me either. Yet I was sexually abused.

Now, as a grown woman, I try to live a holy life and keep a loving attitude, yet inside I am forced to face the shame that overwhelms me because of abuse—the desires of a man's heart that were played out upon me as a child.

Children who have been sexually abused often experience a level of fear that is even difficult to describe. These feelings can go way beyond fear. They have been called 'indescribable.' The closest wording I can come up with is 'debilitating terror.'

I was four years old when my traumatic events

started. *I am now an adult, yet at times I have feelings of such terror that I can barely walk out of the house, let alone be with people.*

My abuser personally came to violate me at a young age while I was sound asleep. As a result, sleeping as an adult became a disturbing event.

Will the abuse ever be repeated? I often wondered. Is it safe for me to close my eyes? There could be trouble again. Perhaps I should stay awake all night watching? Terror stalked me at night. Every rustle or noise made me alert.

These are the awful results on the other side of an addict's desire. This is the human perspective that men who sexually harm others may not have considered. We who were mistreated are not toys or lifeless objects; we are human. We are children, young women, and often, young men. We were helpless and often dependent on the very adults that harmed us.[165]

Letter from a Young Woman

As a child, I looked up to you, and sought your approval and acceptance. I wanted nothing more than to love and to be loved by you. I wanted to be held in your arms and feel the comfort of your protectiveness. For more than thirteen years, you treated me the way I needed to be treated, and I felt loved. In return, I gave you all the unconditional love I could give.

Apparently, my unconditional love was not enough. You wanted more than a child was expected to give. You touched me in places that were inappropriate. Your heart and mind must have enjoyed what you touched, because you touched me there so many times.

To this day, I am unable to handle the physical touch of another human being. I cringe each time I experience any physical contact. Because of this anxiety, I am unable to lower my guard and trust another to let them

> get close. Because of what happened, I have spent seventeen years alone.
>
> I have often felt like giving up. Those hands, fingers and lips didn't only molest my young body; they molested my heart, mind and life.
>
> To this day, I have tried to forget the feelings of those hands, fingers, and lips on my body. I have tried to forget the scent of your liquor you so often breathed on me, and how it was often used as an excuse for this behavior.[166]

Innocent victims deserve justice; but is justice being served? There are no quick or easy answers. One of the main visions of this book is to help create a dialogue among all stakeholders in an effort to help establish such justice. This is a complex issue. But the conflict may be transformed (it must be transformed!) because our present system of justice—even for the offenders of innocents—is still unjust and ineffective.

One of the first steps toward laying the foundation for justice is for ex-offenders who have offended against *innocent* victims to begin taking full responsibility for their actions and doing *whatever is required* to change. Change does not come easily. Addictions are not easily broken; but freedom from offending and from addiction *is* possible. But it requires hard work—a lot of hard and soul-searching work. In my opinion and experience, ex-offenders who resist or refuse counseling and treatment are unlikely to find mercy until they are willing to give justice.

The following is a special word to my brothers—my fellow ex-offenders. In some ways, it may be the most important words I write in this book. In the introduction, I said, "I want us to get this right." I recognize that not all sex offenders are sex addicts; nevertheless, we made deviant decisions and chose to offend. It was not an accident; it was not a mistake. Sometimes we are trying to cover up our own pain. Many of us suffered abuse and neglect ourselves. Yet that does not excuse what we did. It was a deliberately calculated act. Admittedly, we may not have been aware of all of the calculations.

ROLES AND RESPONSIBILITIES OF SEX OFFENDERS

All too frequently one thing leads to another, and we find ourselves enslaved by our desires and trapped in a destructive cycle of deviant thoughts and feelings. We act without thinking. The problem is that once we cross the line, there is no going back without help. We cannot just cover it up and pretend it didn't happen. We have grievously wounded an innocent person. We have committed an act of sexual abuse. We have caused indescribable suffering and harm to a victim, and many others. We must be willing to get help. We must have the courage, judgment, integrity, and dedication to do whatever it takes, as long as it takes, to insure that we do *not* create any more victims.

It is not easy to enter treatment. In many ways, ex-offenders may not be ready to change until they are willing to admit that they are powerless and that their lives have become unmanageable. We must do our part if we expect the community to do theirs. We must work towards building a transparent and accountable community where we can grow and flourish. There is hope and healing, and change is possible.[167]

This is an important point for all who read this book. A ex-offender who molests a child, or deliberately grooms and *illicitly* or *unethically* forces a teenager to engage in sexual conduct for the offender's own perverse and deviant desires, commits a sexual assault. They use power, authority, or manipulation to rob someone, to obtain sexual excitement and take away that person's right to choose.[168] Such individuals are (or were) dangerous sexual predators. *Yet that does not mean that they cannot change. It does not mean they cannot be healed.* Yet while justice often requires prosecution, imprisonment, probation, and some form of registration, we cannot allow fear, prejudice, and ignorance to corrupt and degrade justice into injustice. Unfortunately, as noted in previous chapters, the justice currently being imposed upon ex-offenders is extreme and harmful injustice.

A safe and just society has every reason for protecting themselves from sexual predators. Laws are necessary to establish justice, to insure domestic tranquility, and to secure the blessings of liberty. Yet laws created in a cauldron of fear do not establish justice. Rather they establish and perpetuate a grave injustice. They insure domestic violence and endanger the blessings of liberty for all the citizenry while forfeiting the liberty of many. The path to justice begins when all of the stakeholders (including ex-offenders) commit to creating a dialogue to help victims of sexual abuse find healing, to help establish and protect the truth, and to help find justice and healing for those who commit acts of sexual abuse and those who are labeled as sex offenders.

How do we find ways to develop empathy and compassion on both sides of this issue? How do we create a dialogue among those who are presumed to be enemies? Unless we find a way to end the oppression, ex-offenders will remain wounded, and often suffer from their own history of past abuse while enduring the severe consequences of injustice. Unless we find a way to end the oppression, victims will not find healing.

Both the government and former sex-offenders have a responsibility in establishing justice for all. But the church or spiritual community also has a vital and important role and responsibility in transforming this conflict. For while traditionally the responsibility of the government has been to identify, convict, and imprison the lawbreakers for a time of remediation and correction, the role of the church or faith community has been to seek the redemption and restoration of all—especially prisoners. The next chapter explores the role of the church in this conflict and examines whether the church is fulfilling or failing in its role and responsibility.

8 – *Roles and Responsibilities of the Church*

The church and the state are societal institutions. And just as the state has certain obligations to protect the citizens of a just and civil society, the church has different but equally important obligations. The church is a separate entity from the state and therefore must not join with the state in the punishment and condemnation of lawbreakers. When the punishment imposed on lawbreakers by the state becomes nothing more than revenge and retribution, church leaders and professing Christians must speak out against such extreme injustice. In exhorting professing Christians to rise up against the German state in the early twentieth century, pastor and theologian Dietrich Bonheoffer wrote, "The church has an unconditional obligation towards the victims of any societal order, (and all who endure *injustice* are the victims of the society and of the state), *even if they do not belong to the Christian community. 'Let us do good to all.' (Gal 6:10)*"[169] In addition, Bonheoffer notes, "Individual Christians who know they are called to do so in certain cases [must accuse] the state of inhumanity… [For] either too little law and order or too much law and order compels the church to speak."[170] Furthermore, the role and responsibility of the church and professing Christians (as opposed to those who remain part of the world and the state) is to "do justly, to love mercy and to walk humbly with … God." (Micah 6:8) This then raises the question whether those who know and love God and walk with Him in obedience and faith are seeking the redemption and restoration of all—especially and including former sex-offenders—or do they silently acquiesce and even condone the revenge and retribution inherent in American injustice? Do those who know and love God **love mercy** for others, as well as enjoying it for themselves, or have they forgotten that, "judgment is without mercy to the one who has shown no mercy. Mercy triumphs over judgment"? (James 2:13) Can those who know and love God walk humbly with Him while condemning their neighbors and placing stumbling blocks along their way? (See Romans 14:10-13.) How can a church fulfill its role in society of offering redemption and restoration if it ignores its own Scriptures and conforms its conduct to the standard of the world by silently acquiescing to the state's practice of retribution and revenge?

It is nearly impossible to imagine *repentant* sinners being unwelcome in a local church occupied by many *unrepentant* sinners, because their sins aren't socially acceptable. Yet this is exactly what happens to many former sex offenders. When one man confessed his sins (sexual sins and offense) to the pastor of a nondenominational "megachurch" in Mesa, Arizona, he was informed he was "no longer welcome to attend." They went so far as to prevent him from participating in the *Celebrate Recovery* program offered by the church. Shortly thereafter, a prison ministry leader in one of the largest churches in the southwestern United States wrote, "Because of such fear (of sex offenders), the doors of the organized church are closed." In North Carolina, a thirty-one-year-old man was arrested simply for going to church (based on local laws) because he had been "convicted of indecent liberties with a teenage girl when he was twenty years old."[171] All this was a decade *after* he had served his time for the crime!

Many churches simply prohibit former sex offenders from attending church functions by citing insurance concerns and/or regulations or local laws. Other church leaders limit a former sex offender's presence and participation in the fellowship of the church by developing policies and "covenant agreements" that the ex-offender must agree to and abide by if they want to attend any services. Such covenants allow limited access to the buildings and some of the services, but very little access to the "fellowship of the saints." It is one thing for the secular world (including probation and parole officials) to limit such access, but it is entirely another thing for the church to limit it itself. Apparently, in the eyes of most church leaders, the belief is that "once a leper, always a leper." If church leaders and administrators believe such things, is it possibly any wonder that many people in the church pews do not believe that the blood of Jesus cleanses all sin? Thus smolders the cauldron of discord.[172]

In *The Church Law and Tax Report*, Richard Hammar offers pastors and church leaders guidelines in an article, "Dealing with Sex Offenders Who Want to Attend Your Church: How to Protect Your Most Vulnerable Members." He offers the following steps:

1)   Obtain a record of the sex offender's *prior criminal convictions by conducting a national criminal records check.*

2)   If the sex offender *is on probation, identify his or her probation officer and ascertain the conditions that have been imposed.*

3)   Condition the sex offender's *right to attend church services and activities on his or her signing a "conditional attendance agreement" that imposes the following restrictions:*

- *The* sex offender *will not work with minors in any capacity in the church.*
- *The* sex offender *will not transport minors to or from church, or any church activity.*
- *The* sex offender *will not attend youth or children's functions while on church property, except those involving his or her own child or children, and then only in the presence of a chaperone. (See below.)*
- *The* sex offender *will always be in the presence of a designated chaperone while on church property. This includes religious services, educational classes, activities, and restroom breaks. The chaperone will meet the* sex offender *at the entrance of the church, and accompany the* sex offender *while on church premises until the* sex offender *returns to his or her vehicle.*
- *A **single** violation of these conditions will result in an immediate termination of the* sex offender's *privilege to attend church.*
- *The conditional attendance agreement option will not be available unless the church's insurer is informed and confirms* that the

church's insurance coverage will not be affected.

4) *In some cases, exclusion of the* offender *from the church is the only viable option.*

5) *It is often desirable to draft a short policy addressing the church's response to registered* sex offenders *attending the church, and have it adopted by the church during an annual or special business meeting.*

6) *Seek legal counsel in formulating the church's response.*[173]

Hammar presents a good *legal* (or business) option; but is it a *biblical* and loving option? Unfortunately, Hammar offers little counsel encouraging church leaders to examine the Scriptures, to seek the will of God through prayer and study. This raises the question whether the Scriptures are the foundation for church policy and practice or if there is perhaps some other standard. Creating and following such a policy raises the question as to whether the church is the body of Christ or just another non-profit business. Yet this is nothing new. As far back as 1963, Bible scholar and theologian A.W. Tozer noted:

> *Jesus Christ has today almost no authority at all among the groups that call themselves by His name. By these, I do not mean the Roman Catholics or the liberals, or the various quasi-Christian cults. I do mean Protestant churches generally, and I include those that protest the loudest that they are in spiritual descent from our Lord and His apostles, namely, the evangelicals...*
>
> *He asks, "What church board consults our Lord's Word to decide matters under discussion... Board meetings are habitually opened with a formal prayer or 'season of prayer'; after that the Head of the Church is respectfully silent while the real rulers take over...*
>
> *Who remembers when a conference chairman brought his Bible to the table for the purpose of using it? Minutes, regulations, rules of order (insurance regulations and requirements), yes. The sacred commandments of the Lord, no. An absolute dichotomy exists between the devotional period and the business*

session. The first has no relation to the second.[174]

Marriage and family therapist J. Robert Ross offers a bit more balanced and certainly a more biblical view than Hammar. "A common misconception, aided and abetted by the media, puts all offenders in the same boat. Anyone convicted of a sex offense is automatically labeled as a *sexual predator.*"[175] Such labeling does not distinguish between the child molester, predatory rapist, and those whose victims were either *consenting* or *complicit* in the offense. "Most 'dangerous offenders' are in the minority set of the whole group. Most sex offenses are perpetrated by someone in the home, by someone the victim knows well… Studies indicate that 93 percent of boys and 80 percent of girls are molested by *someone they know.*"[176] The idea of "stranger danger" is often an exaggeration or even a myth.

Ross continues, "When it comes to dealing with sex offenders in the church, there are two distinct problems. The first is how to deal with offenders who have never been identified as such. Many offenses are committed by a staff member or volunteer, and *not* someone previously convicted or on the sex offender registry. **I know of no child being molested in a church by a person already on the sex offender registry."**[177] This last statement by Dr. Ross is particularly significant since he presently serves as marriage and family therapist and worked in a sex offender treatment program for over fifteen years. According to Matt Branaugh, editor of the *Church Law and Tax Group* at *Christianity Today,* "In 2011, allegations involving child sex abuse were the top reason that churches were in state and appellate courts nationwide."[178] Yet few, if any, of these cases involved *previously* convicted sex offenders, but rather were committed by others in the church that *were previously unknown* to the authorities. If sinners—even sexual sinners—were not welcome in the church, who would—or could—attend?

In regards to the second problem, Ross proposes a fourfold purpose in developing a policy towards *welcoming* sex offenders into the church. He recommends a policy that protects children, holds the offender accountable, protects the offender from unwarranted accusations, and ministers to him/her based on his/her unique circumstances. To meet those goals, he puts forward these five steps:

- *Acceptance of total responsibility for his/her offense without minimization or excuse (confession)*
- *Completion of a certified treatment program (accountability)*
- *Participation in a ministry or self-help group (especially for those who show signs of sexual addiction)*
- *Avoidance of contact with children and/or involvement in children's programs*
- *Agreement to be monitored and be accountable to church leaders.*[179]

This is certainly a more balanced approach; yet once again, it is lacking in any significant *scriptural* support. Nevertheless, Ross states, "Let us recognize that excluding offenders from polite company by restrictive laws regarding where they can live and by the rejection of them in public worship *does nothing* to reduce the risk of an offender committing another offense. Research has concluded that residential restriction laws have no effect on whether an offender commits another offense. Indeed, social isolation increases the risk of another offense."[180] Over twenty-five years of research by dozens of social science researchers have concluded that:

> *Sexual offender laws... do little to deter sexual victimization and are not applied in appropriate situations. Instead, such policies create criminal justice systems that are overburdened and unprepared to deal with sex offender populations, both systematically and fiscally. As with all types of programs and treatment initiatives, effective strategies to deal with sex offenders will never be based on anecdote and emotion, they are based on the facts about who the perpetrators and victims are, where they converge in time and space, and how the scenario is best managed. Two decades of legislation and the resulting research should have informed us that our solutions to this problem are misinformed and simply incorrect...Now is the time to be* smart *on sex offending, not just tough.*[181]

Therefore, both the state and the church are engaging in various "protective" practices that are not offering any *protection*. In fact, such policies and practices increase the homelessness and isolation of offenders, thereby actually *increasing* the risk of another offense against innocent and vulnerable victims. What is truly remarkable is that, given the difficulties inherent in the enforced isolation and homelessness of former offenders, the specific recidivism rate, i.e. an ex-offender committing a new sexual offense, is one of the lowest of any major criminal class. More pointedly, as it pertains to the church, a *careful exegesis* of Scripture suggests that, "Whoever causes one of my little ones who believe in me to sin, it would be better for him if a millstone were hung around his neck, and he were drowned in the depths of the sea." (Matthew 18:6)

Ironically, this is the most prevalent Biblical passage suggested by many church leaders and organizations (including *Prison Fellowship* and *Christianity Today*) as their justification for excluding sex offenders from the church. Yet such usage creates a serious error even as a "text out of context creates a pretext for error."

The *Prison Fellowship* webpage featured an article by Prison Fellowship Vice President, Pat Nolan, "How Should We Deal with Sex Offenders":

> One of the most vexing problems facing our society, and more particularly the church, is how to deal with sex offenders. As one pastor expressed to me, 'Jesus taught us to be forgiving. However, he also has made me the shepherd of my flock, and it is my responsibility to protect them from wolves.' As a parent, I am horrified with each press report of an abducted child. I can only imagine the pain those families feel. None of us wants that to happen to any more children. Jesus taught us that 'Whosoever shall hurt one of these little ones that believe in me, it would be better for him to have a millstone hung around his neck and be drowned in the depths of the sea.' Of course, Jesus didn't actually advocate that we actually throw molesters into the sea. However, it is fair to say that most people, **even most Christians**, think that is the minimum they deserve. Fear of such horrifying incidents has led many people

to support tougher penalties for sex offenders.

Nolan's quote was also featured in a 2009 *Christianity Today* article, "Modern Day Leper" (December 3, 2009) and "The 'Monsters' Among Us: Child Sex Abusers in Our Midst" (April 20, 2012). The latter was an editorial, stating, in part:

> *We must prioritize protecting the innocents. In recent years, we've witnessed a movement among churches discerning how to include ex-offenders into the community of faith. No doubt, many lives have been transformed in the process. Still, when the well-being of children and the inclusion of sex offenders conflict, we believe a gospel shaped community should prioritize protecting the most innocent among us, whose violation invites drowning by millstone. (Luke 17:2)*

The editorial concludes:

> *Hear us rightly: restoring molesters doesn't mean full or automatic inclusion in the community life. It certainly means jail time, psychological testing, and an intensive recovery program. It should mean complete barring from children's ministry. But for the gospel shaped community, it will, by God's grace, also mean holding on to the hope that the lives destroyed by the molester—among them his own—will be made new on the Final Day by the loving judgment of Jesus.*

Such a statement, particularly by a conservative Christian publication, begs the question of what is meant by a "gospel-shaped community." How does it differ from a "world-shaped community"? It appears that the church is conforming its practice to the secular worldview more than it is conforming to the truth of the Scriptures.

In actuality (and through diligent exegesis), the text in Matthew 18:6 and Luke 17:2 has nothing to do with anyone who may harm a *child* (although such sin is indeed a serious sin). Here is the biblical passage *in context* from Matthew:

> *At that time, the disciples came to Jesus, saying, 'Who then is the greatest in the kingdom of heaven?'*

Then Jesus called a little child *to him, set him in the midst of them and said, 'Assuredly I say to you unless you are converted and become* as little children, *you will by no means enter the kingdom of heaven. Therefore, whoever humbles himself as this* little child *is the greatest in the kingdom of heaven. Whoever receives one* little child *like this in my name receives me.*

But, whoever causes one of these little ones *who believe in me to sin, it would be better for him to have a millstone hung around his neck and be drowned in the depths of the sea... Take heed that you do not despise these* little ones, *for I say to you that in heaven their angels always see the face of my Father who is in heaven. For the Son of Man has come to save that which was lost... even so it is not the will of the Father that one of these* little ones *should perish.* (Matthew 18:1-6; 10-11; 14)

The terms "little child" (Greek: *paidan*) and "little one" (*mikros*) are not the same. Clearly to "become *as* little children" is not the same as actually becoming a child. Jesus was using this as an example for the disciples who were arguing and debating about who would be the greatest in the kingdom of heaven. He said that they all ought to become *as little children*, i.e., dependent, obedient, and submissive to the Father. In ancient cultures, little children (*paidan*) had no status, power, authority, possessions, personal rights nor agenda. Children depended on their earthly parents (primarily their father). Even so, in *becoming as little children*, Jesus was instructing the disciples to follow this example—of having no status, no power, no authority, no possessions, and no personal rights or agenda and to become wholly dependent on their heavenly Father.

Such a change in stature and in "esteeming others better than oneself" (Philippians 2:3) creates a certain amount of vulnerability and risk. In that day and until now, those who believe in Jesus have faced persecution each day. Jesus said, "In the world you will have tribulation; but be of good cheer. I have overcome the world." (John 16:33) The Apostle Paul wrote:

> *But we have this treasure (the gospel of Jesus Christ) in earthen vessels that the excellence of the power may be of God and not of us. We are hard pressed on every side, but not crushed; we are perplexed, but not in despair; persecuted, but not forsaken; struck down but not destroyed, always carrying about in the body the dying of the Lord Jesus that the life of Jesus might be manifest in our body.* (2 Corinthians 4:7-10)

Christians ought to expect persecution. They ought to expect earthly trials and sorrows. Unfortunately, all too often the organized church appears to care more about protecting its assets and making sure everyone inside is safe from anyone outside than they do about "seeking and saving the lost." When anyone believes the gospel "that Christ died for our sins according to the Scriptures, and that he was buried and that he rose again on the third day, according to the Scriptures," (2 Corinthians 15:3-4) they are saved by grace through faith. They are a child of God, one of his *little ones (mikros)*. And anyone who causes one of the Father's *little ones* (*mikros*) to sin is in serious danger of judgment. (Matthew 18:6)

What happens when the organized church turns away a repentant sinner or even a present sinner who is seeking Christ? How and why does the organized church judge a brother or sister's worthiness based on their *previous* sin, especially when such sin has been confessed and forsaken? What does this say about forgiveness? What does this say about the cleansing power of the blood of Jesus, a power we may sing about but often do not recognize? Would the leper who was healed by Jesus (Mark 1:40-45) be welcomed in the church? What if someone thought the ex-leper was still contagious? If the leper was not welcomed into the community but was forced to continue living "outside the camp,"[182] isn't there a chance that he may become reinfected? What about the demoniac, the one who "for a long time had been homeless and naked, living in a cemetery outside of town"? (Luke 8:26-37) Could he be trusted or welcomed to attend the local church? Why do church leaders insist on viewing people for who they once were rather than who they are in Christ?

Why does the organized church welcome (without question,

concern, or covenant) those who have been (and in some cases still are) fornicators, idolaters, adulterers, homosexuals, sodomites, thieves, the covetous, drunkards, revilers, or extortioners, (1 Corinthians 6:9-11) but insist on a restrictive covenant for a repentant former sex offender to attend services even with an assigned chaperone? Why does the organized church welcome without question a former drug dealer, gang member, arsonist, murderer, and a thief, but have such great concerns about someone *whom the world has labeled* a sex offender?

How can an ex-offender who must "always be in the presence of a designated chaperone while on church property, including religious services, educational classes, activities, and restroom breaks" ever join in the "fellowship of the saints?" How can someone who is "met at the entrance of the church, and accompanied on church premises until returned to his or her vehicle" serve the church body or exercise their spiritual gifts? Is this not akin to what the Apostle James warned against in showing partiality?

My brethren, do not hold the faith of our Lord Jesus Christ, the Lord of glory with partiality. For if there should come into your assembly a man with gold rings and fine apparel [and no criminal record], *and there should also come in a poor man in filthy clothes* [and perhaps even a criminal record]*and you pay attention to the one wearing fine clothes and say to him, 'You sit here in a good place', and say to the poor man, 'You stand there, or sit here at my footstool,' have you not shown partiality among yourselves and become judges with evil thoughts? Listen, my beloved brethren: Has God not chosen the poor of this world to be rich in faith and heirs of the kingdom which he promised to those who love Him? But you have dishonored the poor man. Do not the rich oppress you and drag you into court? Do they not blaspheme the noble name by which you are called? If you really fulfill the royal law according to the Scripture, 'you shall love your neighbor as yourself', you do well, but if you show partiality, you commit sin, and are convicted by the law*

> *as transgressors. For whoever shall keep the whole law and yet stumble in one point is guilty of all. For He who said, 'Do not commit adultery', also said, 'Do not commit murder.' Now if you do not commit adultery, but you do commit murder, you have become a transgressor of the law. So speak and so do as those who will be judged by the law of liberty. For judgment is without mercy to the one who has shown no mercy. Mercy triumphs over judgment.* (James 2:1-13)

Is the church "dishonoring the poor" (former sex-offenders) because of the rich who oppress and are threatening to drag the church into court? Does enforcing a restrictive covenant or completely excluding the ex-offender show "partiality" and therefore constitute sin on the part of the church and its leadership? How does an exclusionary covenant fulfill the "royal law," i.e., loving your neighbor as yourself? If church leaders who endorse such restrictions and exclusions (partiality) were to have a family member or friend fall into sexual sin and such sin led to the commission of a sexual offense, how would they then want the church (the body of Christ!) to respond to them? Would they want to be accepted and loved? The imposition of a restrictive covenant or exclusion is an organizational judgment; it is not merciful. It is not "doing justly, loving mercy, nor walking humbly with your God." (Micah 6:8.)

If the church is to be *the church*—the body of Christ—and not merely an extension of the state, the revenge and retribution of the state must be tempered with the grace and redemption of Christ. The judgment and condemnation of the *state* towards ex-offenders actually creates an opportunity for the *church* to guide one towards "repentance leading to salvation." The abandonment and hatred of the world offers an opportunity for the reaffirmation of Christian love. The mercy and love of Christ may conquer the darkness of the judgment and condemnation of the world with the light and life of Christ by offering hope and a plan for reconciliation and restoration. Experiencing such hope is the key that opens the hardest of hearts and is often the gateway leading to redemption and faith. Christians who have such hope are commanded to, "Sanctify the Lord God in your heart and always being ready to give a defense for the **hope** that is in with you to **anyone who asks**, but in gentleness and fear." (1 Peter 3:15) How can ex-offenders come to repentance leading to salvation, experience the reaffirmation of Christian love and have any hope for reconciliation and restoration when the doors of the church remain closed or when various stumbling blocks are placed in the way of those who are seeking to obtain mercy and find grace?

In other words, those who claim to know and love God must begin practicing *true* Christianity, which the late Chuck Colson (the founder of Prison Fellowship) described as "sacrificial love, concern for all people, forgiveness and reconciliation, and evil overcome by good."[183] For when the prodigal seeks to return to the Father, the church—as the body and presence of Christ in this world—must welcome such a penitent one with a robe, a ring, and rejoicing instead of rejection, restrictive, and exclusionary covenants, and continuing judgment. Unfortunately, as it stands now, too often the organized church and its leaders are more like the "elder brother" than a representative of the loving and forgiving Father.

Those who endorse closing church doors to anyone who has committed a sex offense and who insist on strict adherence to a "covenant" are doing so without any Biblical authority or support. These things are the invention of this world, driven by *fear* rather than empowered by love. Is the body of Christ called to tremble in fear or to live boldly in love? Moreover, how does excluding or limiting a fellow believer edify the body? What are the examples from the early church in both teaching and practice of such behavior?

Paul acknowledged the sinful past of the Ephesians that for many of them included the worship of the Roman goddess Diana. Their practice included "worshiping" with temple prostitutes.[184] He wrote:

> *And you He made alive, who were dead in trespasses and sins, in which you once walked according to the course of this world, according to the prince of the power of the air, the spirit who now works in the sons of disobedience, among whom **we all** once conducted **ourselves** [Paul includes himself] in the lusts of our flesh, fulfilling the desires of our flesh and of the*

mind, *and were by nature children of wrath, just like the others. But God, who is rich in mercy, because of His great love with which He loved us, even when we were dead in trespasses made us alive together with Christ (by grace you have been saved) and raised us up together, and made us sit together in the heavenly places in Christ Jesus, that in the ages to come He might show the exceeding riches of His grace in His kindness toward us in Christ Jesus.* (Ephesians 2:1-7)

He specifically mentions their *sexual* sin.

Be kind to one another, tenderhearted, forgiving one another, even as God in Christ forgave you. Therefore, be imitators of God, dear children, and walk in love, as Christ loved us and gave himself for us, an offering and a sacrifice to God, for a sweet smelling aroma. But fornication *and all* uncleanness *or covetousness, let it not even be named among you, as is fitting for saints; neither filthiness, nor foolish talking, nor coarse jesting which is not fitting, but rather the giving of thanks. For this you know, that no* fornicator, *unclean person, nor covetous man who is an idolater has any inheritance in the kingdom of God.* (Ephesians 4:32-5:5)

The early church was filled with many who had once been *sexual* sinners:

Do you not know that the unrighteous will not inherit the kingdom of God? Do not be deceived. Nether fornicators, *nor idolaters, not* adulterers, *nor* homosexuals, *nor* sodomites, *nor thieves, not covetous, nor* drunkards, *nor* revilers, *nor extortioners will inherit the kingdom of God. And such were some of you. But you were washed, you were sanctified, but you were justified in the name of our Lord Jesus and by the Spirit of our God.* (1 Corinthians 6:9-11)

Therefore, the apostle Paul instructed the church at Ephesus:

I, therefore, the prisoner of the Lord, beseech you to walk worthy of the calling with which you were called,

ROLES AND RESPONSIBILITIES OF THE CHURCH

> *with all lowliness and gentleness, with longsuffering, bearing with one another in love, endeavoring to keep the unity of the spirit in the bond of peace. There is one body and one spirit, just as you were called in one hope of your calling; one Lord, one faith, one baptism, one God and Father of all, and through all, and in all...*
>
> *...And He Himself gave some to be apostles, some prophets, some evangelists, and some pastors and teachers for the equipping of the saints for the work of the ministry, for the edifying of the body of Christ: that we should no longer be children, tossed to and fro and carried about by every wind of doctrine, by the trickery of men, in the cunning craftiness of deceitful plotting, but speaking the truth in love, may grow up into all things into Him who is the head—Christ from whom the whole body, joined and knitted together by what every joint supplies, causes growth of the body for the edifying of itself in love.* (Ephesians 4:1-6, 11-16)

Sexual sin existed in the ancient church and still exists in the church today. Sexual sin is measured by the Scripture, whereas a sexual offense is measured by the state. Yet the state no longer recognizes many sexual sins as sexual offenses. Adultery, homosexuality, sodomy, fornication, cohabitation, premarital sex, and such were once scandalous and even illegal in many jurisdictions, but they are now legal and even encouraged, protected, and celebrated by the state. What is troubling is that those who continue committing such acts *are* welcome in the modern church. In many instances, not only do many church members have a sexually sinful *past*, but they have a sexually sinful *present*. Admittedly, those who are openly struggling or living in sin must not be given positions of responsibility in teaching children and teens; nevertheless, they may still attend all services and participate in "fellowship of the saints." Yet those with a past sexual offense (as measured by the state, but unspecified in Scripture), but who have openly confessed their past sins and completed their prison sentence, who indeed have a broken spirit and a contrite heart, and whose sorrow over such sin led them to repentance and salvation are either excluded from fellowship in the church or subjected to a restrictive covenant! Are these things biblical, or do we have something backwards?

What did the Apostle Paul teach?

> *It is actually reported that* there is sexual immorality *among you, and such sexual immorality that is not even named among the Gentiles—that a man has his father's wife. And you are puffed up, and have not rather mourned, that he who has done this deed might be taken away from among you. For I indeed, as absent in body but present in spirit, have already judged (as though I were present) him who has so done this deed. In the name of our Lord Jesus Christ, when you are gathered together, along with my spirit, with the power of our Lord Jesus Christ, deliver such a one to Satan for the destruction of the flesh, that his spirit may be saved in the day of the Lord Jesus. Your glorying is not good. Do you not know that a little leaven leavens the whole lump? Therefore, purge out the old leaven, that you may be a new lump since you are truly unleavened. For indeed Christ, our Passover, was sacrificed for us.... I have written to you not to keep company with anyone named a brother (or sister) who is sexually immoral, or covetous, or an idolater, or a reviler, or a drunkard—not even to eat with such a person.* (1 Corinthians 5:1-11)

Why are those today who are currently and unashamedly sexually immoral, (e.g., willfully engaging in adultery, homosexuality, sodomy, fornication, cohabitation, premarital sex, abusing various forms of pornography, and so on), welcome in the church, while many former sex-offenders who have confessed and forsaken such sins are still unwelcome? Once again, what do the Scriptures suggest?

> *This punishment, which was inflicted by the majority, is sufficient for such a man, so that on the contrary, you ought rather to* forgive and comfort *him, lest perhaps such a one be swallowed up with too much sorrow. Therefore, I urge you to* reaffirm your love for him. *For*

to this end I also wrote that I might put you to the test, whether you are obedient in all things. Now whom you forgive, I also forgive. For if indeed I have forgiven anything, I have forgiven that one for your sakes in the presence of Christ, lest Satan should take advantage of us; for we are not ignorant if his devices. (2 Corinthians 2:6-11)

A member of the Corinthian church was engaging in serious sexual sin. This was not just another member of the community, but someone who was "named a brother" and who was a member of the local church. Not only had the man sinned, but the church was also sinning in tolerating such sin. Had the man been allowed to continue in such sin, eventually there would have been little difference in the sexual moral values of the church and the community at large. The "leaven" would infect the whole church, much as it has today.

Two of the greatest schemes of the enemy are: first, convincing believers and church leaders that sin is not sin and that one sin is greater than another; second, the problems that exist when church members judge one another without love and compassion. The church is—and has always been—filled with sinners. After all, have not all "sinned and fallen short of the glory of God"? (Romans 3:23) And while it is true that the "wages of sin is death, but the gift of God is eternal life through Christ Jesus our Lord," (Romans 6:23) nevertheless, does God not demonstrate his own love for us, in that "while we were yet sinners, Christ died for us" (including former sex-offenders)? (Romans 5:8) Moreover, we preach that "as many as received Him (Christ Jesus) he gave the right to become children of God, to those who believe in His name: who were born, not of blood, nor of the will of the flesh, nor the will of man, but of God." (John 1:12-13) These truths are among those being taught in jail and prison Bible studies and religious services. These are among the things being believed by the lost, including many who, "desire to come after Jesus Christ, who deny self ... who take up a cross ... and who follow Him" in faith and obedience. (Mark 8:34-35)

How then is it reasonable, merciful, or just to prevent such a brother or sister from joining a church or subject such a disciple of Christ to a restrictive or exclusionary covenant? Does such exclusion or rejection tend to divide or unite the body? Does rejection edify and unify the church? Does isolation demonstrate hospitality? Does it welcome the prodigal? Should the church body welcome the former prisoner (prodigal) as Paul instructed Philemon and the church at Colossae concerning Onesimus? "If then you count me (Paul) as a partner, receive him (Onesimus) as you would me. But if he has wronged you or owes you anything, put it on my account." (Philemon 1:17-18) What if the church were to receive those being released from prison as welcome brothers or sisters, even as they would receive a traveling preacher or famous evangelist? Has such a thing ever been tried? And if not, why not?

The western church struggles with unity—or more likely with *disunity*. Denominational differences divide, and there appears to be a competition for who can put on the best "show."[185] The Apostle Paul wrote to the church at Corinth, which was a very diverse and potentially divided congregation:

> *For as the body is one and has many members, but all of the members of that one body, being many, are one body, so also is Christ. For by one Spirit, we were all baptized into one body—whether Jews or Greeks, slaves or free—and have all been made to drink of one spirit. For in fact, the body is not one member, but many. If the foot should say, 'Because I am not a hand, I am not of the body', is it therefore not of the body? And if the ear should say, 'Because I am not an eye, I am not of the body', is it therefore not of the body? And if the whole body were an eye, where would be hearing? If the whole were hearing, where would be smelling? But now God has set the members, each one of them in the body, just as he pleased. And if they were all one member, where would the body be? But now indeed, there are many members, yet one body. And the eye cannot say to the hand, 'I have no need of you'; or again the head to the feet, 'I have no need of you." No much more, those members of the body*

> *that seem weaker are necessary. And those members of the body, which we think to be less honorable, on these we bestow greater honor; and our unpresentable parts have greater modesty, but our presentable parts have no need. But God composed the body, having given greater honor to that part which lacks it, that there should be no schism in the body, but that the members should have the same care for one another. And if one member suffers, all members suffer with it; if one member is honored, all rejoice with it. Now you are the body of Christ, and members individually.* (1 Corinthians 12:12-27)

It is no small thing to welcome a former sex offender into the fellowship of a local church. Church leaders object because of the perceived risk to the congregation and/or insurance regulations and business practices. But what is the risk of *not* welcoming such a sinner? Beyond the risk to the former offender who may subsequently fall back into sin without the support, encouragement, and exhortation of the body, and correspondingly, beyond the danger to those who cause the former offender (a *little one*) to fall into sin (a punishment worse than a millstone and drowning), there is an even greater danger to the church as a whole. The members of the body who are weaker (i.e., those who have a difficult past) *are, in fact, a necessary part* of the body. **Once again, they are a necessary part of the body!** Those members of the body whom we think are less honorable (ex-offenders), should have bestowed on them a greater honor. The unpresentable parts have greater modesty, that is, they have a greater need for forgiveness, comfort and a reaffirmation of love, but the presentable parts, i.e., the church leaders, pastors and teachers, and "good" members have no such need. The weaker, less honorable and unpresentable parts of the body are, in fact, *what makes the church a diverse and functioning body*. It is what allows for the ministry of love, of edification, and of sanctification. *It is what allows the true nature of Christ's love to be seen by the world.* It is "true" Christianity, "sacrificial love, concern for all people, forgiveness and reconciliation, and evil overcome by good."[186] It is what differentiates the body of Christ from any human social service organization or benevolent non-profit business.

There is a way the church may perform its proper role in society by offering redemption and restoration to ex-offenders. It is by simply obeying the Scriptures. While our brothers and sisters are in prison, the church is commanded to remember and visit them, for when such love and mercy are shown to a prisoner, it is shown to Christ Himself. (Hebrews 13:3; Matthew 25:31-46.) Many prisoners have never heard the gospel, and many may have previously heard, but rejected it at that time. Therefore, in fulfilling the Great Commission, (Matthew 28:19-20) members of the church *ought to visit men and women in prison*. Yet it is far more important to **be** Jesus to a prisoner than it is to merely talk *about* Him. It is the love of God—not a lecture—that instills hope.

According to Baylor University Professor Dr. Byron Johnson, "Religious conversions play a necessary role (in the process of long term change), but their conversions in isolation are insufficient in reforming offenders and bringing about lasting change."[187] "The conversion experience itself is not enough to protect the ex-prisoners from all manner of missteps they might take following release from prison."[188] Most prisoners are isolated from the faith community outside. Many prisoners have never been to church, and the few who have attended previously either have fallen away or have been frequently abandoned by their "fellowship" when they were arrested.

There is a substantial social stigma associated with helping prisoners, and judgment and apathy come much easier than mercy and grace. Johnson also states, "Unless ex-prisoners who happen to become born again Christians get the *social and spiritual support* necessary to develop a deep and lasting commitment—mainly through congregations—they will likely fail in their transition to society."[189] Dr. Ted Roberts notes, "Someone's initial commitment to Christ means the work has just begun. They need to have a place where they can go and get healed and learn to deal with their wounds, traumas and addictions; otherwise, we will just train them to be religious."[190]

Unfortunately, the follow up care and feeding of *ex-prisoners* is seriously lacking. Nevertheless, unless the *gospel according to the scriptures* is preached in jails and prisons, unless the church is intentional about *making disciples*, and unless pastors and teachers are deliberately *"equipping the saints for the work of the ministry,"* the "outside" ministry becomes less important. It is the *inside* ministry (in jails and prisons) where these things must begin. How can ex-offenders receive "social and spiritual support" while they are still inside? "Preaching is crucial, but folks need practical help in ways they never have before. They need mentors and models on how to live. And they need to see them at close range, because the models they had at home have frequently wounded, limited, or confused them. The church, as never before, has to become a healthy family for so many who have experienced unhealthy families and don't even realize it."[191]

Most jail and prison volunteers come from evangelical churches whose congregations believe that prisoners need to hear about Jesus. Unfortunately, these same fellowships are far less inclined to be Jesus—to be His hands, His arms, and His feet—when the prisoner is released. Former prisoners are often unwelcome in the neighborhood, and unwelcome in the church.[192] Since this is true of prisoners in general—of those who have *not* committed a sexual offense—how much more is it true with those who *have* committed such an offense? Those who have been forgiven little and love little often attempt to drive those who have been forgiven much and love much from the fellowship of Christ.

Perhaps it is reasonable to have some form of a covenant agreement between the former sex offender and the church. But what is needed is a different form of covenant, not a covenant driven by exclusion or restriction, and not a covenant for protecting one party at the expense of another as a way of keeping someone out. The great need is for a covenant of inclusion; a covenant of God's forgiveness, mercy, love, and grace, and a covenant modeled after Jesus' example. What if church members were committed to seeking and saving the lost, *especially* those considered by the world to be unforgiveable, unlovable, and untouchable? What if professing Christians deliberately sacrificed to reach out to "the tired, the poor, the huddled masses yearning to breathe free, the wretched refuse, the homeless, the tempest-tost," instead of—or in addition to—the mighty, the noble, the wise, and the wealthy? For has God not *chosen* the foolish, the weak, the vile and the despised—even those who are prisoners and ex-offenders—so that no flesh should glory in his presence? (1 Corinthians 1:26-31)

It is reasonable and wise to establish policies to protect children from sexual harm. Yet the greatest danger is not a sex offender who wants to attend the church. There are many other dangers. One danger is from those who are presently working with children and teens who have not offended—but are tempted—and those who have offended but have not been discovered. It is reasonable to conduct background checks for *all* volunteers who work with children, teens, and other vulnerable populations. It is reasonable to establish good sense and best-practice policies for classes and programs. It is also reasonable for the church to include age-appropriate sexual health education and to facilitate open dialogues and information, especially in light of the onslaught of a media-promoted sexual immorality and especially given the increasing use of smartphones, tablets, and other technologies by children and teenagers.

Yet children and teens are not the only vulnerable populations. The ex-offenders are vulnerable to being discarded by the world, discriminated against in housing and jobs, dehumanized and demonized in the media, endangered by vigilante violence, and often disconnected from their families (particularly when the victim was a close family member). Are these not some of the *little ones (mikros)* whom Jesus came to save, the very same *little ones* that the Father was concerned about perishing? (Matthew 18:14)

But the even greater danger is living in—and conforming to—a sexually salacious and promiscuous world. Children and teenagers, as well as adults, are immersed in a world of pornography and sexually explicit music, movies, television shows, and video games. Often these images run unchecked into our living rooms and bedrooms via the smartphones and other electronic devices that we actually *provide* for our children and teens. Even the best pornography filters will not stop the sexual innuendos and outright sexually explicit messages in advertising and many popular television shows. Sex without conscience or consequence permeates nearly every television drama or sitcom. We immerse and saturate our children's, teenagers' and even our own minds and hearts in a toxic and sexually explicit brine but are then surprised when our brains become pickled!

In my work with the Sex Offender Treatment Program, with the Arizona Department of Corrections, almost all of the students (fellow prisoners and ex-offenders) under the age of forty had been exposed to hardcore and violent pornography, as well as images of child sexual abuse (child porn) when they were preteens or younger. Many such images are created and shared by teenagers "sexting" one another. Sexual sin and the possibility and opportunities for sexual offenses are everywhere in our society—even in the local church. There is an abundance of fear and concern on every side, and perhaps it is reasonable to establish a covenant of protection. But can the church prepare a covenant of grace—a covenant of social and spiritual support for a former sex-offender rather than an exclusionary and restrictive covenant? When is the best time to establish such a covenant?

One of the steps suggested by Richard Hammar is that "the sex offender will always be in the presence of a designated chaperone while on church property… The chaperone will meet the sex offender at the entrance of the church, and accompany the sex offender on church premises until the sex offender is returned to his or her vehicle."[193] Obviously, the intent of such a policy is to protect the church; however, it offers little or no protection to the ex-offenders, except from them not being subject to false accusations while on church property. Such a policy, however, presupposes that the "church" is limited to a building, a specific property, or a program. Is that the New Testament church?

Someone has said that what started in Palestine two thousand years ago as a fellowship went to Greece and became a philosophy, then to Rome and became an institution, and then to Europe and became a culture. But when the fellowship came to America, it became an enterprise or business. The present covenant offered to ex-offenders by the church is a *business* decision. It is not a decision of the *ekklesia*—the body of Christ. Such a decision is not discerning, loving, forgiving, or merciful. It does indicate that we may be in "perilous times," when "men will be lovers of themselves, lovers of money, boasters, proud, blasphemers, disobedient to parents, unthankful, unholy, unloving, unforgiving, slanderers, without self control, brutal, despisers of good, traitors, headstrong, haughty, lovers of pleasure rather than lovers of God, who have a form of godliness but deny its power." (2 Timothy 3:1-5) It corresponds with what has been noted as the ABC's of the organized (or institutional) church: "Attendance, Buildings, and Cash." Such a church is not a New Testament Church. It is not the *ekklesia*—it is not the "body of Christ." It is foolish then to attempt to make a silk purse out of sow's ear.

    A word of caution: I know all too well that generalizations are destructive. Not all sex offenders are the same; as noted, a *small* number of ex-offenders *are* dangerous. Nevertheless, many are not. In the same way, there may be a small number of churches that are obedient to the Scriptures, and hopefully a growing number of professing Christians who are willing to at least engage in a dialogue on these issues. There may be congregations (I am guessing usually smaller ones) for whom Jesus Christ is actually the head of the church, not only in name but also in practice. There may be churches that are willing to consult the Scriptures first—instead of insurance regulations and legal decisions—when facing *spiritual* decisions. There may be churches that are more committed to making disciples than creating converts, that teach and practice spiritual disciplines, and that are willing to reach out to forgive the unforgivable, touch the untouchable, and love the unlovable. Unfortunately, in my experience so far, these bodies are rarely traditional churches; they are more likely the remnant of the authentic New Testament church—the *ekklesia* or the "body of Christ." Perhaps the new covenant of God's forgiveness, mercy, love and grace needs to come from the *ekklesia*. Perhaps it's not the role of the organized church; perhaps it's the role of the *ekklesia*, a role revealed in a later chapter. But first, we must address the question of how we are to transform the conflict.

9 – *Transforming the Conflict*

Up to this point, we have examined injustice and fear, considered the inherent complexities, and identified the participants and some of the deleterious effects of existing paradigms and practices involving sex offenders and related parties. These paradigms and practices constitute a particularly complex problem. Unfortunately, the problem is presently being solved by *force*, (lengthy incarcerations, civil commitments, lifetime registration, shaming and so on) rather than by more productive and peaceful means. Consequently, there is no true justice, and no one is truly satisfied or healed.

Victims remain broken, without healing or understanding. *Offenders* remain broken, declared guilty, judged, and condemned but without being offered opportunities for restoration or reconciliation. Unfortunately, society frequently doesn't allow victims or offenders to ever be anything other than a victim or an offender. They believe victims will always be weak and traumatized; offenders will always be incurable monsters. And because we refuse to see them in a different light, we often inhibit or completely prevent change or transformation.

Inclusion on the sex offender registry guarantees to expose the former sex-offender to a lifetime of social exclusion and living with unrelenting shame. *Society* suffers loss, not because of any significant re-offense, but because of hundreds of millions of tax dollars spent on incarceration and supervision instead of education, innovation, and other community needs. Yet an even greater societal loss is the loss of human capital. After completing their sentence and being released from prison, ex-offenders encounter tremendous difficulties finding suitable employment, especially any *meaningful* employment in accordance with their previous training and expertise. As previously noted, those who commit a sex offense represent a cross section of the outside community. Many former sex offenders are highly educated professionals, teachers, successful business people, and others who often lack the "criminal mindset and habits" so often found in a general population prison environment. What is the societal loss when those who previously practiced various occupations are prevented from utilizing their skills and education in some form of meaningful work? What does this say about the willingness of society or the church to restore and reconcile ex-offenders back into the community?

Victims, offenders, and society all suffer to varying degrees. The destructive and corrosive consequences of sin harm, and ultimately destroy, all of society. In light of such brokenness and chaos, is it possible to transform this complex problem by productive and peaceful means rather than force and social condemnation? Yes, it is!

Albert Einstein once observed, "The world we have made, as a result of the level of thinking we have done this far, creates problems that we cannot solve at the level at which we created them." Justice for *all* will never prevail amidst the current level of hardened emotions, fear and the constrained reasoning of a "justice system" censured with fear, prejudice, and ignorance. Consequently, various attempts at criminal justice fall short of creating reform. Through judgment and condemnation we are treating the results of the disease instead of digging deeper into the cause, i.e., *why* the offense happened. By comparison, trimming the top of a weed does not get at the root, nor does it transform the soil from which the weed has grown. Likewise, a luscious garden will never grow in desert sand and gravel without substantial and dramatic fundamental changes in the soil and environment.

We need fundamental changes in the "soil and environment" and in our understanding of *why* sex offenses happen.   Without such changes, victims will not heal, offenders will remain condemned and unproductive, society as a whole will remain broken, and the church will remain fragmented and divided. Therefore what we need are leaders with the courage to face criticism, even if it means being misunderstood; leaders with the wisdom and judgment to separate the facts from various fictions and myths; and leaders with the dedication and commitment not to take sides but to consider the "side of the whole." We need leaders with the integrity described by Dr. Martin Luther King who said, "The ultimate measure of a man is not where he stands in moments of comfort and convenience, but where he stands at times of challenge and controversy." We need leaders in government and in the church with unwavering courage, integrity, dedication, and judgment.

We know that conflicts arise from complex problems and are an ordinary and necessary part of life. The only question is how we will deal with such conflicts. The complexities of the conflicts surrounding society's response to ex-offenders demand experienced and exemplary leadership. For example, leadership and mediation expert Mark Gerzon notes, "Leading through conflict involves facing differences honestly and creatively, understanding their full complexity and scope, and enabling those involved to move toward original solutions. Such leadership requires going beyond the powerful primordial responses that result in an 'Us vs. Them' mentality."[194] In the present paradigm concerning ex-offenders, an "Us vs. Them" mentality exists. Hard lines are drawn between victims and their advocates and between ex-offenders and their advocates. Both sides fall into the trap of telling rather than listening, closing them off from changing by the world by anything other than force.[195] The only answer is an innovative or new style of leadership.

Gerzon presents the three faces of leadership present in any conflict as the demagogue, the manager or the mediator. **Demagogues** thrive on creating and fueling conflicts. **Managers** work to preserve their own self-interests. **Mediators** employ various tools to lead participants through perils and difficulties of conflict while transforming obstacles and oppression into opportunities, and creating stepping stones towards establishing justice, insuring domestic tranquility, and securing the blessings of liberty for all.

Demagogues are largely responsible for creating and inflaming the conflict involving ex-offenders. According to Gerzon, "This type of leader (demagogue) has contempt for the very idea of transforming a conflict. Instead, they exploit human differences by using a *fear-based stereotype-driven* leadership strategy that:

- *Creates the "Other" by indoctrinating the population that is fragmented and polarized*
- *Distorts reality by refusing to see the actual "system" that connects the perpetrator and victim on so many levels*
- *Is indifferent to the suffering of their victims and dehumanizes both the oppressor and the oppressed*
- *Brands anyone who questions the lies on which their propaganda is based as "traitors" or being one of "them"*
- *Manipulates the means of communication so that no spontaneous feedback is possible.*"[196]

The mainstream media's stereotypical image of sex offenders creates fear and plays into the hands of the demagogues' (legislative leaders' and media pundits') ability to exploit human differences. If the media is to be believed, dangerous sexual predators are lurking everywhere. Moreover, the government's enactment of the AWA and other sex-offender-specific legislation actually enhances the public's fear by creating a second class of citizens (a "demonized other"), thereby fragmenting the population and polarizing neighborhoods and families.

The present justice system facilitates the belief that the offender is "all bad" and the victim is "all good." This ignores the reality that many offenders (at least in part) offend out of their own emotional pain because of previously being victims of sexual exploitation and other forms of neglect and abuse. In addition, it ignores that some victims are themselves either *complicit* or *incompetently* consenting to the crime. The justice system also prevents contact between the ex-offender and the victim, thereby denying opportunities for healthy confrontation, healing, reconciliation, and restoration. Such policies are indifferent to anyone's suffering and lead to the dehumanization of both the former sex offender and the victim.

In an Arizona legislative race, Cecil Ash, an incumbent Republican representative, suggested a reconsideration of the severity of sex offense sentencing as it pertains to child pornography cases.[197] He was unjustly and viciously attacked in the media and by his colleagues (demagogues). Although he was reelected by a very narrow margin, he eventually left office (in part) after growing weary of the futility of effecting change and of being branded as a "traitor" and one of "them." Such is the character and manipulations of demagogues.

Managerial leaders mean well. They "want to contribute to their organization or community… and within firm and fair boundaries they can achieve excellence. Their more narrowly defined focus… enables them to fulfill their responsibilities with skill and often with devotion."[198] Yet on controversial issues, they may be "missing in action" because they:

- *Define themselves by their turf*
- *Pursue only the interest of their group*
- *Compartmentalize their values*
- *Do not think systematically*
- *Are paralyzed by conflict*
- *Disregard the "Other"*
- *Define productivity in terms of 'us', disregarding 'them'."*[199]

Advocates on both sides—ex-offenders and victims—as well as most leaders in the majority of churches and social service organizations often function in a managerial capacity. They define themselves in terms of their own organization, pursuing only the interest of their own group, and do not think systemically or outside the box. They have little regard for the "other." Sex offenders and their advocates often have little regard or empathy for victims; and victims and victim rights groups as well as church leaders have little regard for ex-offenders. Managers view the organization's or church's successes in terms of how well they are doing inside rather than their participation and investment outside—with "them."

Gerzon challenges this managerial mindset:

> *The borders on which you base your leadership and managerial identity are obsolete. Your 'turf' is broadening and you are no longer under control.*

> *Your 'interests' are being redefined, and your world has changed. Your partisan, turf based identity is an anachronism. If you don't change, you will find yourself immersed in conflicts that ultimately lead only to dead ends. To prevent yourself from becoming obsolete, revitalize yourself with the tools of the mediator.*

The third style or face of leadership—and the only one effective in resolving or transforming conflicts—is the **mediator**. This kind of leadership "leads to harmony rather than war, *justice* rather than *oppression*, sustainability rather than destruction, and *respect* rather than *discrimination*. In other words, it will lead to a world where difference and conflict are recognized as parts of the natural order and are seen as opportunities for learning and positive transformation in our relationships, enterprises, and institutions."[200] Perhaps this type of leadership is possible even in our justice system, our society, and our churches.

Unlike the demagogue or even the manager, the mediator:
- *Strives to act on behalf of the whole, not just a part*
- *Thinks systematically and is committed to ongoing learning*
- *Builds trust by building bridges across the dividing lines*
- *Seeks innovation and opportunity in order to transform conflict.*[201]

Where will such leadership arise? Will it arise on the halls of government? Will someone within the social organizations take the lead? What about corrections officials or church leaders? Is this the role of the *ekklesia*? Gerzon teaches that, "Each of us can learn to be a mediator simply by becoming apprentices and learning the tools of the trade. Anyone who sincerely and humbly studies these tools and applies them to his or her life—whether at work in the community or at home—will experience a remarkable, positive shift. Taken together, the tools of the mediator can profoundly change our lives."[202] What are these tools?

The eight tools of the mediator are:
- *Integral vision*
- *Systems thinking*
- *Presence*

- *Inquiry*
- *Conscious conversation*
- *Dialogue*
- *Bridging*
- *Innovation*

Conscious conversation, bridging and innovation are useful tools, but beyond the range of discussion in this book. Therefore, the following discussion focuses on using the tools of integral vision, systems thinking, presence, inquiry, and especially dialogue to help bring transformation to the difficult and complex problem of how to deal with ex-offenders.

Integral vision means "committing ourselves to holding all sides of the conflict, in all their complexity, in our minds and in our hearts, and learning to see beyond boundaries."[203] This is much easier said than done. It requires practice and skill. "The challenge is to recognize that while each of us resides in a 'part,' we can nevertheless seek to identify with the whole."[204] For example, ex-offenders must learn to abandon their tendency towards victim posturing and self-pity and recognize the great harm they have inflicted up on the victims of sexual violence. Victims and their advocates, as well as legislative leaders, must abandon their fear and recognize that offenders do not just suddenly commit a sexual offense. It doesn't "just happen." There is always much more to the story of *why* the offense happened.

When we maintain our own biased and limited perspective and separateness, we create our own prison. The bars on our cell are created by our identification with a particular side. Albert Einstein noted,

> *A human being is part of the whole called by us 'universe'... a part limited in time and space. He experiences himself, his thought and feelings, as separate from the rest—a kind of optical delusion of his consciousness. This delusion is kind of a prison for us, restricting us to our personal desires and to affection for the person nearest us. Our task must be to free ourselves from this prison by widening our circle of compassion to embrace all living creatures.*[205]

"Integral vision means understanding divergent worldviews but not being limited or trapped by them. It means including and transcending different viewpoints, holding diversity in our minds and hearts as part of a larger whole, all the while recognizing that each by itself is partial and incomplete."[206] Fear is the great enemy of integral vision. In a climate or culture of fear, it is especially difficult to be a mediator who does not respond to complexity with stereotypes. Yet even amidst the media's fearful onslaught, such vision and hope is possible.

Systems thinking means identifying all (or as many as possible) of the significant elements related to the conflict and understanding the relationship between them. It involves drawing better boundaries.[207] This requires participants on all sides of the conflict to learn to think (and act) differently. Victims and their advocates, as well as legislators and corrections officials, rarely see an ex-offender in a positive light. Their thinking is limited by their boundaries. At the same time, ex-offenders and their advocates are rarely willing to see the great harm and suffering caused by the offense. "Just as a fish takes water for granted, so we are often unconscious of our boundaries and their implications. Systems thinking is about nothing more, but nothing less, than making this unconscious process conscious and then bringing the awareness to the conflict in our lives."[208]

Unfortunately, as applied to society's complex issues (such as how to deal with sex offenders) the ability or willingness to think systematically is rare. All too frequently, our tendency is to jump to our own conclusions. Unfortunately, when we jump to conclusions, we are usually about as far away from the truth as an outright lie would be.

Engaging in systematic or strategic thinking requires effort. It does not happen automatically. Nevertheless, this tool of a mediator may be exercised when individuals begin thinking systematically about their own role. Everyone has a bias; everyone comes from one side or the other, and may still be more comfortable there. We usually have some bias, some connection that hinders our objectivity. It is not about ridding ourselves of such a position, but becoming consciously aware of it.[209] For those coming from a "managerial" position, it is important to view this conflict from outside of the box. Talking to those who are outside of your "box" and systematically studying their perspectives can bring a new clarity and understanding.[210]

Finally, we begin thinking systematically when we think twice before declaring someone an "enemy."[211] This is crucial. When victims consider an ex-offender as an "enemy" or when ex-offenders consider the police, corrections or probations officials as "enemies," we are dehumanizing and demonizing them. Buddhist monk Thich Nhat Hanh's advice is, "If we divide reality into two camps—the violent and the nonviolent—and stand in one camp while attacking the other, the world will never have peace."[212]

Presence is applying all of our mental, emotional, and spiritual resources to witnessing ourselves and the conflict of which we are now a part, and learning to become awake.[213] The mere mention of the words "sex offender" creates a fearful response. Even among the best of us and at the best of times, strain and tension, fear and defensiveness, pride and rigidity—all are typical reactions. We freak out. Being able to be "present" to one's emotional state is "a tool of the heart, invisible and unmeasureable, and at the same time a tool of the mind with all the discerning power of a sword."[214]

On a personal note, by working with sex offenders in the Arizona Department of Corrections Sex Offender Treatment program (SOETP), I have the opportunity to listen to my brothers. I hear what happened (their offense), but I also am able to come to an understanding of why it happened. I have to work at being "present." This is also an outworking of God's mercy and grace. By being present, we learn to see what Nouwen observed in the "convulsive generation," that,

> *Many people are convinced that there is something terribly wrong with the world in which they live and feel that cooperation with existing models of living constitutes a betrayal of the self. Everywhere we see restless people, unable to concentrate and often suffering from a growing sense of depression. They know what is shouldn't be the way it is, but the see no workable alternative. Thus, they are saddled with frustration, which often expresses itself in undirected, purposeless violence [including sexual offenses] or in*

a suicidal withdrawal from the world.[215]

Consequently, when I listen to what my brother did (his offense), I am also aware of what I have done or recognize that I could have done just as much. Moreover, I am aware of the mercy and grace I have received from God and thankful that I can be "present" to share the same mercy and grace with my brother. Being present helps clarify my motivations and cultivates a quiet existence.

Inquiry is asking questions that unlock essential information about the conflict that is vital to understanding how to transform it. It is the essence of the power of the question.[216] The tool of inquiry is extremely important in transferring this conflict. For the ex-offender as well as for the victims and their advocates, inquiry opens the door to understanding *why* the sexual offense happened.

"Conflicts usually consist of genuine differences compounded by stuck positions, fixed attitudes, hardened identities and closed hearts."[217] The differences between the offender and the victim are obvious; however, those differences are compounded when we *choose* to remain stuck, *maintain* inflexible attitudes, *believe* the stereotypical identities presented in the media, and *lean* more towards judgment than mercy. Honest inquiry allows us to begin choosing differently, to develop and maintain differing points of view, and to seek and believe the truth rather than some inaccurate and prejudicial stereotype.

Gerzon notes, "If you bring the appropriate people together in constructive ways with *reliable information*, they will create authentic vision and strategies for addressing the shared concerns of the organization or community."[218] For example, as noted in Chapter 5 – "Offenses and Offenders," the fact that Adam had sexual contact with Megan when she was a minor is indisputable. She became pregnant with his child; yet that is not all of the reliable information. The back-story describes why the offense happened. It is this back-story—obtained through honest inquiry—that helps justice to prevail without fear or prejudice. Is it possible that reasonable people could create a strategy for addressing the shared concerns of the organization or community in such an instance?

On the other hand, all too often advocacy groups engage in advocacy without reliable information. For example, the case involving "Greg" in Chapter 7 – "Roles and Responsibilities of Ex-Offenders," exposes how advocacy groups defended Greg's *ongoing* deviant sexual conduct without obtaining adequate and reliable information. Before engaging in advocacy, it is crucial to obtain reliable and complete information *and* to have taken into account the feelings of all of the relevant stakeholders. Comprehensive inquiry must precede effective advocacy; otherwise, prejudice and ignorance will continue to corrupt true justice.

Finally, if we only pay attention to the people who are shouting at the microphone (those who believe that anyone who commits a sex offense should be fitted for a millstone and drowned), we are not thinking systematically or developing integral vision. The necessary innovation in some conflicts—and sometime its transformation—may hinge on people whose voices are inaudible (such as sex offenders in prison or civil commitment facilities). Because they are passively silent or actively *silenced* through intimidation and discrimination, the voices of those who are being hurt by the system do not reach us. Ex-offenders are rarely, if ever, called upon to testify before legislative hearings. And even if they are called to testify, their voices may not be *heard* because of the filters of fear, prejudice, and ignorance of injustice.

Dialogue is the most important tool of the mediator, because it increases and facilitates true communication and begins building the human capacity for bridging and innovation. It is moving beyond the "either-or."[219] Establishing a dialogue is the key to transforming any conflict as it is primarily designed for situations in which people have fundamentally different frames of reference. Dialogue is a way of conversing that:

- *Enables a wider range of feelings to be expressed than in debate*
- *Inspires more honesty and forthrightness than other methods*
- *Avoids superficial forced compromises*
- *Generates learning, new options, and innovations*
- *Increases the likelihood that everyone will be heard*
- *Seeks the deeper truth in each perspective.*[220]

Demagogues and managers often attempt to resolve differences by means of decree or debate. Consequently, in attempting to deal with ex-offenders or to advocate on their behalf, both sides engage in debate. The side having the most power (the government) generally imposes their will on the weaker party. They legislate by the golden rule—the one with the gold makes all the rules. Complex conflicts—such as how to deal with ex-offenders—are rarely, if ever, resolved or transformed by decree or debate. Actions imposed in this manner attempt to resolve complexities by force.

As previously discussed, the U.S. justice system attempts to resolve various complexities through force by imprisoning more than two million American citizens—far more per capita than any other country. Many lives are being irretrievably destroyed by the injustices of American justice, specifically by plea bargains. Prison overcrowding leads to human rights abuse and abject suffering. In addition, over 850,000 men, women, and children are listed on the sex offender registry. The consequences of being listed on the sex offender registry are life changing for ex-offenders and their families. Registrants are denied basic human dignity, many personal freedoms, undergo forced isolation, and often experience physical harm. Runaway injustice creates an unjust, ungodly, and *oppressive* environment, if not an actual *criminal war*.

Demagogues and managers do not generally possess or use the tools necessary to help transform complex conflicts. Demagogues are unwilling to yield their power, and managers are unwilling to think outside of their own organization. Leaders skilled at mediation are necessary. Of the eight principal tools of the mediator (described above), perhaps the most important is **dialogue**. Since governments generally enact legislation by debate and because debates have produced more injustice than justice, is there perhaps a better way to resolve complexities? What is the advantage of dialogue over debate?

Gerzon effectively illustrates the power and limitations of debate:

Debate is familiar because we live in debate cultures...
If we want language to lead towards healthier [and more inclusive] and stronger communities and more vibrant, effective organizations, we need language that

promotes progress—not language that maintains the status quo. We need language that lifts us up towards a higher discourse, not language that turns civic and corporate life into a verbal battlefield. While debate is useful for making decisions and taking votes, dialogue is the key to renewal. The power of debate is that two voices are free to speak. *But the power of dialogue is that these voices may actually be* heard.[221]

Dialogue reveals a source of power unavailable in many other forms of communication—the power of our assumptions. Assumptions include unexamined beliefs, biases and stereotypes we embrace about each other and the conflict itself. As we begin examining the "soil and the environment" of the conflict, we also unearth our assumptions exposing them to the light of truth and are suddenly able to see what is helpful and what may be hindering and limiting our community. Unearthing, examining, and releasing these assumptions creates the essential power necessary for transformation and innovative results, just as weeding and fertilizing produces a lush and beautiful garden.

In *Leading Through Conflict*, Gerzon presents the following comparison:[222]

Table 4: Debate versus Dialogue

Debate	Dialogue
• Assuming there is right answer and you have it	• Assuming that many people will have pieces of the answer
• Combative: participants attempt to prove the other side wrong	• Collaborative: participants work together towards common understanding
• About winning	• About exploring common ground
• Listening to find flaws and make counter arguments	• Listening to understand, finding meaning and agreement
• Defending or own assumptions as truth	• Revealing our assumptions for reevaluation
• Seeing two sides to an issue	• Seeing all sides of the issue
• Defending one's own views against others	• Admitting that other's thinking can improve one's own
• Searching for flaws and weaknesses in other's positions	• Searching for strength and value in others' positions
• By creating a winner and loser, discouraging further discussion	• Keeping the topic open even after the discussion ends
• Seeking a conclusion or vote that ratifies you position	• Discovering new options, not seeking closure

Communication—an exchange and acceptance of information—does not come through discussion. As noted, discussions and decisions are useful for "shaking apart "and "cutting off" communication. Dialogue, on the other hand, opens *new* possibilities and seeks *new* options. It is not about planning, "reloading," or proving a point by engaging in angry rhetoric and partisan debates. Rather, it acknowledges that, if we are going to work towards establishing justice for all, we must limit our automatic propensity to engage in fruitless debates and work to increase the opportunities to engage in compassionate dialogues. How can ex-offenders and their advocates, as well as victims and their advocates, government and corrections officials, and anyone else who is affected by these issues, begin working together to establish a dialogue rather than remaining stuck in contentious and unproductive debates?

Dialogue looks good in theory, but it becomes much more difficult to practice. The media has little or no interest in facilitating such a discourse. After all, they thrive on chaos and fear; good news is never "breaking news." They would never report that an ex-offender (especially someone previously guilty of child molestation or predatory rape) who had confessed their crime in brokenness and sorrow, and successfully completed counseling and treatment, is now living a healthy and productive life. Where is the news value in such a "success"? How does this create more fear or divide the community?

The government has little interest in beginning such a dialogue. Politicians can ill afford to be seen as "soft on crime." Any such proposal could make them appear sympathetic towards ex-offenders. For all of the talk about criminal justice reform, very little is actually being done. Any proposed legislation is met with stiff opposition, particularly from those who profit from fear mongering (and private prisons) and from maintaining the status quo. Moreover, most proposals for change concern future sentencing decisions rather than addressing the massive injustice against many of those presently languishing and suffering in prisons or those attempting to live under the shame of the sex offender registry.

Church leaders have the unique opportunity to begin a dialogue, but they seem to have little motivation to do so. There is little sympathy, compassion, or love towards ex-offenders. As previously noted, churches are more likely to comply with insurance regulations, in order to protect their assets and organizations, than they are to be obedient to the Scriptures they preach. Church leaders are inclined to be managers—protecting their own organizations—rather than to risk the potential messiness of mediation. Mediation does not have a predicted outcome. It may by unsafe. It may be miraculous.

For ease in the following discussion, in Table 5 we have labeled ex-offenders and their advocates as *ex-offenders*, and victims and their advocates, as well as government and corrections officials, as the *offended*.

Table 5: Transforming to a Dialogic Community

Ex-Offenders	Offended	Dialogic Community
• Focus on injustice and assume that the answer is shorter sentences, less restrictions and getting rid of the sex offender registry	• Beliefs and actions driven by fear and that the answer is punishment beyond imprisonment and more revenge and retribution	• Offenders and offended come together recognizing that everyone involved has parts of the answer
• Denial, anger, selfishness and other cognitive distortions lead to isolation and victim posturing	• Anger, fear, suspicion, and belief that the offender must be destroyed	• Collaborative: Offenders and offended work together towards common understanding
• Refusal to accept responsibility or consequences for actions and ignorance of the harm caused to the victim and the community	• Belief that the only "safe" community is a community that excludes all ex-offenders	• Offenders and offended explore the common ground of maintaining safe communities for everyone
• Focusing on one's own pain and suffering and lack of empathy towards others	• Thoughts and emotions controlled by fear, abolishing sound reasoning	• Offenders and offended listening to hear, embrace, accept and let go of our own inner clamoring

There is a story of three stonemasons working side by side. The first says, "I am laying bricks." The second says, "I am building a wall." The third says, "I am constructing a magnificent cathedral." Gerzon presents a challenge of turning any conflict into an opportunity.

> *To lead through conflict, we face the challenge of holding the vision of a cathedral, a vision of what is possible. Our challenge is to see the seed or opportunity buried in the soil of conflict. Of course, sometimes the conflict is so entrenched and bitter that we feel helpless. Overwhelmed by grief, sorrow, or rage, we wonder if there will ever be any progress at all. But even in the most tragic of circumstances, the seed of opportunity lies just beneath the surface. These eight tools (of a*

mediator) are designed to unearth it, fertilize it and help it become a reality."[223]

Who can mediate this conflict and begin such a dialogue? The government can't, the organized church won't, and most advocacy groups—whether representing the *offenders* or the *offended*—are blinded by their own prejudices and ignorance and are too entrenched in their own agendas. Where and how is such leadership and mediation possible? It is possible in the *ekklesia*—the subject of the next chapter.

10 – *Ekklesia*

This chapter is personal. First, as an important note and disclaimer: I am very concerned about the church—the *ekklesia*. My criticism of the *organized church* in this chapter and elsewhere is **not** intended to be an attack on the many good and Godly people leading and attending such fellowships. My concern has to do with the institution or the organization commonly referred to as "church." I am greatly concerned that many leaders have been deceived by fear or the enemy or have become entrenched in tradition rather than standing in truth. Therefore they embrace the standards and ways of the world rather than standards of the Scriptures and the way of Christ in decision-making for the body of Christ.

Second, I love God, I love my Lord and Savior Jesus Christ, and I love the Holy Spirit and the Holy Scriptures. I love all of my brothers and sisters in Christ. Yet after many years of experience, prayerful study, and reading, I am unconvinced that the *organized church* is—or has been—the *ekklesia* for many years. Therefore, after much prayer and study, I believe there are things that must be said.

Third, I am grieved when many of my brothers—those whom the world has labeled as sex offenders—have rejected, wandered away, or even abandoned their faith because of the continuing judgment and exclusion from the fellowship of the saints. I am troubled when volunteers from the churches that come into the prison to preach their gospel will not allow an ex-offender to join *their* fellowship after their release from prison. Neither will they meet him or her at the prison gate when they are released. I do not understand when the prison ministry of one of the largest churches in the Southwest writes, "Because of fear (of sex offenders) the doors of the organized church are closed." I am saddened when *most* faith-based prison transition ministries, including *Alongside Ministries*[224], *Teen Challenge, DreamCenter*, and *Church on the Streets*,[225] refuse to assist or minister to former sex offenders when they are released from prison. Murderers, drug dealers, thieves, gang members, arsonists, and others are welcome, but someone labeled as a sex offender is left to fend for themselves. I cannot see this as anything other than a gross and ungodly injustice, and I cannot remain silent anymore. Something must be done.

So far, on this journey, we have considered justice versus injustice, fear versus love, and complexities versus community. We have examined the differences in victims and offenders and revealed how injustice destroys—rather than restores—human lives. We have outlined the type of leadership needed and suggested various steps for transforming conflicts. We have acknowledged the roles and responsibilities of ex-offenders and their advocates and of the *organized church*. Consequently, we may have more information and perhaps a bit more understanding; yet we still do not have a clear path on how to deal with sex offenders.

We have encountered many questions, but few good answers; in fact, there are no easy answers. The attempts to resolve the conflicts or provide a pathway to peace have failed. The only thing we have tried is force. The government once intended to be "of the people, by the people, and for the people" has conspired to imprison and exclude millions of its own citizens. The *organized church* that once welcomed all—"whosoever will may come"—has redefined whosoever to exclude some and limit others from joining in the fellowship of the saints.

Modern society suffers from truth decay. Media organizations and government demagogues manipulate and conceal the truth to protect their power, position, privileges, and most of all, their profit. In an ideal world, the government's practice and propensity for revenge and retribution towards lawbreakers would be balanced by the church's practice and propensity for mercy, forgiveness, reconciliation, and restoration. Yet as discussed in the preceding chapter, the American *organized church* resembles more of a nonprofit business than a place of mercy, love, and forgiveness. Many churches have nearly abandoned the Truth in favor of a convenient religiosity and a commitment to managing their attendance, improving their buildings, and increasing their cash.

In terms of leadership styles, many church leaders act more like *managers* than *mediators*. As previously noted, managers tend to define themselves in terms of their own organization, pursuing only the interest of their own group, and do not think systematically or outside the box. They cannot or will not deal with issues, decisions, or conflicts that cross their own stated boundaries, and they are generally only effective and productive on their own turf.[226] It may not be possible or reasonable to expect the leopard to change its spots; however, we are dealing with human beings, not leopards. Thus, it *may* be possible to resurrect an old idea; an original idea in its day; the original conception of the body of Christ; one that resembles that "Palestinian fellowship" from the first century. We will call it what the early church knew it as: the *ekklesia*.

The American organized church—for most professing Christians and attendees—means little more than going to a building, sitting in a pew, singing a few songs, listening to a sermon, shaking some hands, and racing to the parking lot to beat the other "worshipers" to local restaurants. Any *problem solving* is left to the "leaders." Yet that is *not* what the Scriptures teach.

Jesus established and described the *ekklesia* as a *problem solving community*:

> *Moreover if your brother sins against you, go and tell him his fault between you and him alone. If he hears you, you have gained your brother. But if he will not hear you, take with you one or two more, that by the mouth of two or three witnesses every word may be established. And if he refuses to hear them, tell* it *to the*

> church [ekklesia]. *But if he refuses to hear even the church [ekklesia], let him be to you like a heathen or a tax collector. Assuredly, I say to you, whatever you bind on earth will be bound in heaven, and whatever you loose on earth will be loosed in heaven. Again, I say to you that if two of you agree on earth concerning anything that they ask, it will be done for them by my Father in heaven. For where two or three are gathered in my name, I am there in the midst of them.* (Matthew 18:15-20)

The *body* handles the issue. The concern is brought to the *ekklesia*. In Corinth, Paul instructed the body—the *ekklesia*—to work in unity to resolve issues of division, immorality, lawsuits, and disruptions in their midst. His letters are addressed to the "church [*ekklesia*] of God... to those who are sanctified in Christ Jesus, called to be saints, with all whom in every place call on the name of the Jesus Christ our Lord, both theirs and ours." (1 Corinthians 1:2)

The *ekklesia* involves spiritual commitment with others to pursue the will of Christ.[227] So what is the will of Christ concerning former sex-offenders? What do the Scriptures teach—as opposed to insurance policies or regulations, rules of order, or other requirements? Jesus said, "For the Son of Man has come to save that which was lost… even so it is not the will of the Father that one of these *little ones* should perish." (Matthew 18:14) Jesus spent time with tax collectors and sinners, the lepers and the poor, the downtrodden, and many others who had been marginalized by the government and the religious leaders of that day. Why are these groups not a part of the modern day local church?

The *ekklesia* was what pastor and theologian Dietrich Bonhoeffer referred to as "the Christian community, mean[ing] community through Jesus Christ and in Jesus Christ."[228] Bonhoeffer, in quoting Martin Luther, wrote, "To rule is to be in the midst of your enemies. And whoever does not suffer this does not want to be part of the rule of Christ; such a person wants to be among friends and sit among the roses and lilies, not with the bad people, but the religious people. O you betrayers and blasphemers of Christ! If Christ had done what you are doing who would have ever been saved?"[229]

Bonhoeffer himself continues:

> *When God was merciful to us, we learned to be merciful to one another. When we received forgiveness instead of judgment, we too were made ready to forgive each other. What God did for us, we then owed to others. The more we received, the more we were able to forgive; and the more meager our love for one another, the less we were living by God's mercy and love. Thus, God taught us to encounter one another the way that God has encountered us in Christ, 'Welcome one another, therefore, just as Christ has welcomed you for the glory of God.'*[230]...
>
> *Christian community [ekklesia] is not an ideal, but a divine reality;...Christian community is a spiritual and not an emotional reality.... On innumerable occasions a whole Christian community has been shattered because it has lived on the basis of a wishful image.... Those who love their dream of a Christian community more than the Christian community itself become destroyers of that Christian community even though the personal intentions may be ever so honest, earnest and sacrificial.*
>
> *God hates this wishful dreaming because it makes the dreamer proud and pretentious. Those who dream of this idealized community demand that it be fulfilled by God, by others, and by themselves. They enter the community of Christians with their demands, set up their own law, and judge one another and even God accordingly.*[231]

Pastor and theologian Jon Zens has suggested, "The word 'church' should be purged from our vocabulary. It had its origins in paganism, communicates nothing authentic, masks the life of Christ in the body, and is usually visually connected to buildings that appear every half-mile in America."[232] *Ekklesia* is not a "religious" or even a "Christian" word; it is a Greek word used in ancient times to represent a "duly assembled group of citizens who came together to discuss and take care of common concerns in the community."[233] When Jesus spoke of building his *ekklesia*, (Matthew 18:16; 16:17) he had in view a "duly assembled group of citizens who came together to discuss and take care of common concerns in the community, people gathered together to carry out the whole gamut of Christ's kingdom purposes."[234]

Who then are the *ekklesia*? The *ekklesia* is the *living, breathing body of Christ*. Some have termed it the "organic" church as opposed to the "organized church." Yet in reality, it is more about attitude and spirituality than a religious organization. Members of the *ekklesia* are part of the 6 percent described earlier in this book—those who are more spiritual than religious, who strive to live each day and each moment in accordance with what they say they believe, and are possessed by the Spirit of God. His indwelling presence guides their thought and actions. They live a life characterized by fully loving God, and fully loving each other. No one needs to ask these people what they believe; it is evident in everything they say and do in their public as well as their private world.[235]

In theory and theologically then, the *ekklesia* ought to be a place to find mercy, forgiveness, and grace. It ought to be a place of hospitality. It ought to be a *hospital* with the space where the stranger—even someone labeled as a sex offender—can enter and become a friend instead of an enemy. It ought to be an open space where change can take place. It is not, however, a place to convert someone, to persuade with words of human wisdom, but rather a place of freedom of choice and commitment.[236] The *ekklesia* is where true discipleship begins.

Discipleship—true Christian discipleship—is more caught than taught, and is learned and imitated by following an example rather than reading a book, completing a prescribed course, or even memorizing various Scriptures. For example, learning to love comes by being loved; learning to forgive comes by being forgiven; learning to serve comes by being served; learning to follow Christ comes by someone coming alongside of you and showing you the way. Discipleship is not about giving someone a fish, or even teaching them to fish; it is about making room for them alongside you on the bank of the river and then working together to clean up the filth being dumped into the river upstream.[237] It is about loving and including them *regardless of what they believe or when they believe*. It is about allowing the Holy Spirit to work in their heart in such a way that they ask you about the hope that is in you. (1 Peter 3:15) It is about caring for the lost, the broken, the wounded, and those whose lives have become little more than an existence of unbearable pain and suffering.

Descartes, the French mathematician and philosopher in the 1600s, was noted for his dictum, "I think, therefore I am." The application of this philosophy has reduced the learner to a "thinking thing" in modern education and in modern religious instruction. Consequently, the church's "discipleship" becomes primarily a matter of depositing ideas and beliefs into mind containers.[238] There is no shortage of information and Biblical instruction available to prisoners. Dozens of ministries of various types offer a wide range of correspondence programs. Volunteers come in to teach and preach what they know; yet too often such knowledge does not transfer into a new way of life. For while knowledge abounds, *examples* and *expressions* of love are mostly absent. Prisoners may learn a great deal about the Bible and be able to memorize various scriptures and regurgitate the right answers. However, what if they actually learned much more about *loving by being unconditionally and lavishly loved,* especially by those who teach of Christian love?

The opportunity to love and minister to sex offenders does not begin when they are released from prison. Ideally, it begins when they are first arrested. Yet realistically it begins well *before* their release from prison and should certainly continue once they walk out the gate. Unfortunately, the organized church—rather than the *ekklesia*—is the primary religious or spiritual presence in jail and prison ministries. In addition, it often appears that the agenda of the organized church in jail and prison ministries focuses primarily on getting someone converted or "saved" rather than lovingly serving them and allowing the spirit of Christ to begin the healing process. The emphasis is on *conversions,* rather than on *making disciples*. And even "discipleship" training becomes a matter of information, e.g., memorizing scriptures, Bible studies, listening to sermons, and so on, rather than seeing *examples* of loving and serving one another and allowing the power of the gospel to transform lives.

Prisoners are broken and fearful. One prisoner described being arrested as being "catapulted from one existence to another." Prisoners cannot openly admit or show fear. Showing fear displays weakness, and weakness vulnerability. Consequently, prisoners manifest fear through physicality, hostility, timidity or spirituality. Many prisoners become suddenly interested in spiritual things, begin reading and studying the Bible, attending services, and, most of all, praying for divine intervention in their sentencing. These are all good things; however, they lack authentic *examples* of Christian discipleship.

All people sin, yet some people go above and beyond in their sin and violate the laws of men. Criminal offenses—especially sexual offenses—often grow from disordered hearts and attempts to meet some perceived need, or to medicate some pain. For those who commit a sexual offense, indulging in the sexually toxic culture and the temporary euphoria and ecstatic release that comes from self-gratification or illicit sexual encounters provides a temporary escape from the world and medicates their pain.

Prisoners, particularly sex offenders, often believe the lie that no one cares about them and that no one ever will. Therefore, there is tremendous opportunity for members of the *ekklesia* to build relationships with the broken and fearful simply by demonstrating *care*.

Nouwen describes the foundation for such care:

[W]hen we honestly ask ourselves which persons in our lives mean the most to us, we often find that it is who, instead of giving advice, solutions, or cures, has chosen rather to share our pain and touch our wounds with a gentle and tender hand. The friend who can be silent with us in a moment of despair or confusion, who can stay with us in an hour of grief or bereavement, who can tolerate not knowing, not curing, not healing and face the reality of our powerlessness—that is the friend who cares...

To care means first to be present with each other. From experience, you know that those who care for you become present to you. When they listen, they listen to you. When they speak, they speak to you. And when they ask questions, you know that it is for your sake and not for their own. Their presence is a healing presence because they accept you on your terms, and they encourage you to take your own life seriously.[239]

As it pertains to jail and prison ministries, or intentional interaction with ex-offenders outside of the prison, there is very little such "care." There is an abundance of preaching and teaching and there is plenty of talking, but very little *listening*. The church (or at least the *ekklesia*) ought to be the place to encourage the liberation of fearful hearts, to show compassion, care, and offer healing to the broken hearted, and be places where the Word can find root and bear fruit.[240]

In *Reaching Out: The Three Movements of the Christian Life*, Nouwen writes:

It is obligatory for Christians to offer an open and hospitable space where strangers can cast off their strangeness and become our fellow human beings. [This movement] is hard and full of difficulties. Our society seems to be increasingly full of fearful, defensive, aggressive people anxiously clinging to their property and inclined to look at their surrounding world with suspicion, always expecting an enemy to suddenly appear and do harm. But still—that is our vocation; to convert the hostility *into* hospitality, *the enemy into a guest, and to create the free and fearless space where brotherhood and sisterhood can be formed and fully experienced...*

Maybe the concept of hospitality can offer a new dimension to our understanding of a healing relationship and the formation of a re-creative community in a world so visibly suffering from alienation and estrangement.[241]

Ex-offenders are discarded by the world, discriminated against in housing and jobs, dehumanized and demonized in the media, in danger of vigilante violence, and in many instances disconnected from their families. They are feared, and treated as strangers. The culture of fear creates defensive and even aggressive people looking to protect their neighborhoods, businesses, and churches from the presence of such strangers. Yet if the church remains a hostile place to strangers, are they still a church? The *ekklesia* can convert such hostility into hospitality, the enemy into a guest, and create the free and fearless space where brotherhood and sisterhood can be formed and fully experienced.

How can the *ekklesia* minister to ex-offenders? There is a way the *ekklesia* may perform its proper role in society of offering redemption and restoration to ex-offenders: it is by obeying the Scriptures. While our brothers and sisters are in prison, the *ekklesia* is commanded to remember and visit them, for when such love and mercy are shown to a prisoner, it is shown to Christ Himself. (Hebrews 13:3; Matthew 25:31-46) As mentioned in Chapter 8, Baylor Professor Byron Johnson notes, "Unless ex-prisoners who happen to become born again Christians get the *social and spiritual support* necessary to develop a deep and lasting commitment—mainly through congregations [*ekklesia*]—they will likely fail in their transition to society."[242] And while most jail and prison volunteers come from evangelical (*organized*) churches whose congregations believe that prisoners need to hear about Jesus, these same fellowships are far less inclined to *be* Jesus—His hands, His arms, or His feet—when the prisoner is released. Former prisoners—especially former sex-offenders—are often unwelcome in the neighborhood and unwelcome in the *organized church*.[243] How then do we welcome ex-offenders into the *ekklesia*?

In the previous chapter, we reviewed the restrictive covenants used by some *churches* to *allow* some ex-offenders to attend. Yet there is *no Scriptural basis* for such covenants. Moreover, such covenants tend to isolate rather than include and subject the ex-offender to shame and isolation. How does a former sex offender become a member of the body of Christ if he or she is not allowed to fellowship and participate *fully* with that body? Are there levels of membership in the body of Christ?

Yet what is the responsibility of the ex-offender towards the *ekklesia*? The ex-offender does not have the right to expect the *ekklesia* to include them in the fellowship if he/she is unwilling to be a functioning part of the body. That is, the ex-offender—along with every other member of the body—has an obligation to be growing in Christ-like maturity. This is not a matter of subscribing to some form of legalism so as to avoid doing certain things on manmade lists such as the "dirty dozen, the nasty nine, or the filthy five." Rather it is fulfilling the law of Christ—that is of loving God, loving one another, loving your neighbor, and even loving your enemies. It is learning to walk as the apostle Paul describes to the church at Ephesus: *Walk worthy of the calling with which you were called, with all lowliness and gentleness, with longsuffering, bearing with one another in love, endeavoring to keep the unity of the spirit in the bond of peace.... No longer walk as the rest of the Gentiles, in the futility of their mind... that you put off, concerning your former conduct according to deceitful lusts, and be renewed in the spirit of your mind, and that you put on the new man which was created according to God, in true righteousness and holiness.... Let all bitterness, wrath, anger, clamor and evil speaking be put away from you, with all malice. And be kind to one another, tenderhearted, forgiving one another, even as God in Christ forgave you."* (Ephesians 4:1-3, 17, 22-24, 31-32) This passage, along with many others, teaches about the responsibility of every believer. For a former sex offender to enjoy the benefits of the *ekklesia* they must expect to be a member of the *ekklesia*—a member of the body of Christ, i.e., someone who gives as much or even more than they take so the whole body is edified and built up in love.

Nevertheless, perhaps it is reasonable to have some form of a *covenant* agreement between the ex-offender and the *ekklesia*. What is needed, however, is a different form of covenant, not a covenant driven by exclusion or restriction and not a covenant of protecting one party at the expense of another or a way of keeping someone out. The need is for a covenant of *inclusion*; a covenant of God's forgiveness, mercy, love, and grace; a covenant modeled after Jesus' example. What if church members committed to *seeking* and saving the lost, *especially* those judged and condemned by the world as being unforgiveable, unlovable, and untouchable? Especially those whom the world has labeled as sex offenders.

There is an abundance of fear and concern on every side, and perhaps it is reasonable to establish a covenant of protection. But can the *ekklesia* prepare a covenant of grace—a covenant of social and spiritual support and protection *for* an ex-offender rather than an exclusionary and restrictive covenant of protection *for* the church? We will explore this and other possibilities in the next chapter.

In the Introduction, we set forth a vision for an entirely new idea and a new perspective on an existing issue or conflict. We have examined the way things are and have discovered that solving tough problems by force is unacceptable if indeed we are to be a nation of justice and a community of mercy and love. In the following chapter, "The Vision," we begin to dream the things that have never been—to dream, and see, and hope in the impossible becoming possible.

VISION

11 – The Vision

Silence in the Face of Injustice presupposes injustice. Throughout this book, we have identified the nature of the injustices arising from the culture of fear and the inherent complexities of this conflict. We have begun disentangling the unjust generalizations and potent mythologies concerning sex offenders by delineating the various offenses and types of victims and by humanizing the dehumanized by sharing the "rest of the story" of many typical ex-offenders. We have recognized the necessity of justice for the innocent and, while acknowledging the role and responsibility of the state, have exposed the complicity of the organized church in enabling injustice to continue. We have challenged ex-offenders and their advocates to confess their responsibility for their offenses and corresponding harm, and to open their hearts with compassion and empathy for their innocent victims. We have demonstrated that justice does not arise from fear-mongering demagogues in the government and media; neither does it arise from managers who are intent on protecting their own organization's turf. Rather, justice will only come when leaders from all involved parties come together with courage, dedication, integrity, and judgment, to begin mediating the conflict with care and compassion for all. Miraculous transformations are beyond the capability of the natural; they only exist in the spiritual. Therefore, *the only hope for transforming injustice to justice is a spiritual work.* And the ones most able to begin such transformation are those in whom the spirit of God lives and works—the members of the *ekklesia.*

This book offers no specific solutions, but rather sets forth a challenge and offers hope for transforming the current vengeful and retributive injustice to a redemptive, restorative, and merciful justice. There are unlimited possibilities for transformation for those who are willing to open their minds and hearts. We propose a threefold vision. First, to create an opportunity for impartial mediators to invite all stakeholders to an open dialogue. Second, to encourage members of the *ekklesia* to offer covenants of compassion and care for offenders. Third, to challenge healers—therapists and counselors—to begin moving beyond contemporary clinical techniques and to include ancient and traditional methodologies for healing both victims and offenders within a community of care and compassion.

In setting forth the vision, I recognize that many of the people who read this book may disagree with much of what has been presented. Seeking justice and caring for those who have committed a sexual offense is hardly a popular endeavor. Certainly many good people remain entrapped in the culture of fear or perhaps remain burdened by their own painful experiences or personal sin. It is often the guilty who render the harshest judgments, whereas those who have been forgiven much love much. (Romans 2:1; Luke 7:47) Nevertheless, this vision is not for the majority, but for the 6 percent—the *ekklesia*—who truly love God and are the called according to His purpose. (Romans 8:28)

Yet even among the *ekklesia*, many may struggle with knowing what to do. It is, of course, difficult to forgive the unforgivable, love the unlovable, and reach out to touch the untouchable in the power and strength of men. As children of God and disciples of Jesus Christ, we know what we ought to do, i.e. love one another, our neighbors and even our enemies, but we lack the strength or willingness to carry it out.

Many friendships, marriages, families, communities and even churches become divided because of an unwillingness to love. Such love—*agape*—is an unnatural act. Many ancient philosophers spoke of *agape*. The Greeks referred to *agape* as a general affection or as a "true love" for human kind and a reflection of commitment and belonging in the world. It is the love spoken of by the Apostle Paul in 1 Corinthians 13. *Agape* is an unlimited kindness and compassion toward all others. Loving in this manner fosters a deep sense of self-worth and humility.[244] Such love is the love of God, and the kind of love by which those whom He calls (*ekklesia*) are commanded to love. (Read John 15:12; Luke 10:27-37; Matthew 5:43-48.) Exercising this love, this *agape,* is a spiritual miracle immersed in God's mercy and empowered by His grace—the grace known and practiced by members of His *ekklesia*. How does grace-empowered love shape this vision?

A *dialogue* among members of the *ekklesia* has the potential to create a conversation with a center, not sides, and to take the energy out of our differences and begin channeling it towards something that has never before been created. It lifts us out of a polarization and into a greater common sense.[245] The *covenants* are promises of inclusion and love (*agape*) **from** members of the *ekklesia* **towards** the ex-offender, rather than a covenant of restriction and judgment towards former sex offenders from the church. And the *healings* are what is possible when ancient methods are blended with modern practices to enliven the healing process and restore essential lost elements of ritual, sacredness, community, love, mystery, and Nature's healing forces.

The purpose of a dialogue is to lay the foundation for transformative action.[246] Dialogue is a way of thinking and reflecting together, a living experience of inquiry within and between people. It has the potential to "glue" people together from different walks of life and circumstances to create shared meaning, common understanding, and a *common unity*. The fundamentals and practicalities for creating such a dialogue are beyond the scope of this work. There is, however, an opportunity for those who presume to be leaders to begin working towards establishing such a dialogue. The greatest miracles often come through the greatest difficulties, even as the greatest victories often arrive through the most difficult circumstances. The first part of this vision then is to begin working towards creating such an opportunity. Specific information on techniques of dialogue has been discussed in Chapter 9. In addition, Mark Gerzon's *Leading Through Conflict,* Adam Kahane's *Solving Tough Problems,* and William Isaacs'

Dialogue and The Art of Thinking Together are excellent resources for building opportunities for dialogue.

The organized church often uses restrictive covenants to allow a former sex offender to attend services, even though such covenants have no biblical support. In the previous chapter, we suggested that it is reasonable to have a form of a covenant agreement between the ex-offender and the *ekklesia*—a covenant designed for inclusion, a covenant of God's forgiveness, mercy, love, and grace, and a covenant modeled after Jesus' example. Can the *ekklesia* prepare a covenant of grace—a covenant of social and spiritual support and protection *for* an ex-offender rather than an exclusionary and restrictive covenant of protection for the church? What would such a covenant look like?

There are at least two church groups offering similar covenants: The Church of Jesus Christ of Latter Day Saints (Mormons) and Jehovah's Witnesses. Both of these organizations offer extensive in-prison ministry and transitional support for their members regardless of the nature of their offense, i.e., they minister to prisoners in the general population as well as those convicted of a sex offense. Despite our theological differences, they are doing what most evangelical and mainline Christian churches have been unwilling to do. What if members of the *ekklesia* obeyed the Scriptures by remembering and visiting prisoners and by forgiving, comforting, and reaffirming their love for the ex-offender? (Hebrews 13:3; Matthew 25:31-46; 2 Corinthians 2:7-8)

Prisoners live in fear. They are disconnected from family and friends, dehumanized, demonized in the media, and discarded by the organized church. Only a small percentage of prisoners have any contact with the outside world. Few receive any mail, few have anyone they can call, and even fewer ever receive a visit from a family member or friend. Prison can be a desperately lonely existence. There are a few organizations that will provide some practical assistance for former sex offenders; however, there is little emotional or personal contact between the organization and the prisoner and certainly no true discipleship—no loving example of a Christ-like life. More often than not, there is no one to meet the prisoner at the gate.

What if members of the *ekklesia* made a covenant to minister to prisoners? Such a covenant could look something like this:

Dear Friend,

I heard you were in prison. I am sorry for your troubles. I pray for your safety and that you will decide to use this time to your advantage. Some people go to prison and get bitter, *but some choose wisely, and become* better. *I pray you will become better.*

I offer you my friendship. If you agree, I promise with God's help:
- ✓ *To pray for you daily*
- ✓ *To write to you weekly (or monthly)*
- ✓ *To visit you monthly (or quarterly)*
- ✓ *To help provide you opportunities for personal growth*
- ✓ *With your permission, to reach out in love to your family members*

In addition, when you are released, I promise with God's help
- ✓ *To meet with you upon your release*
- ✓ *To help you find suitable housing*
- ✓ *To help you find suitable employment opportunities*
- ✓ *To help provide you food and clothing and basic necessities*
- ✓ *And to continue our friendship and help you create a circle of support and accountability*

I recognize this is a radical idea and each person has limitations due to time and finances available, distance from home to prison, and family and job obligations. Nevertheless, the disciple who truly cares and wants to be used by God can probably extend the hand of love and offer help to someone in prison in some way. After all, to paraphrase the playwright George Bernard Shaw, some men see things as they are and wonder why, I dream things that have never been, but could be, and ask, "Why not?" There are ways of transforming the hostility of society towards ex-offenders into a compassionate and Christ-like helping hand.

Nouwen writes extensively on this idea:

Maybe the concept of hospitality can offer a new dimension in our understanding of a healing relationship and the formation of a re-creative community in a world so visibly suffering from alienation and estrangement....

Our heart may desire to help others: to feed the hungry, to visit the prisoners and offer shelter to travelers; but meanwhile we have surrounded ourselves with a wall of fear *and hostile feelings, instinctively avoiding people and places where we might be reminded of our good intentions....*

Hospitality therefore, means primarily the creation of a free space where the stranger can enter and become a friend instead of an enemy. Hospitality is not to change people, but to offer them space where change can take place. *It is not to bring men and women over to our side, but to offer a freedom not disturbed by dividing lines. It is not to lead our neighbor into a corner where there are no alternatives left, but to a wide-open spectrum of options for choice and commitment. It is not an educated intimidation with good books, good stories and good works, but the liberation of fearful hearts so that the words can find root and bear ample fruit. It is not a method of making our God and our way into the criteria of happiness, but the opening of an opportunity to others to find their God in their own way.*[247]

There are many who may object to such a radical idea and undoubtedly may question or debate the many logistics and details that yet need to be worked out. What if prisoners take advantage of someone? After all, aren't all prisoners manipulative and hardened criminals? Aren't all prisoners dangerous predators? These are reasonable questions and concerns; nevertheless, if this is a work of God, then all things are possible. Moreover, when Jesus commanded us to visit prisoners, he didn't say to visit the ones we like or the ones that made us comfortable. In fact, some of the prisoners may indeed be enemies of the gospel; nevertheless, isn't this even more reason to love them, to serve them, and to minister the love and mercy of God to them? Consider the words of Jesus:

> *You have heard that it was said, 'You shall love your neighbor and hate your enemy.' But I say to you, love your enemies, bless those that curse you, pray for those who spitefully use you and persecute you, that you may be sons (and daughters) of your Father in heaven; for He makes the sun rise on the evil and on the good and he sends rain on the just and the unjust. For if you love those who love you, what reward do you have. Do not even tax collectors do the same? And if you greet your brethren only, what do you do more than others? Do not even the tax collectors do so? Therefore, you shall be perfect just as your Father in heaven is perfect.* (Matthew 5:43-48)

And the apostle Paul offered the following instructions:

> *Repay no one evil for evil. Have regard for good things in the sight of all men. Beloved, do not avenge yourselves, but* rather *give place for wrath, 'Vengeance is Mine, I will repay,' says the Lord. Therefore, if your enemy is hungry, feed him; if he is thirsty, give him a drink, for in doing so you will heap coals of fire on his head. Do not be overcome by evil, but overcome evil with good.* (Romans 12:17-21)

Establishing compassionate dialogues and creative covenants are two thirds of the vision; the remaining piece is a new kind of healing. In *Ancient Ways*, Geral Blanchard suggests that ancient methods of healing "can successfully be blended with modern practices to enliven the healing process and restore essential lost elements of ritual, sacredness, community, love, mystery and Nature's healing forces."[248] The modern day emphasis on cognitive behavioral therapy (CBT) and its many derivations has allowed us to forget our past and the amazing natural technologies that were once used and are still practiced in a few remaining remote parts of the world.[249] Modern psychotherapy combines talk therapy (counseling) with drug therapy; however, all too frequently when the patient is on the "happy pills" everything is fine, but it does little to equip them to deal with the issues at hand. Tragically, many become dependent on such medications. Healing from the effects of sexual abuse or from having been an abuser is hard work; very hard work. Such healing cannot be accomplished in a standard fifty-minute therapy setting.

Historically, healing wasn't one-dimensional, as is often characterized in modern medicine and psychology. Rather, it was a multi-faceted process that required, first and foremost, that the patient be brought into contact with the larger mind, the infinite intelligence of the Universe.[250] Even with the best use of CBT in its various forms, true healing comes by spiritual means. Helping the ex-offender discover his/her lost spiritual center is the key to healthy living.

Blanchard includes twenty-six essential, active elements that are integral to the healing process and can complement Western medicine and psychology. They involve a diverse and historical spiritual practice. A few Christians may resist a few practices they deem to be unbiblical; however, a closer examination of historical Christianity as well as a loving and discerning spirit should resolve any difficulties. The reality is that modern day conservative evangelical Christianity has done little to help or heal the wounded. The "quick fix" is all too often to persuade someone to "invite Jesus to come into their heart by praying a 'simple prayer'." Sadly, there are many "conversions," but few disciples. Perhaps an expanded vision and tolerance for other ideas outside the mainstream of conservative Christian thought may be helpful in bringing healing to the wounded and to the world.

One of the ancient ways is to "Sacralize (to make sacred) the setting and the healing procedures."[251] Victims of crime and sexual abuse have endured abhorrent and reprehensible trauma, so it is natural and effective to invoke the opposite and corrective forces in a therapeutic setting. A sacred environment can provide an environment where emotional safety may be risked and transformation may occur. "The sacred carries magic, that numinous quality that lifts us beyond the ordinary, moves us beyond previous limitations, and links us to a deeper meaning in an often violent and hurtful world."[252] Nevertheless, it is equally important to recognize that the ex-offender was very likely also subjected to various forms of physical, emotional, and sexual abuse. In addition, since "immoral acts were part of the abuser's world, logically it would follow that spiritual activity would provide a roadmap out of their morass (of pain and suffering and deviant and destructive behavior) as well.... (The healer) must be courageous enough to pass judgments in human conduct (the offense) without at the same time shaming the person who (committed the act.)"[253]

It is much easier and more socially acceptable to employ spiritual methods to help *victims* of sexual offenses begin the road to healing and recovery. It is much more challenging to use these same methods to help *ex-offenders* heal. But are the ex-offenders of any less worth in the eyes of God?

"Sexual assault (abuse) victims often experience long lasting pain from their abuse. They feel hurt, angry, and helpless. Sometimes these feelings don't surface until years have passed. Frequently victims blame themselves because they feel they should have done something to stop or prevent the assault... Nothing crushes a child's self esteem like being abused. Abusers are also emotional vampires who suck innocence and joy from (their victims) through emotional and physical trauma. Such forms of abuse often result in soul theft or soul loss."[254]

When a person experiences trauma such as sexual abuse or assault, they lose part of their soul. They often feel dirty or contaminated by the experience. They feel disconnected from God and wonder why God didn't protect them. The remedy and corrective process for soul loss is soul retrieval. And soul retrieval must include a sacred space and sacred activities. Employing the "sacred" works well with almost any other counseling method. "It invites a reverent homecoming, a way back to parts of self that were momentarily lost, and the best parts of the victim."[255] However, if it works well with the victims of sexual abuse, given that most (if not all) offenders have also experienced various forms of trauma in their past, would it not also work very well in healing the abusers as well? Unfortunately, such healing and grace are rarely offered, although such things are desperately needed.

The current method for dealing with anyone who commits a sexual offense is steeped in revenge and retribution. Some may suggest that such retribution is warranted; however, those who support such a notion are guilty of dehumanizing and demonizing the offenders. Retribution and revenge extract their own form of emotional violence—leading to soul loss. Emotional harm may be inflicted in many ways by probation and parole officers, neighbors, church members, and other community members:

- *Claiming to be right all the time, leaving the offender always in the wrong*
- *Constantly telling them how to live their life*
- *Keeping them off balance, uncertain and intimidated by threats from neighbors and often-unwarranted midnight visits from probation and parole officers*
- *Subjecting them to power games and bullying*
- *Making cutting and sarcastic remarks about someone and making them feel uncomfortable*

The antithesis of such emotional abuse (inflicted by emotional vampires whether they are the abuser towards the victim or society towards the abuser) is "to discharge the toxic vampire energy by treating victims (and victimizers) as sacred people of the earth. Recovery is about noting the strong parts of you that have weathered the storms. It entails nurturing pain like a seed until it transforms into something different, bigger, better, and something that can ultimately nourish the body and the soul. Recovery involves feeding the innate best qualities of a person that are present in everyone, even if they are deeply wounded and buried under years of suffering and shame."[256]

An extensive evaluation of the twenty-six therapies used by Blanchard is beyond the scope of this book; nevertheless, finding a way to implement these things is part of the vision of this piece. Blanchard's books, *Ancient Ways: Indigenous Healing Innovations for the 21st Century*, and *Ancient Ethics* contain extensive information on integrating these methods into current treatment and counseling protocols.

Compassionate dialogues among stakeholders who are members of the *ekklesia*, caring covenants offered to prisoners, and considering new ways of healing are only the beginning. There is much work to do. If you are one of my brothers or sisters of the *ekklesia*, I invite you to pray about how you may become involved in speaking out—not continuing to remain silent—in the face of injustice. This book is a work of His mercy and grace and a milestone on my journey of faith. I close with two passages from Henri Nouwen's works:

> *We cannot change the world by a new plan, project or idea. We cannot even change other people by our convictions, stories, advice, and proposals; but we can offer a space where people are encouraged to lay aside their occupations and preoccupations and to listen with attention and care to the voices speaking at their own center....*
>
> *To convert hostility into hospitality requires the creation of a friendly open space where we can reach out to our fellow human beings and invite them into a new relationship. This conversion is an inner event that cannot be manipulated but must develop from within. Just as we cannot force a plant to grow but can take away the weeds and the stones which prevent its development, so we cannot force anyone to such a personal and intimate change of heart, but we can offer the space where such change can take place.*[257]
>
> *Compassion must become the core, and even the nature of authority [including in the criminal justice system]. Christian leaders [the* ekklesia*] are people of God only insofar as they are able to make the compassion of God with humanity—which is visible in Jesus Christ— credible in their own world.*
>
> *Compassionate leaders stand in the midst of their people but do not get caught in the conformist forces of the peer group [culture of fear], because through their compassion they are able to avoid the distance of pity as well as the exclusiveness of sympathy. Compassion is born when we discover in the center of our own existence, not only that God is God and humans are human, but that also our neighbor [including a former sex offender] really is our fellow human being.*
>
> *Through compassion, it is possible to recognize that the craving for love that people feel resides also in our*

own hearts, that the cruelty that the world knows all too well is also rooted in our own impulses. Through compassion, we sense our hope for forgiveness in our friends' eyes and our hatred in their bitter mouths. When they kill, we know that we could have done it; when they give life, we know that we can do the same. For a compassionate person nothing human is alien: no joy and no sorrow, no way of living and no way of dying.

This compassion is authority because it does not tolerate the pressures of the in-group, but breaks through the boundaries between languages and countries, rich and poor, educated and illiterate, [prisoners and free people.] This compassion pulls people away from the fearful clique into the larger world where they can see that every human face *is the face of a neighbor. Thus, the authority of compassion is the possibility for each of us to forgive our brothers and sisters, because forgiveness is only real for those who have discovered the weakness of their friends and sins of their enemies in their own hearts, and are willing to call each human being their sister and brother.... [Prisoners] look for brothers and sisters who are able to take away their fear and anxiety, who can open the door of narrow-mindedness and show them that forgiveness is a possibility that dawns on the horizon of humanity. The compassionate person who points to the possibility of forgiveness helps others to free themselves from the chains of their restrictive shame, allows them to experience their own guilt, and restores the hope for the future in which the lion and the lamb can lie down together.*[258]

In His Grace—For His Glory.

EPILOGUE

Epilogue

On June 18, 2005, I received an unexpected phone call—a call I never even dreamed possible. One of the associate pastors of the Mesa, Arizona, megachurch I had attended for over fifteen years said, "I am sorry. The Senior Leadership Council met and decided that you are no longer welcome to attend services or to be on the church campus for any reason." I was stunned. My life had already disintegrated over the previous ten days. The dishonest and duplicitous sins in my life had destroyed my marriage, caused me to forfeit my career, and destroyed my plans. And now even God had turned his back on me—or so I thought! Six weeks later, believing I had nothing for which to live, my desperate suicide attempt should have ended my life. But God had other plans.

Thankfully, my time in prison became much more than a punishment or correction; it became an opportunity for education, service, and personal growth. By God's grace and the privilege of working through Exodus Prison Ministry and the Louisiana Baptist University, I received educational opportunities beyond my imagination or dreams. This book is a result of that education.

Along this journey, I have learned much more than I can write as I continue growing and learning each day. Most of all, as a former sex offender myself, I enjoy living and serving among fellow prisoners—

former sex offenders—who have become my closest and dearest friends. The most exciting part of this journey has been serving as a tutor/facilitator in the Arizona Department of Corrections Sex Offender Education and Treatment Program. I work with men who, alongside me, are learning why we did what we did and how we can stop. Yet even more, I have heard the painful stories of my brothers' and friends' own brokenness and sorrow. As previously mentioned, a great number of these men—our brothers—have suffered unspeakable abuse and neglect. I never imagined that men who have been so wounded, so broken, so angry, and so hurting would be carelessly cast aside by society and excluded from the church. I cannot begin to tell all the heart-breaking stories I have heard. Although no one outside these walls may ever hear their stories, God knows the details of every one.

I believe that the key to creating loving, caring, and *safer* communities is in overcoming our fear, prejudices, and ignorance and to remind ourselves that as communities of faith—the *ekklesia*—that we together form the fellowship of the weak, transparent to Him who speaks to us in the lonely places of our existence and says, "Do not be afraid, you are accepted."[259] Nouwen describes this key:

> *To care means first to empty our own cup and to allow the others to come close to us. It means to take away the many barriers that prevent us from entering into communion with the other. When we dare to care, then we discover that nothing human is foreign to us, but that all of the hatred and love, cruelty and compassion, fear and joy can be found in our own hearts. When we dare to care, we have to confess that when others kill, I could have killed too. When others torture, I could have done the same. And when others give life, I could have done the same. Then we experience that we can be present to the soldier who kills, to the guard who pesters, to the young man who plays as if life has no end, and to the old man who stopped playing out of fear of death.*
>
> *As long as we are occupied and preoccupied with our desire to do good but are not able to feel the crying*

EPILOGUE

need of those who suffer, our help remains hanging somewhere between our minds and our hands and does not descend to the heart, where we can care. But in solitude, our heart can slowly take off many of its protective devices and can grow so wide and so deep that nothing human is strange to it.[260]

In closing, I have chosen to share an article written by Megan McKenna, "One of Us," that appeared in the September 2017 issue of *The Sun*. Ms. McKenna travels around the world teaching and preaching on storytelling and the Scriptures and on justice, peace, and community. This is actually an excerpt from her book, *Mary: Shadow of Grace*. She has graciously consented to allow me to close my book with these words. What would change in our world if we treated each other—including those we revile and hate—as if they were "One of Us"?

One of Us

Once upon a time there was an abbot of a monastery who was very good friends with the rabbi of a local synagogue. It was Europe, and times were hard...

The abbot found his community dwindling and the faith life of his monks shallow and lifeless. Life in the monastery was dying. He went to his friend and wept. His friend, the rabbi, comforted him and told him: "There is something you need to know, my brother. We have long known in the Jewish community that the Messiah is one of you."

"What!" exclaimed the abbot. "The Messiah is one of us? How can that be?" But the rabbi insisted it was so, and the abbot went back to his monastery wondering and praying, comforted and excited.

Once back in the monastery, walking down the halls and in the courtyard, he would pass by a monk and wonder if he was the one. Sitting in a chapel praying, he would hear a voice, look intently at a face, and wonder if he was the one, and he began to treat all of his brothers with respect, with kindness and awe, with

> *reverence. Soon it became quite noticeable.*
>
> *One of the older brothers came to him and asked what had happened to him. After some coaxing, he told him what the rabbi had said. Soon the other brother was looking at his brothers differently and wondering. The word spread through the monastery quickly: the Messiah is one of us. Soon the whole monastery was full of life, worship, kindness, and grace. The prayer life was rich and passionate, devoted, and the psalms and liturgy and services were alive and vibrant. Soon the surrounding villagers were coming to the services and listening and watching intently, and there were many who wished to join the community.*
>
> *After their novitiate, when they took their vows, they were told the mystery, the truth that their life was based upon, the source of their strength and life together: the Messiah is one of us. The monastery grew and expanded from house to house, and all of the monks grew in wisdom, age, and grace before others and the eyes of God. And they say still, if you stumble across this place, where there is life and hope and kindness and graciousness, that the secret is the same: The Messiah is one of us.*[261]

Finally, Henri Nouwen shares a similar story from ancient times that has many modern applications:

> *One day a young fugitive, trying to hide himself from the enemy, entered a small village. The people were kind to him and offered him a place to stay. But when the soldiers who sought the fugitive asked where he was hiding, everyone became fearful. The soldiers threatened to burn the village and kill everyone in it unless the young man was handed over to them before dawn. The people went to the minister and asked him what to do.*
>
> *The minister, torn between handing over the man to the enemy and having his people killed, withdrew to*

EPILOGUE

his room to read the Bible, hoping to find the answer before dawn. After many hours, in the early morning, his eyes fell on these words: "It's better that one man should die than the whole people be lost."

Then the minister closed his Bible, called the soldiers and told them where the fugitive was hidden. And after the soldiers led the man away to be killed, there was a feast in the city because the minister had saved the lives of the people.

But the minister did not celebrate. Overcome with deep sadness, he remained in his room. That night an angel came to him and asked, "What have you done?" He said, "I have handed over the fugitive to the enemy." Then the angel said, "But don't you know that you have handed over the Messiah?" "How could I know?" the minister replied anxiously. And the angel said, "If, instead of reading your Bible, you had visited this man and just once looked into his eyes, you would have known."[262]

If members of the *ekklesia* are willing to look into the eyes of ex-offenders, to listen to their stories, and hear the cries of their hearts, perhaps that will be enough to prevent from us from handing them over to the enemy and enable us to help lead them out of their hiding places into the midst of a people—the *ekklesia*—who can help redeem them from their suffering and redeem us from our fears.[263]

In living and working with my brothers, I often wonder if one of them is the one who will change the world. Perhaps *he* is the one who will demonstrate the love of God to a broken and dying world. Perhaps he is the one who will care. Perhaps he is the one whom God will use to restore truth and justice. Perhaps he is the one who will....

I invite you to pray for an abundance of mercy and grace. Join the dialogue; listen, talk, pray with us and come to the throne of grace that together we may obtain mercy and find more grace to help in time of need. (Hebrews 4:16) I do love God and His people, and above all, I want us to get this right.

In His Grace, For His Glory

Acknowledgments

In 2005, when prison appeared inevitable, I made a decision to use the time the best I could. Shortly after arriving on the yard, I read, "Prison will make you bitter or better; you choose. Choose wisely." I chose to become better.

I began pursuing any educational opportunities available. Unfortunately, there are limited educational opportunities and prisoners are ineligible for federal financial aid. There is little or no funding available for prisoners who wish to pursue a college education in prison. Therefore, I began completing various free Bible study correspondence programs. Yet when I signed up for the Exodus Prison Ministry program, I also learned that upon successful completion of their thirty-course program I could apply for acceptance to Louisiana Baptist University's bachelor's degree program in Biblical Studies. Although I didn't have the money, I began studying and praying, and God provided "above and beyond all I could ask or imagine." God provided.

After completing a Bachelor of Arts in Biblical Studies in 2013, I was offered the opportunity to continue my education and earned a Master of Arts in Christian Apologetics in 2014 and ultimately the opportunity to begin the Doctor of Philosophy program in Christian Leadership and Counseling. This book is the result of that opportunity.

ACKNOWLEDGMENTS

Not only did God provide the financial means, He provided me with a network of friends and advisors who were also "above and beyond all I could ask or imagine."

Writing is a challenge; thanking everyone involved is even a greater challenge. First, I thank God for my late parents, Allen and Betty Hardy, who "trained me up in the way I should go," and who patiently loved and prayed for me even after I took a long detour before returning to the faith. Their constant love and faithful encouragement through some very difficult times gave me the strength to persevere. I am also very fortunate to have a wonderful family—Connie, Nancy, Dave, Randy and Cindy who all have shared their love and blessed me in more ways than I can count.

I am indebted to the volunteers at Exodus Prison Ministry and especially their former director, Joyce Hargis. For more than thirty years, Joyce and her husband Weldon, along with many other wonderful volunteers, have invested countless hours helping thousands of prisoners across the country learn the truth of the Scriptures. Even after I completed their program, Joyce became a wonderful friend, advisor, encourager, and thankfully one of the chief editors of this manuscript. She is a precious gift!

A book of this nature requires a lot of research that is not readily available in prison. Moreover, prisoners do not have internet access. Yet once again God provided. Teresa Rogers, Mark Walker, and Pat and Terry Borden spent many hours graciously providing the mountains of research material necessary. In addition, both Teresa and Mark offered me their prayers and wise counsel. Teresa introduced me to the Biblical teachings of her pastor, Dr. G. Michael Corcoris, at the Lindley Church and sent me dozens of his teaching audio CDs and notes. Dr. Corcoris's clear Biblical teaching helped me search the truth of the Scriptures. One of my former pastors, Dr. Michael Tucker, offered his friendship, prayers, and patient encouragement along this journey.

Throughout this time in prison, I have been especially blessed with many wise counselors. Jeff Gay with Heart of America Ministries, Curtis Whalen with Metanoia Ministries, Alice Benson with the Titus House, and Steve and Deb Schmidt with the Eagle's Nest have shared their experience and insight, not only in ministering to prisoners in general, but especially their experience in working with those who have been convicted of a sexual offense. Their friendship, counsel, and encouragement have been invaluable.

My friends and brothers, Gerald Ferguson and William Whitmore, volunteered hours of their personal time and editorial talents in painstakingly and diligently helping shape this manuscript and clarify many of its passages. Any remaining errors are mine.

I am grateful to Dr. Neal Weaver and the trustees and staff at Louisiana Baptist University for making this educational program available to prisoners. One of the greatest blessings has been working with Ms. Amanda Adkins, my primary therapist, through the Sex Offender Education Treatment Program (SOETP) as well as my work supervisor. Most recently, Dr. Matheka has joined the treatment staff in this prison. Together with Ms. Adkins, they are two of the most caring and compassionate people I've ever met. As therapists, they know all of the reasons we are here (in prison), listen to all of our distortions and excuses, and gently and patiently, but firmly, help us work towards healing and learning to begin living healthy and productive lives.

I am indebted to my brothers—my fellow prisoners—in the many SOETP groups and on the yard who have shared their stories with me and granted me insight into their lives, and helped me gain greater insight into my own. Many of them have become my very good friends—men who have made an indelible imprint in my life and without whom this work would not have been possible.

The SOETP inmate facilitator team—Kevin Krout, K.C. Becker, Daniel Mullican, Albert Moraga, William Whitmore, Jason Sanders and Ron Fritz—under the leadership and direction of Ms. Amanda Adkins and Dr. Matheka, has helped me to continue to grow while providing me invaluable feedback and direction. In addition, the men in my primary maintenance group, especially David L., David, R., and Brendan G. share their lives with me, offering me their friendship and counsel.

Prison can be a very lonely place. Friends are difficult to find. I am blessed that my friend and brother, Mike Pryor, has become a consistent voice of reason, wisdom, and strength. Mike is a good friend, who has

ACKNOWLEDGMENTS

offered me Godly counsel, challenged me, scolded me, warned me, protected me, and loved me in more ways than I can count.

I am thankful for the wisdom of many authors. Henri Nouwen, Jon Zens, Geral Blanchard, Dietrich Bonhoeffer, Pat Carnes, John Maxwell, Mark Laaser, Ted Roberts, Mark Gerzon, and Adam Kahane have been particularly insightful and helpful.

Prisons are full of noise. Much of this book was written by listening to the peaceful and inspirational music of John Michael Talbot, Taize, Gregorian Chant, as well as many classical composers.

Above all, I am grateful to my Lord Jesus Christ for saving me and to God who "rescued me because He delighted in me." (Psalms 18:19)

About the Author

Gary W. Hardy completed his PhD in Christian Leadership through Louisiana Baptist University. He is a recovered sex addict, a former sex offender, thief, deceiver, and manipulator; but is he also living proof of the merciful grace of a loving God and that no sinner—no matter how evil—is beyond redemption and usefulness. He is a contributor to *Under the Covers: A Message of Hope*, a book published by ICL Global for use in ministering to sex abusers and offenders. Since 2013 Gary has written the annual Exodus Prison Ministry devotional calendar that is sent to thousands of prisoners around the United States. He also contributes his writings to several prison ministry newsletters and publications. Since 2014 he has served as a peer recovery coach and a group facilitator in the Arizona Department of Corrections Sex Offender Education and Treatment Program. His unofficial work includes helping his brothers in prison find hope and healing even in the midst of troubled pasts and difficult circumstances, through the love and grace of a merciful God. Gary's vision is to challenge and encourage the church—the *ekklesia*—to help bring redemption, reconciliation, and a merciful justice to those who have committed a sex offense and to help insure that there are no more victims. Gary is proof that no one is disposable and no one is beyond the reach of God's grace.

See more about Gary and his work at www.GaryWHardyPhD.com.

APPENDIX A

Appendix A – Population and Prison Statistics

Original 13	Bible Belt	State	2017 State Pop. (1)	St Pop Rank	2015 Prison Pop. (2)	PP Rank	Rate of Incarceration	ROI Rank	Violent Crime Rate	Rank	Property Crime Rate	Rank
	Y	Louisiana	4,710,000	25	36,377	13	776	1	540	5	3353	4
	Y	Oklahoma	3,970,000	28	28,547	16	715	2	422	14	2886	13
	Y	Alabama	4,880,000	24	30,810	15	611	3	472	10	2979	10
	Y	Mississippi	2,990,000	34	18,911	25	609	4	276	35	2834	15
		Arizona	7,030,000	14	42,719	9	596	5	410	17	3033	7
	Y	Arkansas	3,000,000	32	17,707	27	591	6	521	6	3251	6
	Y	Texas	28,400,000	2	163,909	1	568	7	412	16	2831	16
	Y	Missouri	6,120,000	18	32,330	14	530	8	497	9	2854	14
Y	Y	Georgia	10,500,000	8	52,193	5	503	9	378	24	3022	8
	Y	Florida	21,000,000	3	101,424	3	496	10	462	11	2813	18
	Y	Kentucky	4,450,000	26	21,701	20	489	11	219	44	2178	31
Y	Y	Virginia	8,490,000	12	38,403	11	457	12	196	47	1867	41
		Ohio	11,600,000	7	52,233	4	449	13	292	32	2588	27
		Nevada	3,000,000	33	13,071	29	444	14	696	2	2668	22
		Idaho	1,700,000	39	8,052	34	436	15	499	8	2691	21
		Michigan	9,940,000	10	42,628	10	429	16	216	46	1744	46
	Y	Tennessee	6,710,000	16	28,172	17	425	17	416	15	1886	40
Y	Y	S. Carolina	5,030,000	23	20,929	21	414	18	612	4	2936	12
		S Dakota	869,000	46	3,564	43	413	19	505	7	3293	5
		Wyoming	589,000	50	2,424	46	413	20	383	22	1943	37
		Indiana	6,660,000	17	27,355	18	412	21	222	43	1903	38
Y		Delaware	966,000	45	6,654	37	411	22	388	20	2596	26
Y		Penn.	12,800,000	5	49,858	7	387	23	315	29	1813	43
		W.Virginia	1,830,000	38	7,118	36	386	24	338	27	2020	34
		Wisconsin	5,800,000	20	22,975	19	377	25	306	30	1974	36
		Oregon	4,110,000	27	15,245	28	376	26	260	37	2947	11
		Colorado	5,660,000	21	20,168	24	364	27	321	28	2641	23
		Illinois	12,800,000	6	46,240	8	360	28	384	21	1989	35
		Montana	1,050,000	44	3,685	42	355	29	350	25	2624	24
Y	Y	N Carolina	10,200,000	9	36,617	12	352	30	347	26	2750	19
Y		Maryland	6,070,000	19	20,764	23	339	31	457	12	2315	28
		N. Mexico	2,080,000	36	7,169	35	335	32	656	3	3697	2
		California	39,800,000	1	129,593	2	329	33	426	13	2618	25
	Y	Kansas	2,930,000	35	9,857	32	328	34	390	19	2720	20
Y		Conn.	3,580,000	29	1,816	48	312	35	219	45	1812	44
		Alaska	741,000	48	5,338	41	306	36	730	1	2818	17
		Iowa	3,150,000	30	8,849	33	281	37	286	33	2047	33
		Nebraska	1,920,000	37	5,372	40	279	38	275	36	2241	29

Original 13	Bible Belt	State	2017 State Pop. (1)	St Pop Rank	2015 Prison Pop. (2)	PP Rank	Rate of Incarceration	ROI Rank	Violent Crime Rate	Rank	Property Crime Rate	Rank
		Hawaii	1,450,000	40	5,879	39	262	39	293	31	3796	1
Y		New York	19,900,000	4	51,727	6	260	40	380	23	1604	49
		Wash.	7,380,000	13	18,284	26	252	41	284	34	3463	3
		N Dakota	791,000	47	1,795	49	233	42	239	41	2117	32
Y		N Jersey	9,000,000	11	20,849	22	228	43	255	38	1627	48
Y		New Hampshire	1,340,000	41	2,897	45	217	44	189	48	1746	45
		Utah	3,100,000	31	6,492	38	215	45	236	42	2980	9
		Vermont	625,000	49	1,750	50	206	46	118	50	1407	50
Y		Rhode Island	1,060,000	43	3,248	44	204	47	243	39	1898	39
		Minnesota	5,550,000	22	10,798	30	196	48	243	40	2222	30
Y		Massachusetts	6,870,000	15	9,922	31	179	49	391	18	1691	47
		Maine	1,330,000	42	2,279	47	132	50	130	49	1830	42

(1) Retrieved from http://worldpopulationreview.com/states/
(2) Prisoners in 2015 Bureau of Justice Statistics, National Prisoner Statistics Program, 2014-2015
(3) Retrieved from https://nicic.gov statesstats 6/19/17

APPENDIX B

Appendix B – Age of Consent for Various States

State	Legal Minimum Age of Consent for Sexual Activity	Age Differential Between Victim and Defendant if Provided	16 and 25 year old	14 and 18 year old
AL	16	2 years	LEGAL	LEGAL
AK	16	3 or 4 years (depending on the age of the defendant)	LEGAL	*ILLEGAL*
AZ	15/18	If the victim is at least 15, and the defendant is either under 19, attending high school, or is no more than 2 years older than the victim, then the sexual assault is deemed consensual	*ILLEGAL*	*ILLEGAL*
AR	14/16	If the defendant is 20 years or older, the age of consent is 16, otherwise it is 14 with a 4 year differential for victims over the age of 12	*ILLEGAL*	LEGAL
CA	18	Grade of crime depending on age of victim and defendant	*ILLEGAL*	UNKNOWN
CO	18/15	Sexual assault if victim is less than 15 and the defendant is at least 4 years older. If the defendant is at least 10 years older than the victim, the age of consent is raised to 17	*ILLEGAL*	LEGAL
CT	16	If the victim is older than 13, but younger than 16 and the defendant is three years older than the victim, it is sexual assault	LEGAL	*ILLEGAL*
DE	16/18	If the victim is at least 16, but not yet 18 and the defendant is 30 years or older, sexual acts are criminal unless the parties are married.	LEGAL	*ILLEGAL*
FL	16	If a person 24 years or older engages in sexual activity with a person 16 or 17, it constitutes a felony unless the parties are married	LEGAL	*ILLEGAL*
GA	16	If the victim is at least 14, but not yet 16 and the defendant is 18 or younger and is no more than 4 years older than the victim, the penalty is mitigated as a misdemeanor	LEGAL	UNKNOWN
HA	16	If the victim is at least 14, but not yet 16 and the defendant is less than 5 years older than the victim or if the parties are married, the sexual activity is consensual	LEGAL	LEGAL
ID	16/18	When the victim is 16 or 17 and the defendant is 3 years older than the victim it is rape	*ILLEGAL*	*ILLEGAL*
IL	17	A defendant commits an aggravated criminal sexual abuse if the victim is at least 13 years of age but under 17 and the accused is at least 5 years older than the victim	*ILLEGAL*	LEGAL
IN	16	4 years	LEGAL	LEGAL
IA	16	If the victim is 14 or 15 and the defendant is more than 4 years older than the victim, it does constitute sexual abuse	LEGAL	LEGAL
KS	16	4 years	LEGAL	LEGAL
KY	16	N/A	LEGAL	*ILLEGAL*
LA	17	4 years	*ILLEGAL*	LEGAL
ME	16	5 years	LEGAL	LEGAL
MD	16	4 years	LEGAL	LEGAL
MA	16	N/A	LEGAL	UNKNOWN
MI	16	Sexual contact with a person older than 13, but not yet 16 is legal if the defendant is less than 5 years older than the victim	LEGAL	LEGAL
MN	16	If the victim is at least 13, but not yet 16, and the defendant is less than 2 years older than the victim the sexual contact is legal	LEGAL	*ILLEGAL*
MS	16	Sexual intercourse with a victim who is at least 14 but not yet 16 and is at least 3 years younger than the defendant is considered statutory rape, and if the victim is us under 14 and is two years younger than the defendant	LEGAL	*ILLEGAL*
MI	17/14	If the person is over the age of 14, the defendant must be 21 or older for it to be considered statutory rape	*ILLEGAL*	LEGAL
MO	16	4 years	LEGAL	LEGAL
NE	16	Actor must be at least 19	LEGAL	*ILLEGAL*

SILENCE IN THE FACE OF INJUSTICE

State	Legal Minimum Age of Consent for Sexual Activity	Age Differential Between Victim and Defendant if Provided	16 and 25 year old	14 and 18 year old
NV	16	N/A	LEGAL	ILLEGAL
NH	16	4 years	LEGAL	LEGAL
NJ	16	4 years	LEGAL	LEGAL
NM	18/16	Criminal sexual penetration is perpetuated when the victim is over 13, but not yet 16 when the perpetrator is at least 18 and is at least four year older than the child and is not the spouse of the child	ILLEGAL	LEGAL
NY	17	It is considered rape if the defendant is at least 21 years old and the victim is 17, or of the defendant is at least 18 and the victim is 15	ILLEGAL	ILLEGAL
NC	16	4 years	LEGAL	LEGAL
ND	18/15			ILLEGAL
OH	16	N/A	LEGAL	ILLEGAL
OK	16	Persons 14 to 16 can consent to sex as long as the defendant is under the age of 18	LEGAL	ILLEGAL
OR	18	If the victim is at least 15 years of age sexual intercourse is legal if the defendant is less than three years older than the victim	ILLEGAL	ILLEGAL
PA	16	4 years	LEGAL	LEGAL
RI	16	If the victim is between 14 and 16, sex is consensual unless the defendant is over the age of 18	LEGAL	ILLEGAL
SC	16/14	If the defendant is under 18 sex is consensual if the victim is at least 14	ILLEGAL	ILLEGAL
SD	16	3 years	LEGAL	ILLEGAL
TN	18/15	4 years	ILLEGAL	LEGAL
TX	17/14	3 years	ILLEGAL	ILLEGAL
UT	16/18	Sexual conduct with a 16 or 17 year old is unlawful if the defendant is 10 or more years older than the victim	ILLEGAL	ILLEGAL
VT	16	If the defendant is less than 19 and the victim is at least 15, the sex is consensual	LEGAL	ILLEGAL
VA	18/15	N/A	ILLEGAL	ILLEGAL
WA	16	4 years	LEGAL	LEGAL
WV	16	4 years	LEGAL	LEGAL
WI	18	N/A	ILLEGAL	ILLEGAL
WY	16/13	Range depending on age of victim and age of defendant	ILLEGAL	ILLEGAL
DC	16	4 years	LEGAL	LEGAL

Appendix C – Sex Offender Probation Terms

STATE OF ARIZONA
SEX OFFENDER TERM AND CONDITIONS OF PROBATION

1) Do not initiate, establish or maintain contact with any male or female child under the age of 18, including relatives, or attempt to do so, without the prior written approval of the APD. Sign and abide by the APD definition of "no contact."
2) Have no contact with victim(s) without prior written approval of the APD.
3) Do not go to or loiter near schools, school yards, parks, playgrounds, arcades, swimming pools or other places primarily used by children under the age of 18, or any other location as deemed inappropriate by the APD, without the prior written approval of the APD.
4) Do not date, socialize, or enter into a sexual relationship with any person who has children under the age of 18 without prior written approval of the APD.
5) At the discretion of the APD, attend, actively participate, and remain in sex offender treatment. Authorize therapists to disclose to the Court and the APD information regarding your attendance and progress in treatment.
6) Submit to any program of psychological or physiological assessment at the direction of the APD, including but not limited to, the penile plethysmograph and/or the polygraph, to assist in treatment, planning and case monitoring.
7) Any temporary or permanent changes to residence, employment, and education must have the advanced written approval of the APD.
8) Do not travel outside Maricopa County without the advance written approval of the APD.
9) Abide by any curfew imposed by the APD.
10) Do not possess any sexually stimulating or sexually oriented material, in any form, without the prior written approval of the APD. Do not patronize any adults-only establishment where such material or entertainment is available.
11) Do not possess children's clothing, toys, games, videos, etc. without prior written approval of the APD.
12) Be responsible for your personal appearance, to include the wearing of undergarments and clothing when in locations where another person might see you.
13) Do not hitchhike or pick up hitchhikers.
14) Do not operate a motor vehicle without prior written approval of the APD.
15) Do not use any computer equipment or access the Internet without prior written approval of the APD. If granted use or access, abide by the APD computer usage guidelines.

Appendix D – Recommended Reading for Ex-Offenders

Ex-offenders who are seeking to change and grow may find these books helpful. Many of them are used in sex offender treatment programs around the country. They have been extremely helpful in my own journey of healing, recovery, and ministry.

Anderson, Cordelia. The Impact of Pornography on Children, Youth, and Culture. *Holyoke: NEARI Press, 2011.*

Anonymous. "Letter From a Woman: To the Man Who Injured Me." In Under the Covers: A Message of Hope, *by Joy L. Matthews, 121. Kansas City: ICL Global, 2015.*

Bays, Laren, and Robert Longo. Enhancing Empathy. *Holyoke: NEARI Press, 2000.*

Bradshaw, John. Healing the Shame That Binds You. *Houston: Bradshaw.*

Carnes, Patrick. Out of the Shadows, 3rd edition. *Minnesota: Hazelden, 2001.*

Delmonico, David L., and Elizabeth Griffin. Illegal Images: Critical Issues and Strategies for Addressing Child Pornography Use. *Holyoke: NEARI Press, 2013.*

Department of Justice: Federal Bureau of Prisons. Starting Over. *Carson City. NV: The Change Companies, 2004.*

Grant, Jonathan. Divine Sex: A Compelling Vision for Christian Relationships in a Hypersexualized Age. *Grand Rapids, MI: Brazos Press, 2015.*

Laaser, Mark. Healing the Wounds of Sexual Addiction. *Grand Rapids, MI: Zondervan, 2004.*

Lachelle. "Dealing With Terror: Should a Child Even Have To." In Under the Covers: A Message of Hope, *by Joy L. Matthews, 119. Kansas City: ICL Global, 2015.*

Longo, Robert E, and Lauren Bays. Why Did I Do It Again and How Can I Stop? *NEARI Press: Holyoke MA, 2004.*

Longo, Robert E, Lauren Bays, and Steven Sawyer. Enhancing Empathy. *Holyoke: NEARI Press, 2011.*

—. Who Am I and Why Am I in Treatment? *Holyoke MA: NEARI Press, 2011.*

Maltz, Wendy and Larry. The Porn Trap: The Essential Guide to Overcoming

Problems Caused by Pornography. *New York: Harper Collins, 2008.*

Morin, John, and Jill Levenson. Road to Freedom. *Fort Lauderdale: Center for Offender Rehabilitation and Education, 2002.*

Roberts, Ted. Pure Desire. *Ventura, CA: Regal, 2008.*

Thompson MD, Curt. The Anatomy of the Soul. *Carrolton: Tyndale Momentum, 2010.*

Yates, Pamela, and David Prescott. Building A Better Life: a Good Lives and Self Regulation Workbook. *Brandon VT: Safer Society Press, 2011.*

Appendix E – Recommended Reading for Justice

These are helpful and informative books addressing the injustice and challenges concerning ex-offenders in America. Only a few of them are referenced in this book; however, these books provide valuable and important information in creating a compassionate and transformational dialogue.

Crawford, William B. Justice Perverted: How the Innocence Project at Northwestern University's Medical School of Journalism Sent an Innocent Man to Prison. *Amika Press: Los Angeles, 2015.*

Hanley, Paul. Roller Coaster to Hell and Back: A True Story of Sexual Abuse and New Hope. *Atlanta: CreateSpace Independent Publishing, 2017.*

Haralson, J., and J. Cordiero. Unprecedented: How Sex Offender Laws are Impacting Our Nation. *Dallas: PCG Legacy, 2012.*

Janus, Eric. Failure to Protect: America's Sexual Predator Laws and the Rise of the Preventative State. *New York City: Cornell University Press, 2009.*

Jenkins, Philip. Moral Panic: Changing Concepts of the Child Molester in Modern America. *New York City: Yale University Press, 2004.*

Lancaster, Roger. Sex Panic and the Punitive State. *Los Angeles: University of California Press, 2011.*

Leon, Chrysanthi S. Sex Fiends, Perverts, and Pedophiles: Understanding Sex Crime in America. *New York City: NYU Press, 2011.*

Logan, Wayne. Knowledge as Power: Criminal Registration and Community Notification Laws in America. *Los Angeles: Stanford Law Books, 2009.*

Rigby, Alan. It's Okay, We're Only Sex Offenders. *Atlanta: Xlibris, 2008.*

Strub, Whitney. Perversion for Profit: The Politics of Pornography and the Rise of the New Right. *Columbia University Press: New York City, 2013.*

Wright PhD, Richard G., ed. Sex Offender Laws: Failed Policies, New Directions. *New York City: Springer Publishing, 2009.*

Zilney, Laura. Perverts and Predators: The Making of Sexual Offending Laws. *Boston: Rowman and Littlefeld Publishers, 2009.*

Bibliography

Anderson, Cordelia. The Impact of Pornography on Children, Youth, and Culture. *Holyoke: NEARI Press, 2011.*

Anderson, Kurt. "How America Lost Its Mind." *The Atlantic, September 2017: 76-91.*

Anonymous. "Letter From a Woman: To the Man Who Injured Me." *In* Under the Covers: a Message of Hope, *by Joy L. Matthews, 121. Kansas City: ICL Global, 2015.*

Barna, George. America at the Crossroads: Explosive Trends Shaping America's Future and What You Can Do About It. *Grand Rapids: Baker Books, 2016.*

Bays, Laren, and Robert Longo. Enhancing Empathy. *Holyoke: NEARI Press, 2000.*

Blanchard, Geral. Ancient Ways: Indigenous Healing Innovations for the 21st Century. *Holyoke: NEARI Press, 2011.*

Bonhoeffer, Dietrich. "Life Together." In *The Bonhoeffer Reader, by Dietrich Bonhoeffer, edited by Clifford Green and Michael P. DeJonge, 514-561. Minneapolis, MN: Fortress Press, 2013.*

Bonhoeffer, Dietrich. "The Church and the Jewish Question." In *The Bonhoeffer Reader, by Dietrich Bonhoeffer, edited by Clifford Green and Michael Dejonge, 373-375. Minneapolis: Fortress Press, 2013.*

Bradberry, Travis. "How to Win an Argument Every Time." *Forbes. 4 23, 2015. http://onforb.es/1DSLPAy (accessed 6 1, 2015).*

Bradshaw, John. Healing the Shame That Binds You. *Houston: Bradshaw.*

Carnes, Patrick. Out of the Shadows, 3rd edition. *Minnesota: Hazelden, 2001.*

Carter, Venedita. "Opening Remarks." Rally Against the Prostitution of Women. *St. Paul, October 11, 2011.*

Cassin, Rene. "Preamble." Universal Declaration of Human Rights. *1948.*

Colson, Charles, and Harold Ficke. Faith: Given Once for All. *Nashville: Zondervan, 2012.*

Crawford, William B. Justice Perverted: How the Innocence Project at Northwestern University's Medical School of Journalism Sent an Innocent Man to Prison. *Amika Press: Los Angeles, 2015.*

Delmonico, David L., and Elizabeth Griffin. Illegal Images: Critical Issues and Strategies for Addressing Child Pornography Use. *Holyoke: NEARI Press, 2013.*

Department of Justice: Federal Bureau of Prisons. Starting Over. *Carson City. NV: The Change Companies, 2004.*

Ellman, Ira Mark, and Tara Ellman. ""Frightening and High": The Supreme Court's Crucial Mistake about Sex Crime Statistics." Constitutional Commentary, *Fall 2015.*

Franklin, Karen. "Invasion of the Hebophile Hunters." *June 19, 2017.*

Fujita, Stephen. "Japanese Americans." Microsoft Encarta. *2002-2003.*

Gerber, Rudolph. "On Dispensing Justice." Arizona Law Review, *2001: 135-172.*

Gerzon, Mark. Leading Through Conflict. *Bostom MA: Harvard University Business School Press, 2006.*

Glassner, Barry. Culture of Fear. *New York City: Basic Books, 1999.*

Godfrey, Dr. W. Robert. "Understanding Personhood." TableTalk, *April 2013.*

Gore, Albert. Assault on Reason. *New York City: Penguin Books, 2007.*

Grant, Jonathan. Divine Sex: A Compelling Vision for Christian Relationships in a Hypersexualized Age. *Grand Rapids, MI: Brazos Press, 2015.*

Hammar, Richard. "Dealing With Sex Offenders Who Want to Attend Your Church: How to Protect Your Most Vulnerable Members." Church Law & Tax Report.

Hanh, Thich Nanh. For A Future to be Possible: Commentaries on the Five Wonderful Precepts. *Berkley: Parallax Press, 2003.*

Hanley, Paul. Roller Coaster to Hell and Back: A True Story of Sexual Abuse and New Hope. *Atlanta: CreateSpace Independent Publishing, 2017.*

Hanson, R. Karl, Andrew J.R. Harris, Leslie Helmus, and David Thorton. "High Risk Offenders May Not Be High Risk Forever." Journal of Interpersonal Violence, *November 2013.*

Haralson, J., and J. Cordiero. Unprecedented: How Sex Offender Laws are Impacting Our Nation. *Dallas: PCG Legacy, 2012.*

Harlem, Georgia. "Unjust and Ineffective." The Economist, *August 6, 2009: 35-39.*

Hoffman, Gene Knudsen. Compassionate Listening. *Portland: Friends Bulletin Corporation, 2003.*

Holcomb, Justin. "Ethics of Personhood." TableTalk, *April 2013.*

Issacs, William. Dialogue and the Art of Thinking Together. *New York: Currency - Doubleday - Random House, 1999.*

Janus, Eric. Failure to Protect: America's Sexual Predator Laws and the Rise of the Preventative State. *New York City: Cornell University Press, 2009.*

Jenkins, Philip. Moral Panic: Changing Concepts of the Child Molester in Modern America. *New York City: Yale University Press, 2004.*

Johnson, Byron. More God, Less Crime. *West Conshohocken, PA:*

Templeton Press, 2011.

Kahane, Adam. Solving Tough Problems. *San Francisco: Berret-Koehler Publishers, 2004.*

Kassin, Saul. "Social Psychology." Encarta. *Microsoft Corporation, 2002-2003.*

Laaser, Mark. Healing the Wounds of Sexual Addiction. *Grand Rapids, MI: Zondervan, 2004.*

Lachelle. "Dealing With Terror: Should a Child Even Have To." In Under the Covers: A Message of Hope, *by Joy L. Matthews, 119. Kansas City: ICL Global, 2015.*

Lanagan PhD, Patrick A., Erica Schmit, and Matthew R. Durose. Recidivism of Sex Offenders Released from Prison in 1994. *Washington DC: Bureau of Justice Statistics, 2003.*

Lancaster, Roger. Sex Panic and the Punitive State. *Los Angeles: University of California Press, 2011.*

Leon, Chrysanthi S. Sex Fiends, Perverts, and Pedophiles: Understanding Sex Crime in America. *New York City: NYU Press, 2011.*

Levenson, Jill, Gwenda M. Willis, and David S Prescott. "Adverse Childhood Experiences in the Lives of Male Sex Offenders: Implications for Trauma Informed Care." Sexual Abuse: A Journal of Research and Treatment *28(4) (June 2016): 340-357.*

Logan, Wayne. Knowledge as Power: Criminal Registration and Community Notification Laws in America. *Los Angeles: Stanford Law Books, 2009.*

Longo, Robert E, and Lauren Bays. Why Did I Do It Again and How Can I stop? *NEARI Press: Holyoke MA, 2004.*

Longo, Robert E, Hogen Laren Bays, and Steven Sawyer. Enhancing Empathy. *Holyoke: NEARI Press, 2011.*

Longo, Robert E, Lauren Bays, and Steven Sawyer. Enhancing

BIBLIOGRAPHY

Empathy. *Holyoke: NEARI Press, 2011.*

—. Who Am I and Why Am I in Treatment? *Holyoke MA: NEARI Press, 2011.*

Maltz, Wendy and Larry. The Porn Trap: The Essential Guide to Overcoming Problems Caused by Pornography. *New York: Harper Collins, 2008.*

McKenna, Megan. "One of Us." The Sun, *September 2017: 5.*

McKune v. Lile. *536 U.S. 24, 34 (United States Supreme Court, 2002).*

Merriam Webster. 11th Collegiate Dictionary. *Merriam Webster, Inc., 2003.*

Morin, John, and Jill Levenson. Road to Freedom. *Fort Lauderdale: Center for Offender Rehabilitation and Education, 2002.*

Nouwen, Henri J.M. Out of Solitude: Three Meditations on the Christian Life. *Notre Dame: Ava Maria Press, 1974.*

—. Reaching Out: The Three Movements of the Spiritual Life. *New York: An Image Book Published by Doubleday, 1975.*

—. "With Care." Sun Magazine, *December 2014: 16-17.*

—. The Wounded Healer: Ministry in a Contemporary Society. *New York: Image Doubleday, 1972.*

Parsons, Burt. "Proclaiming Life to the Captives." TableTalk, *April 2013: 2.*

Ragusa-Salerno, Laura M., and Kristen Zgoba. "Taking Stock of Twenty Years of Sex Offender Laws and Research." Journal of Crime and Justice, *2012: 335-355.*

Rigby, Alan. It's Okay, We're Only Sex Offenders. *Atlanta: Xlibris, 2008.*

Roberts, Ted. Pure Desire. *Ventura, CA: Regal, 2008.*

Ross Jr., Bobby. "Modern Day Lepers." Christianity Today,

December 2009.

Ross, J. Robert. "Sex Offenders in the Church." Christian Standard, 2016.

Rozek, Sandy. "Do Public Parks Belong to All of the Public?" The Digest. *Albuquerque: NARSOL, October 2017.*

—. "#Tent in the Woods." NARSOL Digest, *February 1, 2017.*

—. "Storm of the Century." The Digest. *Albuquerque: NARSOL, October 2017.*

Selby, Tom. "The Intimacy Cycle." *Family Transitions, 2016.*

Smith, James K. A. You Are What You Love. *Grand Rapids: Brazos Press, 2016.*

Sproul Jr, R.C. "Blood in the Streets." TableTalk, *April 2013.*

Sproul, Dr. R.C. "Against the Sophist." TableTalk, *April 2017: 5.*

—. "The Voice of the Church." TableTalk, *April 2013.*

Strauss, Neil. "The Age of Fear." Rolling Stone, *October 20, 2016: 42 - 56.*

Strickland, Darby. "Counseling in the Brambles." Edited by David Powlinson. Journal of Biblical Counseling *(Christian Counseling Education Foundation), 2017: 24-26.*

Strickland, Darby. "Identifying Oppression in Marriage." Edited by David Powlinson. Journal of Biblical Counseling *(Christian Counseling and Education Foundation) Volume 30, no. 2 (2016): 7-21.*

Strub, Whitney. Perversion for Profit: The Politics of Pornography and the Rise of the New Right. *Columbia University Press: New York City, 2013.*

The Economist. "Paedophilia: Shedding Light on the Dark Field." The Economist: International Version, *August 13, 2016.*

The Sentencing Project. Trends in U. S. Corrections. *Washington DC:*

BIBLIOGRAPHY

The Sentencing Project, 2016.

Thompson MD, Curt. The Anatomy of the Soul. *Carrolton: Tyndale Momentum, 2010.*

Tozer, A.W. "Final Words in 1963." In Jesus is Family, *by Jon Zens, 101-106. Orange: Quoir, 2017.*

Wright PhD, Richard G., ed. Sex Offender Laws: Failed Policies, New Directions. *New York City: Springer Publishing, 2009.*

Yates, Pamela, and David Prescott. Building A Better Life: a Good Lives and Self Regulation Workbook. *Brandon Vt: Safer Society Press, 2011.*

—. Building A Better Life: a Good Lives and Self Regulation Workbook. *Brandon VT: Safer Society Press, 2011.*

Yoder, Steven. "What's the Real Rate of Sex-Crime Recidivism?" Pacific Standard, *May 2016.*

Yoffe, Emily. "Innocence is Irrelevant." The Atlantic, *September 2017: 66-74.*

Yung, Corey Rayburn. "The Emerging Criminal War on Sex Offenders." Harvard Civil Liberties - Civil Law Review, *2010: 436-481.*

Zens, Jon. Jesus is Family: His Life Toegther. *Orange: Quoir, 2017.*

Zilney, Laura. Perverts and Predators: The Making of Sexual Offending Laws. *Boston: Rowman and Littlefeld Publishers, 2009.*

NOTES

Foreword
1   (Barna 2016), pp. 63-69

Introduction
2   (Nouwen, Out of Solitude: Three Meditations on the Christian Life 1974), p. 35 (italics added)
3   (Kahane 2004), p. 4
4   *Ekklesia*, is a transliteration of the Greek word "Εκκλεσια" and which is frequently translated in the Bible as "church"; however, it more accurately reflects the spiritual body of Christ instead of a particular structure or hierarchical organization.
5   This quote is attributable to German theologian and martyr Dietrich Bonheoffer, however, it is not found in his writings.
6   (Cassin 1948)
7   I am indebted to Debra Hirsch who wrote something very similar in her excellent book *Redeeming Sex: Naked Conversations about Sexuality and Spirituality;* Intervarsity Press, Downer Grove, 2015.

Chapter 1 – Silence In the Face of Injustice
8   (Issacs 1999), p. 6
9   (Merriam-Webster 2003)
10   Institute of Criminal Policy Research (ICPR), World Prison Brief, 11th edition
11   Research conducted by Stephen W. Tweedle, an Associate Professor Emeritus in the Department of Geography at Oklahoma State University, identifies two Bible Belts. One includes Florida, Alabama, Tennessee, Kentucky, Georgia, North Carolina, South Carolina, and Virginia, and the second includes Texas, Arkansas, Louisiana, Oklahoma, Missouri, Kansas, and Mississippi
12   Prisoners in 2015 Bureau of Justice Statistics, National Prisoner Statistics Program, 2014-2015.
13   *Ex Post Facto* is attempting to pass a law that makes a

NOTES

previous act criminal.

14   In 2017, the Pennsylvania Supreme Court ruled that sex offender registration is *punitive* (at least in the state of Pennsylvania and given certain circumstances.) This may open the door for other legal challenges.

15   See (Yung 2010)

16   (Yung 2010), p. 473

17   (Sproul, Against the Sophist 2017)

18   Benjamin Franklin expressed his concern at the Constitutional Convention when he said, (If this form of government is not well administered) it "can only end in despotism, as other forms have done before it, (for) when the people shall become so corrupted as to need despotic government, (they become) incapable of any other… [W]hen you assemble a number of men, to have the advantage of their joint wisdom, you inevitably assemble with those men all their prejudices, their passions, their errors of opinion, their local interests, and their selfish views."

19   Minimum sentencing laws set a statutory minimum sentence for certain criminal offenses. The judge is not permitted to deviate from this sentence.

20   Mandatory sentencing stipulates that probation is not available. The offender must be imprisoned.

21   Presumptive sentencing sets a higher than minimum sentence that must be imposed if mitigating circumstances do not warrant the imposition of the minimum sentence.

22   Three-strike laws require imprisonment if the most recent offense is the third strike. Consequently, many repeat offenders are imprisoned for charges that would otherwise warrant probation or other interventions.

23   (Gerber 2001), p. 136

24   Ibid, p. 136

25   Ibid, p. 137 (Emphasis added.)

26   Ibid, p. 139 (emphasis added.)

27   State v. Barger, 167 AZ 563.810 P.2d 191 (App. 1990)

28   (Yoffe 2017), p. 70

29   The "Prison Industrial Complex" includes private for-profit

prisons as well as a growing network of businesses that benefit from cheap or free prison labor and/or companies that sell goods and services to prisoners at exorbitant rates. As an example, a package of ramen noodles–a staple in many college dormitories and prison cells–sells for 64 cents in prison, while available outside for 10 – 15 cents. In addition, an intrastate (local) phone call costs inmates and/or their families 20 cents a minute. Many of the companies providing such goods and services also provide commissions or incentives (kickbacks) to prisons.

30   (Gerber 2001), p. 141
31   Ibid, p. 146
32   (Yoffe 2017), p. 70
33   Although President Barak Obama moved to limit the use of military equipment by the police, Donald Trump has reinstated the practice begun under President Ronald Reagan. Such practice is dangerous even as power corrupts and absolute power corrupts absolutely. When the tools of waging war also become the tools and weapons of waging law enforcement, are we not in grave danger of creating a militaristic government rather than sustaining a democracy?
34   (Gerber 2001), p. 165
35   (Yoffe 2017), p. 74
36   In most cases, only murderers are imprisoned for life without the possibility of parole; however, because of minimum mandatory and consecutive sentencing, many sex offenders in Arizona are serving *de facto* life sentences with hundreds and even thousands of years remaining on their sentence.
37   (Yoffe 2017), p. 70
38   Ibid, p. 70
39   Ibid, p. 72
40   (The Sentencing Project 2016)

Chapter 2 – The Culture of Fear
41   (Glassner 1999), p. 210
42   Ibid, p. 210
43   (Strauss 2016), p. 44

44 Ibid, p. 44
45 Ibid, p. 45 (Emphasis added.)
46 (Kassin 2002-2003)
47 (Strauss 2016), p. 44
48 (Glassner 1999)
49 (Strauss 2016), p. 44 (Emphasis added.)
50 (K. Anderson 2017), p. 86
51 Ibid, p. 87 (Emphasis added.)
52 Ibid, p. 67
53 Ibid, p. 45
54 The reasons for the decline in sexual morality in America are discussed in more detail in the next chapter—*Complexities*.
55 (Fujita 2002-2003)
56 (Harlem 2009)
57 Netflix offers the NC-17 movie *Showgirls* as well as other adult-only content.

Chapter 3 – Complexities
58 (Kahane 2004), p. 1
59 Ibid, p. 2
60 Ibid, p. 4
61 Ibid.
62 (Issacs 1999), p. 17
63 (Merriam-Webster 2003)
64 Ibid.
65 These differences will be discussed in more detail and application in Chapter 7.
66 (Issacs 1999), p. 45
67 *Psychology Today* does not claim to be, nor is it recognized as a professional or academically credible journal; nonetheless, Longo's comments in the article continue shaping the legislative agenda in this country concerning sex offenders.
68 (Yoder 2016)
69 (Ellman and Ellman 2015), p. 2 (Emphasis added.)
70 (McKune v. Lile 2002) (Emphasis added.)
71 (Ellman and Ellman 2015), p. 4

72   Ibid, p. 6
73   (Hanson, et al. 2013), p. 3
74   *Static 99* is one measure used by therapist and law enforcement for differentiating levels of risks for various sex offenders. Not all sex offenders have the same risk.
75   (Hanson, et al. 2013), p. 1 (Emphasis added.)
76   *The Journal of Interpersonal Violence* is a respected professional journal, unlike *Psychology Today* which appeals to a more contemporary but unprofessional audience.
77   (Harlem 2009)
78   Information in table derived from tables 22 and 23 in (Lanagan PhD, Schmit and Durose 2003).
79   (Ellman and Ellman 2015), p. 6
80   (Issacs 1999), p. 10-12
81   Gore, p. 5
82   (Levenson, Willis and Prescott 2016), p. 340
83   Ibid, p. 350
84   Ibid, p. 353
85   (Grant 2015), p. 15
86   Ibid, p. 121
87   (C. Anderson 2011), p. 2
88   (Maltz 2008), p. 25
89   (C. Anderson 2011), p. 4
90   Ibid, p. 6
91   (Carter 2011)
92   I am using "Child Sexual Abuse Images" (CSAI) in place of the more recognizable term "child pornography" to avoid glossing over the fact that children cannot give legal consent and to increase the awareness of the lifelong traumatizing impact the production of these images has on a child. Thanks to David Delmonico and Elizabeth Griffins' introduction of this concept in *Illegal Images: Critical Issues and Strategies for Addressing Child Pornography Use*.
93   (Franklin 2017)
94   (Carnes 2001), p. 82-85
95   (The Economist 2016)

NOTES

96   (Kahane 2004), p. 43
97   Ibid, p. 2
98   Ibid, p. 75
99   Ibid, p. 76
100   Ibid, p. 83
101   Ibid, p. 92
102   (Nouwen, Out of Solitude: Three Meditations on the Christian Life 1974), p. 16

Chapter 4 – Victim Profiles

103   (Longo, Bays and Sawyer 2011), p.73
104   "Incompetent consent" differentiates in that although a minor may not **legally** consent to sex, i.e. they are legally "incompetent," they often eagerly and willingly participate in the offense without any coercion, force, or enticement.
105   It is worth considering the impact of the decline of sexual mores and morals in society and the impact on a sexually-charged culture described in Chapter 3.
106   For a complete state-by-state breakdown, see the appendix "Age of Consent."
107   In Arizona, any sexual conduct with a minor under the age of 15 is considered a "dangerous crime against children," and subjects the offender to a minimum of ten years in prison. In addition, if there was more than one act, and there usually is, each act counts as a separate offense and must be served **consecutively**.
108   "Dangerous crimes against children" allow prosecutors to seek longer sentencing and enhancements such as requiring multiple charges with the same victim to be served **consecutively.** The sentencing range for a single offense of a fourteen- and eighteen-year-old engaging in *consenting* sexual activity is a minimum of thirteen years, a presumptive of twenty years and maximum of twenty-seven years in prison. Therefore, an eighteen-year-old convicted of a **single offense** would be imprisoned at least until the age of thirty-one and possibly until forty.
109   "*Illicit consent*" differentiates, that although a minor may technically consent to sex, such consent is gained through illicit

grooming and without any loving or noble intentions on the part of the offender.

110   *"Unethical consent"* differentiates, that although a minor may technically consent to sex, such consent is gained through illegal and *unethical* means such as power and control, coercion, force, or other enticements.

111   To be guilty of a crime, the person must also have had the intent to act in a harmful way. This element is sometimes called the requirement of mental fault or *mens rea*, a Latin term that means "guilty mind." Thus, many crimes are defined in terms of intentionally, knowingly, maliciously, willfully, recklessly, or negligently acting or bringing about a result, or of conducting oneself with intent to accomplish a specified consequence. The *mens rea* requirement distinguishes between inadvertent or accidental acts and acts for which a person is criminally liable. (see Dresibach, Daniel; Criminal Law; Microsoft Encarta 2011)

112   (Gerber 2001), p. 139

113   (Grant 2015), p. 121

Chapter 5–Offenses and Offenders

114   (Hoffman 2003), p. 312

Chapter 6–Effects of the Sex Offender Registry

115   See Chapter 4, "Victim Profiles," for a discussion of incompetent consent.

116   See "Age of Consent" in the appendix.

117   (Yung 2010), p. 436

118   This cultural phenomenon is described in detail in Johann Hari's excellent exposition on the genesis and futility of the drug wars, in *Chasing the Scream.*

119   In various publications, former United States Senators John F. Kennedy (MA), Mark Hatfield, (OR) and Barak Obama (IL) have all expressed disappointment upon first entering the senate, that in the greatest legislative body in the world, *no one is listening.*

120   (Gore 2007), p. 5

121   As I am writing this paper, Republicans and Democrats in

NOTES

Congress are engaged in a contentious and partisan debate over healthcare. Political gridlock is becoming the rule, and nothing constructive is being accomplished.

122   For example, the families of Adam Walsh, Jacob Wettlering, Megan Kanka, and other innocent victims who have been molested, kidnapped, raped and murdered.

123   (Harlem 2009)

124   See Chapter 4.

125   (Rozek, #Tent in the Woods 2017)

126   (Yung 2010), p. 448

127   (Cassin 1948)

128   Thankfully, a rare **unanimous** decision by the United States Supreme Court overturned a North Carolina law banning sex offenders from commercial social networking sites. In the majority opinion, Justice Anthony Kennedy wrote, "A fundamental First Amendment principle is that all persons have access to places where they can speak and listen and then, after reflection, speak and listen once more. Today, one of the most important places to exchange views is cyberspace, particularly social media that offered relatively unlimited low cost capacity for communication of all kinds. (*Reno v. American Civil Liberties Union 521 U.S. 844, 870....* Social media allows users to gain access to information and communicate with one another on any subject that might come to mind. With one broad stroke (the state) bars access to what for many are the principle sources for knowing current events, checking ads for employment, speaking and listening in the modern public square, and otherwise exploring the vast resources of human thought and knowledge. Foreclosing access to social media altogether thus prevents users from engaging in legitimate exercise of First Amendment rights. Even convicted criminals–and in some instances especially convicted criminals–might receive legitimate benefits from these means for the access to the world of ideas, particularly if they seek to reform and to pursue lawful and rewarding lives." 582 US ____(2017)

129   (Rozek, Storm of the Century 2017)

130   (Rozek, Do Public Parks Belong to All of the Public? 2017)

131   (Strickland, Identifying Oppression in Marriage 2016), p. 11

132   Ibid.
133   Ibid, p. 31
134   (Strickland, Counseling in the Brambles 2017), p. 29
135   (Strickland, Identifying Oppression in Marriage 2016), p.11
136   (Parsons 2013), p. 1
137   Ibid. (Emphasis added.)
138   As previously noted in the chapter on Victim Profiles, "Compared with males in the general population, sex offenders had more than three times the odds of *childhood sexual abuse* (CSA), nearly twice the odds of physical abuse, thirteen times the odds of verbal abuse, and more than four times the odds of emotional neglect and coming from broken homes."
139   See Matthew 25:31-46.
140   Florida, where Ligionier Ministries is based, has the tenth highest rate of incarceration in the country.
141   (Johnson 2011), p. 157
142   (Holcomb 2013), p. 16
143   Ibid, p. 18
144   (Sproul, The Voice of the Church 2013), p. 26
145   Ibid.
146   Ibid, p. 28
147   Ibid, p. 26
148   (Godfrey 2013), p. 8
149   (Sproul Jr 2013), p. 28
150   Ibid, p. 29
151   See John 6: 1-14, esp. v. 12.

Chapter 7 – Roles and Responsibilities of Sex Offenders
152   This state (Arizona) prosecutes each image as a separate offense, the minimum sentence is ten years, and all sentences must run consecutively. Therefore, 20 images * 10 years = 200 years.
153   Seventeen years is the presumptive sentence for one image of child porn in Arizona.
154   By *complicit,* we mean minor victims who intentionally misrepresent their age either by possessing a fake ID, misstating their age on the internet, or engaging in certain "adult" activities in public

NOTES

places, or minors who post and share sexually explicit pictures of themselves.

155   See Chapter 3 for a further discussion of the decline of sexual mores and standards in this country.

156   As previously noted, some appellate courts have overturned convictions where the offender and the victim had not met in person and the offender had no other way to determine the victim's true age.

157   See in Chapter 1.

158   *Incompetent* consent is a term used to help differentiate that, although a minor may not **legally** consent to sex, i.e. they are legally "incompetent"; they often eagerly and willingly participate in the offense without any coercion, force, or enticement.

159   *Illicit* consent is a term used to help differentiate that, although a minor may technically consent to sex, such consent is gained through illicit grooming and without any loving or noble intentions on the part of the offender.

160   *Unethical* consent is a term used to help differentiate that, although a minor may technically consent to sex, such consent is gained through illegal and *unethical* means such as power and control, coercion, force, or other enticements.

161   Celebrate Recovery is a twelve-step recovery program following eight biblical principles for individuals with "hurts, habits, and hang-ups."

162   See the references in Chapters 3 and 6 as well as the "Age of Consent" table in the appendix.

163   Financial justice in such cases is requiring the child's father to pay child support in accordance with state laws.

164   The book, *Under the Covers: A Message of Hope* is available at www.goingunderthecovers.com

165   (Lachelle 2015)

166   (Anonymous 2015)

167   Treatment is available and is often required for sex offenders as a condition of their probation or parole. Some states offer treatment in prison. Appendix D lists numerous resources that I recommend and have found helpful in my own journey.

168   (Morin and Levenson 2002), p. 3

Chapter 8 – Roles and Responsibilities of the Church
169   (Bonhoeffer, The Church and the Jewish Question 2013), p. 374
170   Ibid, p. 373
171   (Ross Jr. 2009)
172   See, for example, Proverbs 6:16-19.
173   (Hammar n.d.) (Emphasis added.)
174   (Tozer 2017), pp. 103-104
175   (Ross 2016)
176   Ibid. (Emphasis added.)
177   Ibid. (Emphasis added.)
178   Ibid.
179   Ibid.
180   Ibid.
181   (Ragusa-Salerno and Zgoba 2012), p. 352
182   See Leviticus 13.
183   (Colson and Ficke 2012) p. 21
184   See Acts 19.
185   An Arizona church recently hired a former Broadway lighting director and purchased professional lighting and sound equipment for morning worship services.
186   (Colson and Ficke 2012) p. 21
187   (Johnson 2011), p. 164
188   Ibid, p. 158
189   Ibid, p. 158 (Emphasis added.)
190   (Roberts 2008), p. 48
191   Ibid, p. 59
192   Ibid, p. 157
193   (Hammar n.d.)

Chapter 9 – Transforming the Conflict
194   (Gerzon 2006), p. 4
195   (Hoffman 2003), p. 311-312
196   (Gerzon 2006), p. 18
197   Arizona prosecutes each image as separate offense, the minimum sentence is ten years, and all sentences must run

consecutively. For example, twenty images means two hundred years in prison. The Representative was not attempting to decriminalize possession of child porn; he was simply suggesting that Arizona could be more in line with other states and federal sentencing guidelines.

198   (Gerzon 2006), p. 32
199   Ibid, p. 32
200   Ibid, p. 48
201   Ibid, p. 50
202   Ibid, p. 52
203   Ibid, p. 61
204   Ibid, p. 64
205   Albert Einstein, letter, cited in Warren Bennis, *On Becoming a Leader*, (Warren Bennis Inc, 1989)
206   (Gerzon 2006), p. 65
207   Ibid, p. 81
208   Ibid, p. 85
209   Ibid, p. 92
210   Ibid, p. 92
211   Ibid, p. 94
212   (Hanh 2003)
213   (Gerzon 2006), p. 97
214   Ibid, p. 99
215   (Nouwen, The Wounded Healer: Ministry in a Contemporary Society 1972), p. 38
216   (Gerzon 2006), p. 119
217   Ibid, p. 120
218   Ibid, p. 122
219   Ibid, p. 167
220   Ibid, p. 168
221   Ibid, p. 171
222   Ibid, p. 170
223   (Gerzon 2006), p. 225

Chaptern 10 – The *Ekklesia*
224   *Alongside Ministries* is a Phoenix Arizona faith-based "in

prison" mentoring and transitioning program assisting general population inmates; however, they refuse to offer any assistance to sex offenders.
225 *Church on the Streets* is a faith-based prison transition ministry that also refuses any assistance to sex offenders.
226 (Gerzon 2006), p. 33
227 (Zens 2017), p. 34
228 (Bonhoeffer, Life Together 2013), p. 517
229 (Bonhoeffer, Life Together 2013), p. 515
230 Romans 15:7
231 (Bonhoeffer, Life Together 2013), pp. 521-522
232 (Zens 2017), p. 31
233 (Zens 2017), p. 32
234 (Zens 2017), p. 32
235 (Barna 2016), pp. 63-69
236 (Nouwen, Reaching Out: The Three Movements of the Spiritual Life 1975), p. 71
237 Adapted from *Advocating for Justice: An Evangelical Vision for Transforming Systems and Structures;* Offut, Stephen et al.
238 (Smith 2016), p. 6
239 (Nouwen, With Care 2014), pp. 38-39
240 (Nouwen, Reaching Out: The Three Movements of the Spiritual Life 1975), p. 72
241 Ibid, p. 65
242 (Johnson 2011), p. 158 (Emphasis added)
243 Ibid , p. 157

Chapter 11 – The Vision
244 (Selby 2016)
245 (Issacs 1999), p. 19
246 (Gerzon 2006), p. 8
247 (Nouwen, Reaching Out: The Three Movements of the Spiritual Life 1975), pp. 67-71
248 (Blanchard 2011), p. xviii
249 Ibid, p. 3
250 Ibid, p. 5

251 Ibid, p. 6
252 Ibid, p. 17
253 Ibid.
254 Ibid, p. 10
255 Ibid, p. 9
256 Ibid, p. 11
257 (Nouwen, Reaching Out: The Three Movements of the Spiritual Life 1975), p. 76
258 (Nouwen, The Wounded Healer: Ministry in a Contemporary Society 1972), pp. 45-46

Epilogue
259 (Nouwen, Out of Solitude: Three Meditations on the Christian Life 1974), p. 28
260 Ibid, p. 45
261 (McKenna 2017)
262 (Nouwen, The Wounded Healer: Ministry in a Contemporary Society 1972), p. 29
263 Ibid, p. 30

SILENCE IN THE FACE OF INJUSTICE

www.ingramcontent.com/pod-product-compliance
Lightning Source LLC
Chambersburg PA
CBHW051539020426
42333CB00016B/2000